Public Opinion and American Foreign Policy

Analytical Perspectives on Politics

Political Science is developing rapidly and changing markedly. Keeping in touch with new ideas across the discipline is a challenge for political scientists and for their students.

To help meet this challenge, the series Analytical Perspectives on Politics presents creative and sophisticated syntheses of major areas of research in the field of political science. In each book, a high-caliber author provides a clear and discriminating description of the current state of the art and a strong-minded prescription and structure for future work in the field.

These distinctive books provide a compact review for political scientists, a helpful introduction for graduate students, and central reading for advanced undergraduate courses.

Robert W. Jackman, *Power without Force: The Political Capacity of Nation-States*

Linda L. Fowler, *Candidates, Congress, and the American Democracy*

Ole R. Holsti, *Public Opinion and American Foreign Policy*

Public Opinion and American Foreign Policy

Ole R. Holsti

Ann Arbor

THE UNIVERSITY OF MICHIGAN PRESS

Copyright © by the University of Michigan 1996
All rights reserved
Published in the United States of America by
The University of Michigan Press
Manufactured in the United States of America
⊗ Printed on acid-free paper

1999   1998   1997   1996   4   3   2   1

A CIP catalog record for this book is available from the British Library

Library of Congress Cataloging-in-Publication Data

Holsti, Ole R.
    Public opinion and American foreign policy / Ole R. Holsti.
        p.   cm. — (Analytical perspectives on politics)
    Includes bibliographical references (p.) and index.
    ISBN 0-472-09619-2 (cloth : acid-free paper). — ISBN
0-472-06619-6 (pbk. : acid-free paper)
        1. United States—Foreign relations—1989–   —Public opinion.
    2. United States—Foreign relations—1945–1989—Public opinion.
    3. Public opinion—United States.   I. Title.   II. Series.
E840.H592   1996
327.73—dc20   96-10151
                                                                CIP

For Ann, Maija and Chuck, Kal and Marilyn

Preface

Ours is appropriately called the "age of polling." Few aspects of contemporary life have eluded the public scrutiny of the survey. Polls are regularly conducted to determine what the general public thinks about issues, parties, candidates, presidents, institutions, and other countries, to say nothing of products, pastimes, and popular personalities. As this is being written, the public is being asked whether the Miss America Pageant should continue to judge contestants in bathing suits and how retired general Colin Powell would fare as a presidential candidate in 1996. Other surveys rely on expert opinion to answer some variant or another of America's favorite question: "Who is number one?" Which college football team is the best this week in the opinion of sports writers and coaches? How do academic specialists rank graduate programs in their disciplines?

Foreign affairs, once considered the private preserve of small groups of knowledgeable and interested elites, have also been the subject of repeated surveys. Although those surveys have consistently revealed that the average American is poorly informed about international affairs, opportunities for the public to become engaged in foreign policy have increased. For example, new communications technologies permit the public to observe important events as they unfold. The Cable News Network (CNN) brought the Persian Gulf War into the world's living rooms in real time, and it did the same with the mission of Jimmy Carter, Sam Nunn, and Colin Powell to persuade Haiti's ruling junta that stepping down voluntarily was the only way to avert an American military invasion to force it out of power. These technologies can also make the public a quasi participant in such episodes by almost simultaneous polling to determine reactions to and assessments of events as they take place.

The impact and consequences of these developments are not free of controversy, but many of the issues that have surfaced are in fact variants of venerable debates about the role of the public in international affairs. Is foreign policy "different" from other aspects of public policy? How can a poorly informed public make any coherent sense of the complex issues that constitute international relations? Can it make any constructive contribution to foreign policy? Can great powers in the nuclear age afford to take public sentiments into account when the consequences of policy choices may determine the continued existence of the country, or perhaps even of the human race? Can they afford not to? Has the end of the Cold War increased the likelihood that public passions will drive governments into well-meaning but hopeless undertakings that have little relationship to the national interest? Conversely, will a public suffering from "compassion fatigue" insist that an agenda of domestic problems be given priority over the vision briefly articulated by former President Bush—a "new world order" in which the United States would play a leading role?

More basically, what is the proper role of public opinion in the conduct of foreign affairs in a democratic polity? What do we know about the nature and impact of public opinion on foreign and defense policy? Philosophers have debated the first question for centuries, but twentieth-century conflicts have played a crucial role in framing the key questions and research agendas in the search for answers to the second one. World War I transformed the question of public participation in foreign affairs from a theoretical issue into a practical one that many postwar leaders had to confront. World War II was equally significant. For many leaders and public opinion analysts, a key question arising from that conflict was whether the public would permit the United States to play a constructive leadership role in the postwar international order. Answers to many of the normative and empirical questions that emerged from extensive research during the two decades following World War II came to be reexamined as a consequence of the long and failed U.S. effort in Vietnam. The end of the Cold War has raised new questions, including the extent to which our understanding of American public opinion and foreign policy may need to be modified in the light of a world that has in many ways been transformed since the late 1980s. The chapters that follow will attempt to examine and evaluate some of the theory and evidence concerning these issues.

John Zaller (1992) has appropriately argued that our knowledge about public opinion has suffered from a tendency to organize research around policy issues, including foreign policy. While this book is focused on opinions about international affairs, I have also made some effort to draw upon theory and evidence from other issues and such related aspects of political behavior as voting.

In the course of writing this book I have received invaluable help from many persons and institutions. John Aldrich, Ronald Hinckley, Layna Mosely, and Jim Rosenau read the entire manuscript in draft form and provided many helpful comments, cogent criticisms, and constructive suggestions for improving it. Peter Feaver did the same for the final chapter. Jim Rosenau has also been a collaborator for more than two decades on a related project concerning the political beliefs of American opinion leaders. This book, which originated in a suggestion by John Aldrich, is far better than it would have been without their help.

I am also indebted to those who read and commented on an earlier and much briefer effort to review the literature on public opinion and foreign policy: Stephen Earl Bennett, Bill Chittick, Thomas Graham, Jon Hurwitz, Ben Page, Mark Peffley, Philip Powlick, Bruce Russett, and Gene Wittkopf. Many stimulating conversations with Gene Wittkopf about most of the topics discussed here have invariably been enlightening.

Four National Science Foundation (NSF) grants made it possible for me to conduct surveys of American opinion leaders in 1980, 1984, 1988, and 1992. Some of the resulting data are reported in chapters 4 and 5. The NSF also provided a Research and Training Grant (RTG) in political psychology to the Mershon Center at the Ohio State University. The frequent meetings of faculty and doctoral students under the auspices of the Mershon RTG have provided an exceptional inter-university, multidisciplinary, and cross-generational setting in which to further my education.

The Duke Arts and Sciences Research Council provided a grant to undertake the initial survey of opinion leaders in 1976, and since that time it has frequently provided additional support for my research on American public opinion and foreign policy.

Any reader will quickly come to appreciate that this book could not have been written without the efforts of many people who have written about public opinion and foreign policy. It is thus appropriate for me to express my gratitude to all of the authors cited in the bibliography. Three of them—Ronald Hinckley, Alan Kay, and Steven Kull—also have generously shared the results of their own surveys with me.

For many years I have relied on the expert programming skills of Daniel F. Harkins. As the entire computing system at Duke has undergone immense changes on an almost annual basis, Dan's patience and ingenuity have been almost as important as his immense technical abilities. The many drafts of the manuscript and tables were skillfully typed by Rita Dowling. Not even the most daunting table ever caused her to lose her excellent sense of humor. Layna Mosely and Elizabeth Rogers provided outstanding assistance in searching through memoirs and biographies of presidents and secretaries of state for materials related to public opinion. Justine Lapatine diligently checked the quotations and citations.

Finally, I wish to thank several persons at the University of Michigan Press: Colin Day, Malcolm Litchfield, and Charles T. Myers, who supported this project from its inception.

All those who have so kindly contributed to this book are, of course, absolved from blame for any remaining deficiencies.

The dedication is offered with gratitude and affection for many reasons, none of which have anything to do with either public opinion or foreign policy.

Contents

Tables

Figures

CHAPTER 1

Introduction

In one of several public addresses on the appropriate prerequisites for deployment of American combat forces abroad, Secretary of Defense Caspar Weinberger in 1984 specified six requirements for any such U.S. military intervention. According to Weinberger, one of those preconditions was that "there must be some reasonable assurance that we will have the support of the American people" (*New York Times*, November 29, 1984, A5: 1). His cabinet colleague, Secretary of State George Shultz, publicly disagreed with the "Weinberger Doctrine," characterizing it then, and later in his memoirs, as an unreasonably stringent set of preconditions that would rarely, if ever, be met. Consequently, Shultz argued, these restrictions effectively would serve as an excuse for inaction, even when vital American interests abroad were potentially threatened (Shultz 1993, 84, 103, 649–51). The public disagreement between Weinberger and Shultz may be seen as one of many arguments about the ends and means of foreign policy that have marked the decades since the American intervention in Vietnam ended in defeat. Varying interpretations of the Vietnam War, why it was lost, and the appropriate "lessons" to be drawn from that conflict, especially with respect to the deployment of troops abroad, have continued to generate heated debate more than two decades after the last Americans were evacuated from Saigon.

The differences between Weinberger and Shultz may be seen as part of the "Vietnam Syndrome"—the propensity to perceive and assess international undertakings through the prism of the war in Southeast Asia. They also may be viewed as part of a more basic and venerable debate about a central issue regarding the theory and practice of democratic government: namely, what is the proper role of public opinion in the conduct of foreign affairs? Understandably, a great deal of research on public opinion and foreign policy has been driven by issues of the moment. Almost any dramatic international development will give rise immediately to surveys directed at discovering public attitudes and preferences for dealing with it. Indeed, each of the three major U.S. television networks conducts regular surveys in cooperation with a national newspaper, and it is now even

possible to report how the public is reacting to events as they unfold.[1]

One of the themes to be developed in this and the following two
chapters is that research and theory on public opinion and foreign
policy have been heavily influenced by major international developments and by normative preferences for the ways the United States
should deal with them. Despite the heavy emphasis in most surveys
sponsored by the popular media on public reactions to current issues—or, perhaps, because of it—there is value in linking the issue of
public opinion and foreign policy to broader questions about the conduct of public affairs. This examination of the linkage between public
opinion and foreign policy will begin with a review of the historical
controversy over the issue. A good starting point is the long-standing
debate between proponents of two quite different philosophical approaches to international relations.

Public Opinion in the Realist-Liberal Debate

Although other major theoretical contenders have claimed to provide empirical and/or normative guides to international relations—
twentieth-century examples have included several variants of Marxist-
Leninist and dependency theories—the rival assertions by proponents
of realism and their liberal critics have tended to dominate debates
among theorists, reformers, and policymakers. Realists can properly
claim the longest intellectual lineage, tracing their roots to Thucy-
dides, if not earlier. Most liberal theories are of more recent vintage,
dating to the seventeenth century and more or less coinciding with the
creation of the modern state system with the Treaties of Westphalia in
1648. Although realist-liberal differences extend across virtually all
central questions of foreign policy, international relations and statecraft, the appropriate role for public opinion in foreign policymaking
is at the center of persisting debates between these two approaches to
international affairs. Is public opinion a force for enlightenment—
indeed, a necessary if not sufficient condition for sound foreign policy
and, thus, a significant contributor to peaceful relations among nations—as celebrated by Woodrow Wilson and many other liberals?
Alternatively, is the public more appropriately described as a source
of emotional and shortsighted thinking that can only impede the effective pursuit and defense of vital national interests?

There is a long liberal tradition, dating back at least to Jeremy
Bentham, that places public opinion at the center of legitimate and
effective public policy. Bentham described public opinion, or "The

Public-Opinion Tribunal," as "the sole remedy" for many problems of government. His "Plan for an Universal and Perpetual Peace" also proposed removing the veil of secrecy from the conduct of foreign affairs: "That secresy [*sic*] in the operation of the foreign department ought not to be endured in England, being equally repugnant to the interests of liberty and those of peace" (Bentham 1962, 8:561, 2:547). James Mill effectively summarized the liberal case for public opinion as a repository of wisdom.

> Every man, possessed of reason, is accustomed to weigh evidence, and to be guided and determined by its preponderance. When various conclusions are, with their evidence, presented with equal care and with equal skill, there is a moral certainty, though some few may be misguided, that the greatest number will judge aright, and that the greatest force of evidence, wherever it is, will produce the greatest impression. . . . [W]hen all opinions, true and false, are equally declared, the assent of the greater number, when their interests are not opposed to them, may always be expected to be given to the true. These principles, the foundations of which appear to be impregnable, suffice for the speedy determination of every practical question. (Mill 1913, 16, 18)

Rousseau and Kant developed similar themes specifically with respect to foreign policy and war. Monarchs may engage in wars for reasons that have nothing to do with the interests of their subjects. In contrast, the foreign policies of republics are more peaceful, at least in part because the public can play a constructive role in constraining policymakers; accountability to the public can restrain any warmaking proclivities of leaders. Kant based his argument on the constraints that republics and nonrepublics face when they contemplate engaging in war. The former are likely to be more peaceful because the public, which bears most of the costs, will be cautious about engaging in war: "If (as must inevitably be the case, given this form of constitution) the consent of the citizenry is required in order to determine whether or not there will be war, it is natural that they consider all its calamities before committing themselves to so risky a game." The situation is quite different under nonrepublican constitutions, according to Kant, because:

> The easiest thing in the world to do is to declare war. Here the ruler is not a fellow citizen, but the nation's owner, and war does

not affect his tables, his hunt, his places of pleasure, his court festivals, and so on. Thus, he can decide to go to war for the most meaningless of reasons, as if it were a kind of pleasure party, and he can blithely leave its justification (which decency requires) to his diplomatic corps, who are always prepared for such exercises. (Kant 1983, 113)

Among nineteenth-century statesmen, William Gladstone most explicitly adhered to the liberal vision "which favors the pacific, not the bloody settlement of disputes, which aims at permanent and not temporary adjustments; above all, which recognizes as a tribunal of paramount authority, the general judgement of civilized mankind" (quoted in Kissinger 1994, 164). The essence of the liberal thesis is thus a distinction between the peaceful public and leaders who may, for a broad range of reasons, pursue policies that lead to war. British Foreign Minister Ernest Bevin succinctly summarized the Kantian case for public opinion as a barrier to war when he told Parliament in November 1945: "There has never been a war yet which, if the facts had been put calmly before ordinary folk, could not have been prevented. The common man is the greatest protection against war."[2]

Although the liberal position on the desirability of engaging the public in the conduct of foreign affairs boasts a distinguished lineage, an equally formidable array of theorists and statesmen in the realist tradition has taken a much more skeptical stance on the public's contribution to enlightened and effective diplomacy. In contrast to most liberal theories, realism has generally been grounded in a pessimistic theory of human nature, either a theological version (for example, St. Augustine and Reinhold Niebuhr), or a secular one (for example, Machiavelli, Hobbes, and Hans Morgenthau). Man is by nature self-regarding and is largely motivated by such passions as greed and fear, qualities that are not lost when men are aggregated into political units such as nation-states.

Because realists are skeptical of institutional arrangements for promoting international cooperation in an anarchical system, to say nothing of philosophers' blueprints for regulating international relations or ensuring peace, they typically rely upon balance-of-power strategies for defending national interests. Viscount Palmerston's widely quoted aphorism that Great Britain has no permanent friends or enemies, only permanent interests, summarizes a cardinal rule of realist statecraft. But the flexibility required to pursue balance-of-power politics effectively may run contrary to public sentiments. Because the public is likely to be interested in "nationality, justice, or traditional friendships and enmities," selling the proposition that yesterday's friend is today's enemy, and vice versa, may not be easy (Wright 1965, 265). Realists have typically viewed both friends and enemies from an instrumental perspective; they are means to the common end of defending vital national interests. In contrast, according to realist critics, the public is more likely to view relations with other countries as ends in themselves. Thus, realists usually describe public opinion as a barrier to any thoughtful and coherent foreign policy, hindering efforts to promote national interests that may transcend the moods and passions of the moment.

The skepticism of the realists could also be found among the founding fathers who formulated and debated the U.S. Constitution. Alexander Hamilton and others expressed grave doubts about the wisdom of the general public. The authors of the *Federalist Papers* argued that the Senate (an appointed body until early in the twentieth century) rather than the directly elected House of Representatives was the body best suited to playing a key role in the conduct of foreign affairs. Because a reliable and stable member of the government is necessary in order to gain "the respect and confidence of other nations," the Senate is to be preferred to the "numerous and changeable" House. "Without a select and stable member of the government, the esteem of foreign powers will . . . be forfeited by unenlightened and variable policy." Moreover, in order to enact foreign policies that will be in the interest of the country as a whole, it is best to rely on a body of the legislature that is not so directly responsible to the public, as is the House. In foreign policy matters, the Senate can serve as a "defence to the people against their own temporary errors and delusions." Senators are also in a better position to gain the expertise and preserve the secrecy essential to the effective conduct of foreign policy. Finally, according to Hamilton, the fluctuating character of the House makes it the less suitable body for ratifying treaties. "Accurate and comprehensive knowledge of foreign politics; a steady and systematic adherence to the same views; a nice and uniform sensibility to national character; decision, *secrecy,* and dispatch, are incompatible with the genius of a body [the House of Representatives] so variable and so numerous." Taken together, these arguments add up to a concise statement of the realist case for shielding the nation's foreign and security policy from the assumed vagaries of the public and the institution, the House of Representatives, which most directly represented it (Hamilton, Jay, and Madison 1937, nos. 62–64, 75).

Several decades later, Alexis de Tocqueville, a sympathetic French analyst of American society and politics, questioned whether democracies could satisfy the requirements for the effective conduct of diplomatic affairs. After admitting that it is "very difficult to ascertain, at present, what degree of sagacity the American democracy will display in the conduct of . . . foreign policy," he nevertheless expressed his own judgment in terms applicable not only to the United States but to all democracies: "As for myself, I do not hesitate to say that it is especially in the conduct of their foreign relations that democracies appear to be decidedly inferior to other governments." His analysis went on to identify the "propensity that induces democracies to obey impulse rather than prudence, and to abandon a mature design for the gratification of a momentary passion" as the essential barrier to effective foreign policymaking. In contrast to the aristocracy—"a firm and enlightened body"—the "mass of the people may be led astray by ignorance and passion" (Tocqueville 1958, 1:243–45). These putative qualities of the general public identified by Tocqueville—ignorance and passion—lie at the heart of virtually all realist critiques of public opinion.

At this point it is appropriate to introduce a question that I will also revisit later. Do domestic and foreign policy differ sufficiently so that they require separate normative and empirical theories? More specifically, do these differences extend to the role of public opinion in these two realms of policy? Realists and liberals often vary in their approaches to this question as well. Realists generally answer the question in the affirmative, asserting that foreign affairs are indeed sufficiently unlike domestic issues to require differences in the processes by which policy is formulated; even some liberals, for example, John Locke, would accept this distinction.[3] According to realists the public might be sufficiently informed and motivated to deal with schools, zoning, and other local issues that impinge on their daily lives, but foreign affairs are too far removed from their experiences and, in any case, they have little time or inclination to become sufficiently informed about such complex and remote issues. Moreover, realists may sometimes concede that the quality of domestic policy might be enhanced by public deliberations but the benefits of public participation do not extend to foreign affairs. The effective conduct of diplomacy must often be based on sensitive intelligence or other confidential information that cannot be shared with the public. It usually requires secrecy, flexibility, speed of action, and other qualities that would be seriously jeopardized were the public to have a significant impact; and public passions would often make it impossible to conduct sensitive negotiations with either friends or adversaries abroad.

Thus, to permit the public a strong voice in policy would be to place democracies at a distinct disadvantage in their relations with other nations; doing so would perhaps even put the stability of the international system at risk. In this vein, Theodore Lowi (1967) has argued that democracies perform most effectively during crises, precisely the circumstances that reduce the impact of domestic "politics as usual." They perform less effectively in other circumstances; therefore, an important challenge is to "make democracy safe for the world." Hans Morgenthau summarized the case against an active role for public opinion in words that would gain the approval of most realists: "The rational requirements of good foreign policy cannot from the outset count upon the support of a public opinion whose preferences are emotional rather than rational" (Morgenthau 1978, 558).

These differences between liberals and realists often have been intensified by wars and major conflicts. Historians of various perspectives still argue about many questions relating to the impact of public opinion. Did angry farmers drive the Madison administration into an unnecessary war with Great Britain in 1812? Did public opinion, aroused by William Randolph Hearst, Joseph Pulitzer, and other masters of "yellow journalism," push the United States into war with Spain in 1898? Did the public, still scarred by the horrors of World War I, prevent Britain and France from realistically facing up to the threats posed by the expansionist dictatorships during the 1930s? Was Franklin Roosevelt forced to back off from his efforts to warn the world about the growing dangers of fascism—for example, by his "quarantine" speech in 1937—because of an outpouring of negative reactions from some prominent opinion leaders and several isolationist segments of the American public? Was the Truman administration "compelled by stiffening American opinion—vocally expressed in the Republican-controlled Eightieth Congress—to adopt the containment strategy"? (Crabb 1976, 91). In his efforts to gain public support for aid to Greece and Turkey in 1947 and other aspects of the containment policy, did Truman help to create a hypervigilant public mood that ultimately made him a captive of his own rhetoric?

World War I, which might be described as the first public relations war, was an especially significant event in the liberal-realist debate on the proper role of public opinion in diplomacy. From the war's inception, the Allied and Central Powers tried to win over "world opinion" in various ways, including publication by many foreign offices of highly selective document collections—the so-called color books—all of which were intended to absolve them from responsibility for the war while placing the entire blame on their adversaries. The propaganda war during the conflict was almost as intense as that on the battlefield. As the most powerful nonbelligerent, the United States was an especially important target of vigorous propaganda efforts by both sides until it entered the war in April 1917.[4]

President Wilson's hopes for a new postwar world order depended significantly on democratizing foreign affairs and diplomacy. In his war message of April 2, 1917, he declared that "A steadfast concert for peace can never be maintained except by partnership of democratic nations. No autocratic government could be trusted to keep faith within it or observe its covenants. It must be a league of honor, a partnership of opinion . . . Only free people can hold their purpose and their honor steady to a common end and prefer the interests of mankind to any narrow interest of their own" (Wilson 1917, 1:1). "Open covenants openly arrived at," an important feature of Bentham's blueprint for perpetual peace, was the first of Wilson's Fourteen Points and among his most important procedural prescriptions for reforming an international order in which secret diplomacy allegedly had dragged nation after nation into the catastrophic war against the will and interests of its ordinary citizens. The last of the Fourteen Points, the creation of a general international organization, had a similar goal of bringing diplomacy within the purview of world public opinion. During the war Wilson had stated:

> The counsels of plain men have become on all hands more simple and straightforward and more unified than the counsels of sophisticated men of affairs, who still retain the impression that they are playing a game of power and are playing for high stakes. That is why I have said that this is a people's war, not a statesman's. Statesmen must follow the clarified common thought or be broken.[5]

Wilson's faith in the public was not limited to abstract political theory. Throughout his career he had looked to the public as the court of final appeal for his most important projects. When faced with Senate opposition to the Treaty of Versailles, within which the League of Nations Covenant was embedded, he believed that direct appeals to the public would force the Senate to accept the treaty without the modifications proposed by Senator Henry Cabot Lodge and many other Republicans.

In September 1919, the president undertook a nationwide speaking tour, intending to go over the heads of the Senate by taking his case for the League of Nations directly to the people.[6] However, three weeks after leaving Washington, after a well-received speech in

Pueblo, Colorado, Wilson suffered a serious stroke. His illness ended the tour and reduced his effectiveness for the remainder of his presidency. The initial Senate vote on the treaty defeated it by a vote of thirty-nine to fifty-five, as forty-two Democrats loyally followed Wilson's request to reject it because of the Lodge reservations. In a later Senate vote, the Versailles Treaty was approved by a margin (forty-nine to thirty-five) that fell short of meeting the constitutional requirement of a two-thirds favorable majority, again in large part because of the president's unwillingness to accept the Lodge package of reservations on the league covenant.

Yet Wilson optimistically staked his hopes for a reversal of that verdict by relying once again on the public. The 1920 presidential election would serve, he hoped, as "a great and solemn referendum" on the League of Nations. In fact the campaign predictably revolved around a wide variety of issues, ranging from prohibition to independence for Ireland. The 1920 Democratic platform and presidential candidate supported the league, but the Republican platform was sufficiently ambiguous such that both supporters and opponents of the league could believe it expressed their preferences. The resulting landslide victory for the Republican ticket headed by Warren G. Harding effectively ended the debate on American participation in the League of Nations.

Although Wilson's faith in the wisdom and power of public opinion did not save the Treaty of Versailles, his hopes for the beneficial effects of democratizing foreign policymaking were not merely the lonely, utopian longings of a former college professor. Elihu Root, arguably the most distinguished Republican foreign policy leader of the time—he was a former secretary of war, secretary of state, and U.S. Senator, as well as the winner of the 1912 Nobel Peace Prize— effectively summarized the reasoning of those who welcomed an increasing role for the public in the conduct of foreign affairs. In the lead article of the initial issue of *Foreign Affairs,* published by the Council on Foreign Relations, Root eloquently expressed the case for democratizing foreign policy.

> When foreign affairs were ruled by autocracies or oligarchies the danger of war was in sinister purpose. When foreign affairs are ruled by democracies the danger of war will be in mistaken beliefs. The world will be the gainer by the change, for, while there is no human way to prevent a king from having a bad heart, there is a human way to prevent a people from having an erroneous opinion.

By more effective international education, "the people themselves will have the means to test misinformation and appeals to prejudice and passion based on error."[7] Root was not alone among notable conservatives in placing emphasis upon public opinion as a force for peace. Frank Kellogg and Henry Stimson, Republican secretaries of state, counted on public opinion as a pillar of support for the Kellogg-Briand Pact (also known as the Pact of Paris).

But not all observers of postwar world affairs joined Wilson and Root in applauding the prospect of popular diplomacy. A young journalist, Walter Lippmann, was among the leading skeptics. Lippmann had accepted an appointment in the Wilson administration during World War I that gave him insight into the uses and effects on public opinion of wartime propaganda. Disillusioned by the compromises that President Wilson made at the Paris Peace Conference, he and his colleagues at the *New Republic* unanimously opposed the Versailles Treaty on grounds quite similar to those of the most irreconcilable isolationists in the Senate: "Americans would be fools if they permitted themselves now to be embroiled in a system of European alliances" (Steel 1980, 159).

During the next few years, Lippmann undertook a full-scale attack on the liberal case for public opinion. In two book-length treatises that adopted a sociopsychological perspective on politics, he challenged the core premises of classical liberal democratic philosophy. Liberal theory assumed that, if given the facts, the public could and would make reasonable decisions. In contrast, Lippmann most emphatically questioned whether the average citizen could make any constructive contribution to world affairs (Lippmann 1922, 1925). "He lives in a world which he cannot see, does not understand, and is unable to direct" (Lippmann 1925, 14).

Liberal theory was, according to Lippmann, wrong on several counts. The common man is too fully involved in the requirements of earning a living and in otherwise attending to his most immediate needs to have the time or inclination to satisfy the heroic, but what he argued were the clearly unrealistic assumptions about the informed and engaged citizen celebrated in classical democratic theory. The chasm between theory and reality is especially wide in the realm of foreign affairs, which are typically far removed from the direct experiences of the general public. Because the "pictures in the head" of the average citizen are unlikely to have much correspondence to the real world of international affairs, according to Lippmann, even were the public inclined to take an active part in foreign affairs, it could scarcely make an informed and constructive contribution. In fact, these "pictures" are likely to be little more than stereotypes that, in turn, color the manner in which reality is perceived. Thus, average citizens are not unlike those portrayed in Plato's allegory of the cave; instead of observing reality directly, they can see only indirect and inadequate representations of it. His remedy was also not unlike Plato's: the salvation of the democratic polity requires greater reliance upon the experts.

Finally, journalist Lippmann was not notably sanguine when he contemplated the role that his profession could play in bridging the gap between the real world and the average citizen's stereotypes. In a short book published in 1920, he had outlined the inadequacies of the press and questioned "whether government by consent can survive in a time when the manufacture of consent is an unregulated private enterprise. For in an exact sense the present crisis of western civilization is a crisis of journalism" (Lippmann 1920, 5). He also presented some proposals for improving the performance of the media.

With his *New Republic* colleague Charles Merz, Lippmann also undertook an empirical analysis of the press, focusing on the Russian Revolution as depicted on the pages of America's "newspaper of record"—the *New York Times*—during the period 1917–20. As a standard against which to measure the performance of the *Times,* their assessment included only events that unquestionably had occurred: failure of the July 1917 Russian offensive in Galicia; overthrow of the Kerensky Provisional Government by the Bolsheviks in November 1917; the Russian-German peace treaty of Brest-Litovsk in March 1918; failure of the White Generals' campaign against the Bolsheviks; and maintenance of power by the Bolsheviks through March 1920. The study did little to assuage Lippmann's pessimism about the ability of the media to serve as a source of valid information about the world for the public. Lippmann and Merz concluded that coverage of these events was inadequate and misleading: "In the large, the news about Russia is a case of seeing not what was, but what men wished to see. . . . From the point of view of professional journalism the reporting of the Russian Revolution is nothing short of a disaster. On the essential questions the net effect was almost always misleading, and misleading news is worse than none at all. . . . The Russian policy of the editors of the *Times* profoundly and crassly influenced their news columns" (Lippmann and Merz 1920, 2, 3, 42).

Although Lippmann's books were written long before public opinion polling had become a "science" and a pervasive feature of American society—and before he had achieved the status of a widely

read, frequently quoted, and immensely influential syndicated columnist—they have had an extraordinary and continuing impact on students of public opinion and the role of the media. As a recent reviewer
put it, "Lippmann's theories are the diving board from which scholars
in these two disciplines take their plunge."[8] (Isaacs 1994, 2–3).

As has often been the case, the ebb and flow of the liberal-realist
debate depended at least as much on the course of contemporary
world events as on the eloquence and logic of supporters and critics
for one side or the other. The events leading up to the outbreak of
World War II, which seemed to raise serious questions about the
optimistic Wilsonian premises while apparently providing compelling
empirical confirmation for the realist approach to international politics, further tipped the balance in the debate on public opinion and
foreign policy in favor of the skeptics. Hitler's ability to arouse public
support for breaking out of the international order established at the
Versailles Peace Conference, as well as for more aggressive steps
later; the tepid response of the British and French publics to Japanese,
German, and Italian expansion during the 1930s; and American isolationism in the face of mounting evidence that the post–World War I
international order was collapsing—were all among developments
cited by realists to sustain their doubts about the ability of general
publics to contribute constructively to foreign policy.

The realist British diplomat and historian, Edward Hallett Carr,
wrote perhaps the most savage attack on Wilsonian liberalism and its
nineteenth-century intellectual foundations, with a special emphasis
on what he called the liberal "doctrine of salvation by public opinion"
(Carr 1941, 33). While his polemics were aimed at a wide array of
liberal targets, including those who supported the League of Nations
or who asserted that world public opinion would provide an effective
sanction against aggression, Carr's most powerful attacks were directed at the Wilsonians and their faith in public opinion.

> Woodrow Wilson's "plain men throughout the world," the
> spokesmen of "the common purpose of enlightened mankind,"
> had somehow transformed themselves into a disorderly mob
> emitting incoherent and unhelpful noises. It seemed undeniable
> that, in international affairs, public opinion was almost as often
> wrong-headed as it was impotent. . . . Governments of many
> countries acted in a sense precisely contrary to this [expert] ad-
> vice [on how to conduct foreign policy], and received the en-
> dorsement of public opinion at the polls. . . . The breakdown of
> the post-War utopia is too overwhelming to be explained merely

in terms of individual action or inaction. Its downfall involves the bankruptcy of the postulates [about public opinion] on which it is based (Carr 1941, 50–53).

The Inception of "Scientific" Opinion Polling

The period encompassing World War II and its immediate aftermath coincided with the inception of "scientific" public opinion polling. The 1936 presidential election provided something of an unplanned critical experiment on two approaches to polling. The *Literary Digest* magazine used a method that had enabled it correctly to predict the winner in several previous presidential elections, including Franklin Roosevelt's victory over Herbert Hoover in 1932. In the 1936 Roosevelt-Landon election it sent out ten million ballots. The magazine described its poll as "the most extensive straw ballot it the field—the most experienced in view of its twenty-five years of perfecting—the most unbiased in view of its prestige—a Poll that has always been correct." From its returns of more than two million ballots, it confidently forecast a Landon victory of landslide proportions: the Kansas governor was predicted to win 57 percent of the popular vote and 370 votes in the electoral college (*Literary Digest* 1936, 5–6). In fact, Landon carried only Maine and Vermont, and the *Literary Digest* folded before it could try to salvage its reputation in the 1940 presidential election.[9]

In contrast, the recently established American Institute of Public Opinion, more popularly known as the Gallup poll, used a sampling design that yielded far fewer respondents but a more representative sample. Gallup correctly predicted the outcome but even his poll underestimated the magnitude of the Roosevelt electoral avalanche. Nevertheless, we can date the beginning of the era of scientific surveys from the establishment in 1935 of the Gallup poll or of the *Public Opinion Quarterly* three years later.[10]

Polling also became a part of the policy process. In an effort to influence public attitudes on foreign policy, the State Department had established a Division of Information before World War I. The State Department later undertook its own polling to assess public attitudes (see Elder 1957; White 1959; Chittick 1970; and Foster 1983). President Roosevelt was a pioneer in the use of a professional public opinion consultant—Hadley Cantril, one of the founding fathers of the new science—for guidance on policy on both domestic and foreign policy. Roosevelt had an extraordinary interest in public opinion and there is ample evidence that his foreign policy actions were significantly shaped and constrained by his sense of what was politically feasible, given the climate of domestic opinion (Dallek 1979). Virtually all presidents since Roosevelt, even those who have expressed disdain for "policy by polls," have engaged the services of public opinion specialists. Cantril not only advised FDR in this capacity, but he went on to serve as a consultant to the Eisenhower and Kennedy administrations.

Theory and research on international relations have almost always been shaped by contemporary events in the real world. It is impossible to understand the agenda that dominated research and writing on public opinion and foreign policy during the first quarter century after the inception of scientific polling without reference to the central policy question of the period: namely, what role would the United States play in the postwar international system? Members of the Roosevelt administration and many others who felt that an irresponsible American isolationism after 1919 had contributed to the breakdown of the Versailles world order and the consequent outbreak of war feared that after World War II, the public mood might trace out a pattern resembling the experience of the earlier conflict: that is, wartime idealism and internationalism, followed soon thereafter by cynicism and disenchantment with active American leadership in efforts to create a new and more stable international order, and concluding, ultimately, with withdrawal.

During the decade before Pearl Harbor, the essential lessons of World War I for many Americans could be summarized by two words: never again! When war broke out in Europe in 1939, an overwhelming proportion of the public favored the Western allies over Germany—even a Soviet victory was seen as preferable to a German one—but sentiments for staying out of the war were even stronger.[11] Isolationists, Anglophobes, revisionist historians, and the congressional hearings conducted by Senator Gerald Nye had persuaded many Americans that the nations's entry into World War I—a "war to end all wars"—had more to do with the machinations of American munitions makers, bankers, and other wealthy holders of British bonds than with the prudent pursuit of national interests. Consequently, many Americans came to hold highly skeptical views of the nation's participation in that conflict and a resulting determination never again to become embroiled in war for reasons short of a direct attack on the United States. Indeed, a 1937 Gallup poll revealed that fully 70 percent of the respondents answered in the affirmative when asked, "Do you think it was a mistake for the United States to enter the World War?" That opinion remained virtually unchanged as late as a month after the German invasion of Poland in 1939, when 68 percent stated that it had been a mistake.

Perhaps of even greater importance, much of the public looked to the experience of World War I as a rich source of "lessons" to guide U.S. foreign policy. During the 1930s Congress had regularly passed neutrality legislation that was aimed at preventing a recurrence of the policies and actions that, according to many isolationists, had led the United States into war in 1917. The Ludlow Amendment to the Constitution, which required a national referendum before any declaration of war unless it was in response to an invasion of the United States, failed in the House of Representatives by only a handful of votes despite diligent lobbying against it by the president and Secretary of State Cordell Hull. A series of Gallup surveys conducted between 1935 and 1939 revealed consistently strong support for several key propositions that, according to isolationists, would prevent the nation from being unwisely dragged into war, as it was in 1917.[12] These were, specifically:

Restraints on the executive

In order to declare war, the Congress should be required to obtain approval of the people in a national referendum. Seventy-five percent of respondents to a September 1935 Gallup survey agreed with this proposition, and it gained the approval of 71 and 73 percent of those taking part in surveys during the next two years. By February 1939, after the Ludlow Amendment had been defeated in the House of Representatives and seven months before World War II began in Europe, this proposal still had the support of almost sixty percent of the public.

In March 1939, 61 percent supported a constitutional amendment to require a national vote before Congress could draft men to fight overseas. Support for such an amendment declined to 51 percent six months later.

According to more than two-thirds of those taking part in a 1937 survey, Congress is more to be trusted than the president to keep the United States out of war.

Restraints on Americans abroad

Americans should not be permitted to engage in certain types of risky behavior because doing so might drag the United States into war. For example, only 18 percent agreed in September 1939 that American citizens should be allowed to travel on ships of warring countries. The same survey revealed that even fewer respondents (16 percent) agreed that American ships should be allowed to carry goods anywhere rather than be kept out of war zones.

American citizens in China should be warned to leave and the troops protecting them should be withdrawn, according to 54 percent of respondents in August 1937. A similar proposal garnered even higher support (70 percent) four months later.

Restraints on arms and arms makers

The manufacture and sale of war munitions for private profit should be prohibited according to 82 percent of those to whom the question was posed in January 1936.

In surveys conducted in 1937 and 1938, two-thirds of the public favored a world disarmament conference.

Almost two-thirds of the public opposed arms shipments to China in February 1938. Five months earlier an overwhelming 95 percent had opposed any bank loans to China or Japan.

By early 1939, a very small majority (52 percent) agreed that the United States should sell arms to Britain and France. However, after war had broken out in Europe in September 1939, 90 percent of respondents wanted Great Britain and France to pay cash, rather than be given credit, for American goods. An even greater proportion (94 percent) agreed that those countries should be required to carry the goods away on their own ships.

Internationalists regarded the outbreak of World War II as the direct result of a shortsighted and futile isolationist agenda. Even some devout isolationists experienced a conversion. For example, Senator Arthur Vandenberg, a leading isolationist and Republican presidential hopeful, began his diary on December 7, 1941, with the observation that "In my own mind, my convictions regarding international cooperation and collective security for peace took form on the afternoon of the Pearl Harbor attack. That day ended isolationism for any realist" (Vandenberg 1952, 1). But there could be no assurance that others would read the lessons of the interwar period in the same manner. Because rejection by the Senate of the Treaty of Versailles symbolized for many internationalists the abdication of a responsible U.S. role in the postwar international order, a central question was whether the United States would join or again turn its back on membership in a general international organization after World War II.

Interest in the postwar state of American public opinion was reflected in the frequency with which the Gallup and other polling organizations asked respondents general questions about the United States taking an active role in or staying out of world affairs and more specific queries about support for or opposition to American membership in a general international organization. These surveys seemed to indicate that substantial majorities among the general public in fact rejected a return to isolationism after the war. A February 1943 Gallup survey revealed that, by a margin of 76 to 14 percent, Americans preferred taking "an active role" rather than "staying out" of postwar international affairs. The same question was posed five additional times between February 1944 and November 1946, a period spanning the Normandy invasion, the defeat of Nazi Germany, the atomic bomb attacks on Japan, the end of World War II, and the first signs that wartime cooperation among the victorious Allies would not extend into the postwar period. Responses to each of those surveys indicated, by margins ranging between three to one and four to one, that the public rejected an American retreat from an active international role. Further evidence that the public might reject isolationism emerged from a question posed just as the guns were being stilled in Europe. A strong majority of Americans supported the reciprocal trade agreement program as well as its use for further reductions of tariffs in the United States and abroad (Gallup 1972, 505).

Public sentiments on another key issue should also have provided some comfort for internationalists, as Gallup surveys revealed comparably strong support for U.S. membership in some kind of general international organization. As early as July 1941, several months before the attack on Pearl Harbor brought the United States into the war, almost three-fourths of the general public favored American entry into such an organization. Although the nature of the organization and the specific obligations of membership could not have been known at that time, these results appear to have reflected a rather sharp shift in public sentiment since the mid-1930s. Interestingly, only a month later a survey of leaders drawn from *Who's Who in America* revealed that support among elites for U.S. participation in an international organization fell somewhat short of that among the general public.

A June 1944 Gallup poll also suggested that President Roosevelt's efforts to avoid some of Woodrow Wilson's mistakes in dealing with the League of Nations issue were bearing fruit; 72 percent of the respondents favored American membership in a successor to the League of Nations, and differences between Democrats and Republicans were negligible (Gallup 1972, 451–52). Wilson had broken a tacit wartime agreement to mute partisanship by asking the electorate to support him with Democratic House and Senate majorities in midterm elections held just as peace was settling over Europe in 1918; he failed to include any prominent Republicans in the American delegation to the Versailles Peace Conference; he allowed his deep personal animosity toward Republican Senator Henry Cabot Lodge, chairman of the Foreign Relations Committee after the 1918 elections gave the Republicans majorities in both the House and Senate, to color his strategy for guiding the Versailles Treaty through the Senate; and, finally, he rejected even moderate compromises to the treaty in the hopes of ultimately winning on all its features. As he put it, "I would rather be defeated in a cause that will ultimately triumph, than to win in a cause that will ultimately be defeated" (quoted in Kegley 1993, 131).

Unlike Wilson, Roosevelt had engaged such leading Republicans as John Foster Dulles in planning for a postwar international organization, and he avoided casting the issue in partisan terms. Indeed, the agreement between Secretary of State Cordell Hull and Dulles, the foreign policy adviser to Republican candidate Thomas Dewey, to keep the United Nations issue out of the 1944 presidential campaign is often cited as the genesis of "bipartisanship" in foreign policy. The June 1944 Gallup survey revealed Republicans were scarcely less inclined than Democrats to support American membership in the United Nations. Even respondents from the Midwest, often considered the most congenial region for isolationism, did not in fact differ on this issue from those living in other sections of the country.

This reassuring survey evidence notwithstanding, fears of a postwar return to isolationism persisted. Roosevelt's concerns in this respect were amplified by a memorandum that Hadley Cantril gave the president just before he left for the Yalta Conference with Churchill and Stalin early in 1945. According to Cantril:

> Although the overwhelming majority of the American people now favor a strong international organization necessarily dominated by the big powers, it is unrealistic to assume that Americans are international-minded. Their policy is rather one of expediency, which, at the moment, takes the form of internationalism. The present internationalism rests on a rather unstable foundation: it is recent, it is not rooted in any broad or long-range conception of self-interest, it has little intellectual basis. (Cantril 1967, 76)

This advice reinforced Roosevelt's own judgment. He said privately, "Anybody who thinks that isolationism is dead in this country is crazy. As soon as this war is over, it may well be stronger than ever" (quoted in Schlesinger 1995, 4). Roosevelt also told his allies that public opinion would not permit American occupation troops to remain in Europe for more than two years after the end of the war.

Although attended only by the soon-to-be victorious Allies, the 1945 San Francisco conference from which the United Nations Charter emerged was marked by disagreement on a number of issues. American participation in the UN nevertheless won overwhelming support in the Senate as only two dissenting votes were cast. Thus, the United States joined the United Nations when that organization came into existence in October 1945. Despite success in the campaign to bring the United States into the United Nations, proponents of an active American role in postwar international affairs continued to worry that there might soon be a reversion to withdrawal, and they usually focused their attention on public opinion as the most likely driving force behind any return to isolationism. Consequently, research on the relationship of public opinion to foreign policy emerged as a growth industry during the period immediately following World War II. Much of the analysis and writing on the question was marked by two features: an *empirical* approach that relied heavily on the growing body of polling data, and a *normative* concern that mood swings among the public might lead the United States to repeat the failed isolationist policies of the interwar years. Both these features may be found in three of the pioneering works on public opinion and foreign policy: Thomas A. Bailey's *The Man in the Street* (1948), Lester Markel's *Public Opinion and Foreign Policy* (1949), and Gabriel Almond's *The American People and Foreign Policy* (1950). Each of these works examined the growing body of evidence produced by the Gallup Poll, the Office of Public Opinion Research at Princeton, the National Opinion Research Center (NORC), and other major survey organizations. Finding very little in the data to assuage their concerns, they came to share a distinctly skeptical view of the man in the street and his potential contributions toward the conduct of postwar American foreign policy. Fears that an ill-informed and emotion-driven American public would force the country back into an irresponsible isolationism generated a substantial postwar research effort.

An Overview

The consensus that emerged from much of this research during the two decades following the end of World War II, which I will review in chapter 2, painted an unflattering portrait of the general public. Public opinion was described as not only ignorant about international realities, but also as volatile, reflecting unstable moods of the moment rather than an understanding of international realities, as well as lacking in any structure or coherence. Although some observers feared that a feckless public would severely damage the prospects for a coherent foreign policy, others assured these critics that, in fact, public opinion seldom if ever has a significant impact on actual policy decisions.

Just as the two world wars of this century stimulated interest in the public's impact on foreign policy, the Vietnam War served as a catalyst for serious reexamination of the post-World War II consensus on the nature and effects of public opinion. Although these more recent studies continued to show that the public is often poorly informed about international affairs, the evidence nevertheless challenged the theses that public opinion on foreign policy issues is volatile, structureless, and without significant impact on policymaking. Following a summary of these research efforts, chapter 3 then turns to some further evidence about the nature of public opinion by examining survey data on attitudes toward several of the most important clusters of issues of the Cold War era: namely, the nature of the Soviet Union and its foreign policy goals; prospects for conflict or cooperation between Washington and Moscow in general, as well as on such specific issues as arms control; and appropriate U.S. foreign policy goals.

Chapter 4 compares the general public and opinion leaders—the relatively small stratum of the public that is most likely to be interested in, informed about, and influential upon the way in which the United States copes with international challenges and opportunities. The chapter first examines data on the *content* of opinions about several international issues, including the appropriate U.S. role in the world, trade and protectionism, economic and technical assistance, military assistance, deployment of U.S. troops abroad, and foreign policy goals. The analysis then turns to the *structure* of foreign policy beliefs, presenting evidence about appraisals of the international system, future threats to U.S. national security, the Persian Gulf War, and the sources of change in Eastern Europe and the former Soviet Union. Chapter 4 concludes with an examination of the relationship between *domestic* and foreign policy beliefs among opinion leaders.

Chapter 5 focuses on the *sources* of foreign policy beliefs among both the general public and opinion leaders. The hypothesis that partisan and ideological differences have, since the Vietnam War, increasingly become the driving forces behind debates on the conduct of American foreign policy is examined in some detail. The chapter also

presents evidence about other background factors that are often identified as important sources of foreign policy attitudes, including generation, gender, education, region, and race.

Chapter 6 addresses the question: "Where do we go from here?"
It develops the thesis that public opinion is likely to play a more rather
than less potent role during the post–Cold War era, at least in part
because the "new" issues that are likely to gain prominence on foreign
policy agendas—including but not limited to trade, immigration, the
environment, and civil wars arising from nationalism, religion, and
ethnicity—are more likely to be resistant to executive arguments that
the requirements of secrecy, speed, and flexibility justify excluding
the public and its representatives from the policy process. The chapter
then turns to some of the ways in which our understanding of public
opinion and its impact might be strengthened. The conclusion adduces
some anecdotal evidence to suggest that, although there is compelling
evidence that the public is often ill informed about specific aspects of
world affairs, we nevertheless have more to fear from processes and
policies that blatantly disregard public sentiments than from those that
make a serious effort to engage the public in discussions of such
central questions as the scope and nature of American interests in
developing situations.

CHAPTER 2

The Post–World War II Consensus

Among the social scientists enlisted into the effort to win World War II were survey researchers. They undertook projects ranging from studies of morale among American soldiers (Stouffer et al. 1949) to the impact of strategic bombing on Germany (U.S. Strategic Bombing Survey 1947). Julian Woodward (1945, 245), who had worked in the Office of War Information, believed that ultimately such surveys would become a routine function of government.

> Sooner or later the government itself will have to go into the polling field and provide both its administrators and its legislators with adequate and sound information on what the public thinks. Eventually this sort of information will become as necessary as census data and will be provided by an agency with a reputation for unbiased research equal to that now enjoyed by the Census Bureau.

The inception of scientific public opinion polling was not universally applauded, however. Congress, suspicious of the political and social uses to which surveys could be put, dismantled much of the wartime apparatus for such studies. Even George Gallup, whose surveys had underestimated the Democratic vote in 1944—as they had also done in 1936 and 1940—was called before Congress to explain the errors of his ways (Jean Converse 1987, 207–10). Skeptics of surveys also existed outside Congress. One of them, Lester Markel, welcomed the startling failure of the Gallup and other polls to predict Harry Truman's victory over Thomas Dewey in the 1948 presidential election, and he ventured the judgment that as a result the practice of polling would be permanently discredited: "The poll, then, fortunately, has been dethroned from its high place. Government, Congress and the people will be better off" (Markel 1949, 31). But even Markel conceded that surveys might be useful for gaining some insight into the average citizen's knowledge, or lack thereof, about international affairs.

All of the many surveys undertaken during the years immediately following World War II to assess the level of public knowledge about international affairs came to essentially the same two conclusions. First, among the general population there is a wide variation in the level of factual information about world affairs, and the average citizen is remarkably uninformed, even about institutions, events, and personalities that have been the focus of current news and controversies. Soon after the United States joined the United Nations as a charter member, a National Opinion Research Center (NORC) survey in Cincinnati revealed that few citizens had much interest in or knowledge about that international organization. Even a rather simple six-question test found that 30 percent of the respondents were "uninformed" about the UN, and another 27 percent were "poorly informed" (National Opinion Research Center 1947).[1] Other evidence indicated that the citizens of Cincinnati were not unusual in this respect (Cottrell and Eberhart 1948).

In the same manner, Thomas Bailey's (1948) pioneering study of public opinion and foreign policy, based on the growing archives of survey evidence at the Gallup Organization and elsewhere, sketched a distinctly unflattering portrait of *The Man in the Street*. His chapter titles—for example, "The Perils of Apathy," "The Incubus of Ignorance," "The Curse of Caprice," and "The Fruits of Isolation"—provide ample clues to the substance of Bailey's main fears and findings. Martin Kriesberg (1949) undertook a similar study of the survey evidence and, in a chapter entitled "Dark Areas of Ignorance," he emerged with conclusions that sustained those of the Cincinnati and Bailey studies. Gabriel Almond's *The American People and Foreign Policy* (1950), the most important and systematic analysis of survey data on the topic to that point, reinforced the conclusion that despite the dramatic events of the previous decade—including World War II, the start of the nuclear era, the nation's emergence as a world leader, and the onset of the Cold War—many Americans remained remarkably uninformed about even the most elementary aspects of international affairs.

Research undertaken by educators would be unlikely to applaud widespread ignorance about the world and, indeed, all these studies pointed to the need for better international education. The mere fact of public ignorance, however, was not the sole reason for worry. Concerns about the lack of basic information about international affairs were reinforced, perhaps even magnified, by a second finding that emerged consistently from the survey data. One's level of knowledge about the world was typically correlated with attitudes toward many important aspects of international affairs, including global institu-

tions, other nations, and appropriate U.S. foreign policies for coping
with postwar issues. For example, the Cincinnati study found that
among the better-informed respondents, 76 percent thought that
America should take an active part in world affairs, 55 percent mentioned an international problem as among those confronting the
United States, and 61 percent agreed that they would benefit person-
ally from increased foreign trade. Among the "uninformed," the comparable figures were 41 percent, 29 percent, and 41 percent (National
Opinion Research Center 1947).

More generally, respondents within the least informed strata of
the public were also most likely to be isolationist, chauvinist, suspicious of other nations, and generally opposed to policies that involved international cooperation, whether in the United Nations,
through the Marshall Plan, or in the North Atlantic Treaty Organization (NATO). Conversely, the most informed strata of the public also
tended to provide the strongest support for the wide array of international undertakings that constituted what was often described as the
post–World War II "revolution in U.S. foreign policy."

In short, much of the research during the years immediately
following the end of the World War II was driven by the same normative concerns that had engaged internationalists during the war—the
fear that the public would in fact validate Hadley Cantril's warning to
President Roosevelt, cited in the previous chapter, by retreating from
its temporary and shallow enthusiasm for an active international role
once the fighting had ended. Thomas Bailey (1950, 907) expressed
views that more or less represented a shared outlook among many
pioneers in the study of public opinion and foreign policy.

The statesmen in charge of American foreign policy, as well as
the better-informed citizens, know that isolation is not only dead
but dangerous; that we must learn to see the other nation's problems as they appear to its eyes; that we must cultivate tolerance
and understanding; that we must sublimate suspicion and ill-will;
that we must yield pride and prestige; that we must meet the other
fellow half way, sometimes more than half way; and that we must
invest some of our precious sovereignty in effective world organization—perhaps some kind of world government. But the average citizen—indifferent, ignorant, or misled by ill informed and
sometimes unscrupulous editors, columnists, radio commentators, and politicians—does not see all these things. Yet, as we
have repeatedly observed throughout this book, American public

opinion in the long run determines basic foreign policies. If the American people, through their Congress, insist upon isolation, non-cooperation, ruinous tariff barriers, and other impediments to world recovery, they will have their way—with consequent disaster.

The availability after World War II of growing archives of polling data and the institution of systematic studies of voting behavior, combined with the assumption of a leadership role in world affairs by the United States, served to stimulate many additional analyses of public opinion. A general consensus about the nature, structure, and impact of public opinion seemed to have emerged from those who focused their attention on international affairs during the period between the end of World War II and the escalation of the American military effort in Vietnam. It centered on three major propositions.

> Public opinion is highly volatile and thus provides very dubious foundations upon which to develop and sustain sound foreign policies.
> Public attitudes on international affairs are so lacking in structure or coherence that they might best be described as "nonopinions."
> At the end of the day, however, perhaps the deficiencies of the general public will not be so damaging because public opinion has a very limited impact on the conduct of foreign policy.

Let us examine each of these propositions and the evidence upon which they rest in more detail.

Public Opinion Is Volatile

In an early analysis of the sources and nature of public opinion, Gabriel Almond argued that most Americans invest their intellectual and emotional energies in private pursuits, to the neglect of public policy concerns. Policy issues that impinge directly on their daily lives may generate some interest and attention among the public, but remote international events rarely do so. Consequently, foreign policy issues give rise to mass indifference, punctuated by occasional apprehension or anger in response to international crises. Almond described these "superficial and fluctuating responses" as "plastic moods which undergo frequent alteration in response to changes in events" (Almond 1950, 53). Lacking any firm foundations in knowledge of or interest in international affairs, these moods are highly unstable but not necessarily random or unpredictable. Owing to some central tendencies in the American national character, Almond suggested that public mood swings would take place along several dimensions of direct relevance to foreign policy:

Withdrawal/intervention
Unstructured moods/policy simplification
Optimism/pessimism
Tolerance/intolerance
Idealism/cynicism
Superiority/inferiority

Almond proposed the hypothesis that these mood fluctuations are related to the business cycle. Specifically, he suggested that an economic depression would impair national self-confidence, weaken foreign policy resolution, result in feelings of international overextension, and lead ultimately to withdrawal (Almond 1950, 54–65).

To substantiate the thesis that public moods are highly volatile, Almond turned to one of the questions that had been posed repeatedly by Gallup surveys during the 1935–49 period: "What is the most important problem facing the United States today?" The evidence revealed striking shifts in the percentage of respondents who identified any foreign policy issue as "most important." Between November 1935 and January 1939 that figure ranged between 11 and 26 percent. During the first year after Hitler's invasion of Poland the figure rose to just under half of the respondents, and by November 1941 (just prior to Pearl Harbor), fully 81 percent of the public placed a foreign policy issue first on the agenda of the nation's most important problems. A month after the Japanese surrender in 1945, domestic issues again took top priority for an overwhelming proportion of the public as only 7 percent identified a foreign policy issue as the most important problem. During the next four years, the comparable figures ranged from a low of 11 percent in June 1946 (ten months after the Japanese surrender but before the Cold War) to a high of 73 percent less than two years later, when the Soviets had just instituted the Berlin blockade.[2]

Interpreting these data, however, is not unlike deciding whether a glass is half full or half empty. From Almond's perspective, the surveys revealed a fickle public whose limited attention span precluded a steady focus on important international problems. But the same figures do not automatically exclude an alternative and somewhat more flattering interpretation of shifts in public identification of the most

serious problems: the public reasonably focuses its attention on external problems when wars, crises, and confrontations pose a major
threat to the United States. When these international threats appear to
have faded or disappeared—for example, with the Japanese surrender
that ended World War II—public attention turns to more proximate
problems and threats that originate in the domestic arena; for example, unemployment, inflation, race relations, crime, and the like.

The explanation for these mood swings resembled those proposed by Tocqueville in the nineteenth century and Lippmann during
the 1920s. It could be found, according to Almond (1950, 76), in
general American value orientations:

> The average American is so deeply and tensely involved with
> immediate, private concerns that any diversion of attention meets
> with powerful resistance. When political issues impinge, or
> threaten to impinge, upon these concerns, public attention
> broadens to include them. But the moment the pressure is re-
> duced there is a swift withdrawal, like the snapping back of a
> strained elastic.

Although the half decade prior to Almond's study had witnessed
a number of major international commitments by the United States,
including membership in the United Nations and the North Atlantic
Treaty Organization, the Truman Doctrine, and the Marshall Plan,
Almond drew some sober policy conclusions from his analysis. The
possibility of a relapse into mindless isolationism could not be ruled
out because only a thin veneer of postwar internationalism covered a
thick bedrock of indifference to the world. Most leaders might understand that isolationism is no longer a viable option for the United
States, but public opinion could serve as a volatile and mood-driven
constraint upon foreign policy. "The undertow of withdrawal is still
very powerful. Deeply ingrained habits do not die easy deaths. The
world outside is still very remote for most Americans; and the tragic
lessons of the past decade have not been fully digested"(Almond
1950, 85). Consequently, "Perhaps the gravest general problem confronting policymakers is that of the instability of mass moods, and
cyclical fluctuations which stand in the way of policy stability" (Almond 1950, 239).

Six years later, Almond restated his thesis, citing not only the
instability of public moods but other deficiencies of public opinion as
well. He told an audience at the National War College, "For persons

responsible for the making of security policy these *mood* impacts of the mass public have a highly irrational effect. Often public opinion is apathetic when it should be concerned, and panicky when it should be calm" (Almond 1956, 59).[3]

Expressions of concern about the instability of public opinion were not limited to such academic analysts as historian Thomas Bailey and political scientist Gabriel Almond. George F. Kennan, a diplomat whose "long telegram" from Moscow in 1946 and subsequent "X" article in 1947 often have been depicted as the intellectual foundations of the American policy of containment, delivered a series of lectures in 1950 that examined the bases, assumptions, and practices of American diplomacy. Kennan's diagnosis, like those of Tocqueville and Almond, focused broadly on American society rather than solely on public opinion. From a realist perspective on world affairs, he raised some questions about the ability of a democratic society imbued with moralistic and legalistic values to conduct its external relations effectively. Using the metaphor of a dinosaur, Kennan (1951, 59) vividly depicted his views on the inept ways in which democracies attempt to cope with their international environments.

> But I sometimes wonder whether in this respect a democracy is not uncomfortably similar to one of those prehistoric monsters with a body as long as this room and a brain the size of a pin: he lies there in his comfortable primeval mud and pays little attention to his environment; he is slow to wrath—in fact, you practically have to whack his tail off to make him aware that his interests are being disturbed; but, once he grasps this, he lays about him with such blind determination that he not only destroys his adversary but largely wrecks his native habitat.

Kennan recognized that it would be impossible to eliminate altogether the impact of public opinion, but his prescription, like those of Bailey and Lippmann, placed a heavy emphasis on giving foreign policy experts a greater degree of latitude in the conduct of policy.

Walter Lippmann, who by the 1950s had become America's most influential political columnist, delivered still another attack on public opinion, charging that democracy run amok had come to threaten the possibility of formulating and implementing effective foreign policies. During the interwar period Lippmann had described the average citizen as indifferent and ill informed about the world and thus unable to play the role required by classical democratic theory. Moreover, he had repeatedly expressed doubts that the mass media could or would bridge the chasm between the public's stereotypes and international reality.

Three decades later, at the height of the Cold War, Lippmann had become even more alarmed about the prospects for democratic government because the "spirit of Jacobinism" had destroyed the proper balance between rulers and the ruled, resulting in "excesses of democracy" and "misrule by the people." While public opinion remained ignorant, in his view it had grown into an almost uncontrollable monster. "Where mass opinion dominates the government, there is a morbid derangement of the true functions of power. The derangement brings about the enfeeblement, verging on paralysis, of the capacity to govern." The consequences are no less than "the precipitate and catastrophic decline of Western society" (Lippmann 1955, 15). Tracing the roots of the problem to the need of democratic governments to pander to the public during World War I, Lippmann asserted that legislatures, representing the will of the public, had infringed seriously upon the proper prerogatives of the executive with disastrous consequences for the quality of foreign policy. Whereas his earlier analyses had emphasized the public's indifference and ignorance, by 1955 Lippmann (1955, 20) had come to see public opinion as a virtually irresistible, highly irresponsible, and potentially catastrophic element in the conduct of foreign affairs.

> The unhappy truth is that the prevailing public opinion has been destructively wrong at the critical junctures. The people have impressed a critical veto upon the judgments of informed and responsible officials. They have compelled the government, which usually knew what would have been wiser, or was necessary, or what was more expedient, to be too late with too little, or too long with too much, too pacifist in peace and too bellicose in war, too neutralist or appeasing in negotiations or too intransigent. Mass opinion has acquired mounting power in this country. It has shown itself to be a dangerous master of decision when the stakes are life and death.

Although Lippmann's book was intended to be a broad-ranging treatise on the philosophical foundations of all democratic governments rather than a commentary on contemporary American foreign policymaking, it is somewhat ironic that it was published during the first Eisenhower administration, a period when executive dominance of foreign policy had perhaps reached its peak. Congressional challenges to the executive role in the conduct of foreign relations, in the form of the Bricker Amendment on treaty powers, and Senator Joseph McCarthy's shotgun attacks on the State Department, Foreign Service, the U.S. Army, General George Marshall, and Presidents Truman and Eisenhower, to name just a few of his more prominent targets, had recently been beaten back. Indeed, formal censure by his colleagues effectively ended the power of the Senator from Wisconsin to wreak havoc upon American diplomacy. More generally, although Democrats regained control of Congress after the 1954 elections, the most vitriolic congressional attack on Eisenhower's foreign policies often came from right-wing Republicans. Although there were certainly partisan differences in congressional policy debates and votes, many disagreements of the period revolved around means, strategies, and tactics for achieving ends shared by most members on both sides of the aisle. (On this point, compare Wittkopf 1990 and Holsti and Rosenau 1984.) Moreover, it would be hard to find serious evidence that, during the Eisenhower years, public opinion was so significantly at variance with the main features of American external policies that it seriously hampered the ability of the White House to conduct foreign relations. Few foreign policy issues of the Eisenhower era divided the public along primarily partisan lines (Campbell, Converse, Miller, and Stokes 1964, 113–14; see also chap. 5). If the term *internationalist foreign policy consensus* was ever a valid description of the domestic bases of American foreign policy, it would appear to have been most applicable to the period between the traumas of the Korean and Vietnam Wars.

Many others contributed to the view that public opinion on foreign policy issues is highly volatile. By the mid-1960s, if not before, that conclusion had become a standard part of virtually all treatises and textbooks on the domestic sources of American foreign policy. Guided by Almond's (1950, 69) hypothesis that superficial attitudes are "bound to be unstable since they are not anchored in a set of explicit values and means calculations or traditional compulsions," studies directed at locating the sources of public volatility seemed to find the answer in the structure—or more precisely, in the lack of structure—of mass political beliefs.

Public Opinion Lacks Structure and Coherence

The growing volume of data on public opinion and voting behavior, as well as increasingly sophisticated methodologies, enabled analysts not only to describe aggregate results and trends but also to delve into the structure of political beliefs. Owing to immediate policy concerns about the U.S. role in the postwar era, many of the early studies were largely descriptive, focusing on attitudes toward such issues as participation in international organizations and alliances, the deployment of troops abroad, security commitments, foreign aid, protectionism, and the like. Would the United States accept internationalist and cooperative policies to deal with these and other issues, or would it retreat into a more isolationist stance? The underlying premise was that a single internationalist-to-isolationist dimension would serve to structure foreign policy beliefs, much in the same way that a liberal-to-conservative dimension was assumed to underlie preferences on domestic issues.

Challenges to the notion that there were ideological underpinnings to political thinking among the public that gave rise to coherent and consistent issue voting emerged most prominently from studies of American voters and the bases of their electoral decisions (Lazarsfeld, Berelson, and Gaudet 1944; Berelson, Lazarsfeld, and McPhee 1954; and Campbell, Converse, Miller, and Stokes 1964). In a classic study based on evidence from the late 1950s and early 1960s, Philip Converse (1964) analyzed the correlations across responses to questions on domestic and foreign policy issues, as well as between these two policy areas. Finding only very low correlations, he concluded that the political beliefs of the mass public lack any "constraint" or underlying ideological consistency that might provide genuine structure or coherence to political thinking and to the act of voting. It is worth noting that Converse's results did not yield much support for those who had argued that foreign policy attitudes constitute a special case because this issue area was more remote from the daily concerns of the average citizen. In contrast to these findings about the general public, his analyses of elites—congressional candidates—revealed substantially higher correlations across responses to various domestic and foreign policy issues. Moreover, Converse found that both mass and elite attitudes on a given issue had a short half-life. Responses to a question in 1956 only modestly predicted answers to the same question two years later, much less in 1960. These findings led him to conclude that mass political beliefs are best described as "nonattitudes" (Converse 1970).

Although Converse's findings were later to become the center of an active debate, it should be emphasized that his was not a lone voice in the wilderness. His results contributed additional evidence in support of hypotheses developed by Almond and others about the absence of intellectual foundations for the public moods, and they also provided a plausible explanation for the putative volatility of public attitudes. Moreover, Converse's findings were only one of the most widely quoted results emerging from the voting studies. Other students of electoral behavior came to essentially the same conclusions about the absence of structure, coherence, or persistence in the political beliefs of the mass public—especially on foreign affairs (Miller 1967). For most Americans, they asserted, the bases of voting decisions were not be found in structured or ideological assessments and responses to policy issues. A concise summary of the primary findings that emerged from the voting studies has been offered by Campbell, Converse, Miller, and Stokes (1964, 280–81): "What psychological dimensions of voting are of greatest importance to the political system? Our discussion will focus on the low emotional involvement of the electorate in politics; its slight awareness of public affairs; its failure to think in structured, ideological terms; and its pervasive sense of attachment to one or the other of the two major parties." Thus, whether analyzed as a respondent to Gallup or other surveys, or as a voter, the portrait of the average American citizen that emerged from study after study was a rather pale imitation of the informed and engaged citizen celebrated in classical democratic theory and countless civic textbooks. Indeed, he was sometimes depicted as ignorant of, indifferent about, and perhaps even a threat to the most fundamental tenets of democratic society (Prothro and Grigg 1960).

Thus, unlike some of the earlier analysts who had focused on foreign policy attitudes as a special case, at least some of these studies of public opinion and voting behavior tended to regard the lack of information and structure on foreign policy issues as part of a broader problem—the gap between the ideal and actual American citizen.

Public Opinion Has a Limited Impact on Foreign Policy

The most important reason for interest in public opinion on foreign affairs arises from the assumption that in some ways and at least some of the time public attitudes have an impact, for better or worse, on the conduct of the nation's external policy.

For students of foreign policy and international relations, the central questions were not merely whether one party or the other controlled the White House or Congress. The United States was armed with atomic weapons, as was its primary adversary after 1949, and it was the political leader of a Western coalition attempting to contain the USSR. The U.S. economy produced half of the world's goods and services soon after World War II, and, as the core country in a network of international institutions that was intended to prevent a replay of the "beggar-thy-neighbor" economics of the decade prior to World War II, its impact on trade and financial issues was enormous. Even if Almond, Bailey, Kennan, Lippmann, and other critics did not always agree on specific U.S. policies and undertakings, they were united by the fear that the public would render ineffective the efforts of foreign policy elites to provide enlightened global leadership in the quest for a more stable world order. These fears even appear to have provoked some prescriptive overreactions. For example, Thomas Bailey, a fervent "small-d" democrat whose frequent jibes at "low blow Joe" McCarthy and other demagogues enlivened his enormously popular classes at Stanford, nevertheless felt sufficiently alarmed about the potential impact of the public to justify distinctly undemocratic leadership behavior: "Franklin Roosevelt repeatedly deceived the American people during the period before Pearl Harbor. . . . He was like the physician who must tell the patient lies for the patient's own good. . . . Because the masses are notoriously shortsighted and generally cannot see danger until it is at their throats, our statesmen are forced to deceive them into an awareness of their own long-run interests" (quoted in Shogan 1995, 278).

Certainly it is not hard to find expressions by policymakers avowing the importance of public opinion. In his August 21, 1858, debate with Stephen Douglas, Abraham Lincoln asserted that "Public sentiment is everything. With public sentiment nothing can fail; without it nothing can succeed" (Angle 1991, 128); and in 1936, Secretary of State Cordell Hull stated that "Since the time when Thomas Jefferson insisted upon a 'decent respect to the opinions of mankind,' public opinion has controlled foreign policy in all democracies" (Hull 1936, 47). Similar assertions have been made at one time or another by almost all presidents and secretaries of state.

Such hyperbolic statements, depicting an unalloyed direct democracy or "bottom-up" model of government, are unlikely to withstand serious empirical scrutiny. Not the least limitation of assertions such as those by Lincoln and Hull is that they neglect the role of institutions that may shape, mobilize, transmit—and perhaps distort—public preferences. These include the media, opinion leaders, interest groups, parties, and legislators. Moreover, the impact of public opinion cannot be assessed merely by describing its content. Nor should we assume that its impact is constant across administrations, circumstances, and issues. Policymakers may vary widely in their answers to some important questions: What is the appropriate role of public opinion in the formulation of foreign policy? Under what circumstances and for what issues should it play a greater or lesser role? What are the most appropriate indicators of public sentiments? The media? Interest groups? Prominent opinion leaders? Congress? Opinion surveys? What strategies should be used by policymakers to gain public support for policies? I shall return to these questions in chapter 6.

As we have seen, the driving force behind many of the analyses of public opinion during and after World War II was the fear that an ill-informed and emotional mass public would serve as a powerful constraint on the conduct of American diplomacy, establishing unwise limits on policymakers, creating unrealistic expectations about what is feasible in foreign affairs, and otherwise doing serious mischief to American diplomacy and, given the American role in the world after 1945, perhaps even to international stability (compare Lowi 1967 and Waltz 1967 on this point). In contrast to these fears, some analysts came to the conclusion that an ill-informed and largely indifferent public could not be taken very seriously by policymakers, limiting its impact on policy. As a leading social psychologist stated the point, "A public opinion so impoverished can hardly have a major impact on foreign policy decisions" (Kelman 1965, 580). In line with this reasoning, by the middle of the 1960s a consensus in fact seemed to emerge on a third point: public opinion has little if any impact on foreign policy. The weight of the research evidence cast doubt on the potency of public opinion as the driving force behind, or even a significant constraint upon, foreign policymaking.

Bernard Cohen's (1973) research most directly attacked the proposition that the public significantly affected foreign policy or that it even established limits beyond which policymakers would not dare to venture. In a critical review of the literature he argued that assertions about the constraining role of public opinion far outnumbered any empirical demonstration of that relationship. Indeed, he argued that the often-cited "limits" proposition was rarely if ever even put to a serious test. His own interview study of the foreign policy bureaucracy indicated that State Department officials had a rather modest interest in public opinion, and to the extent that they even thought about the public, it was as an entity to be "educated" rather than as a lodestar by which to be guided in formulating and implementing foreign policy. Or, as one State Department official put it, "To hell with public opinion. . . . We should lead, and not follow" (Cohen 1973, 62).

Elections are intended to provide an opportunity for the public to have an impact on policy. According to the "electoral retribution" model, officeholders will be sensitive to public opinion for fear of alienating voters to the point of losing office at the next election; vigilant voters will "throw the rascals out" if they fail to respond to public preferences. A core finding of virtually all the election studies was that there was so little issue-based voting as to raise serious questions about the classic views of accountability to the public on policy issues. As the authors of one of these studies noted, "the quality of the public's review of policy formation is that the electoral decision gives great freedom to those who must frame the policies of government" (Campbell, Converse, Miller, and Stokes 1964, 282). Moreover, the evidence indicated that while public officials might find it prudent to respect their constituents' preferences on domestic issues, they felt largely free of such constraints on votes pertaining to foreign affairs. A classic study of the public-legislator relationship revealed that constituents' attitudes on foreign policy issues had less impact on members of the House of Representatives than did their views on domestic issues (Miller and Stokes 1963). Research that focused on the presidency came to similar conclusions. The proposition that the president has "almost a free hand" in the conduct of foreign affairs received support from diverse studies (Caspary 1970; Graebner 1983; LaFeber 1977; Lipset 1966; Paterson 1979).

This period also witnessed a proliferation of case studies of key foreign policy decisions.[4] With some exceptions,[5] however, they tended to make few references to the impact of public opinion. But it is not always clear whether that is because public opinion was irrelevant as an explanation for the decisions under analysis. Some alternative reasons for the omission might include the following: decision makers quietly anticipated public opinion without consciously considering it; public opinion was excluded from the research design and thus no effort was made to assess its impact; or disproportionate research attention to international crises—events that are usually characterized by short decision time—tended to exclude episodes in which decisions are the culmination of a long and complex political process. All other things being equal, the more protracted the decision process, the more likely are policymakers to be subjected to the impact of public opinion through the activities of Congress, interest groups, the media, and opinion leaders. Finally, analyses of recent events must necessarily rely more on interviews of foreign policy officials than on archival research. To the extent that there is a bias among policymakers toward attributing their own decisions to "doing what is right" rather than to pressures or constraints from the public, such research might underemphasize the actual impact of public opinion.

These studies did not answer all of the questions about the impact of the public on foreign policy processes and outcomes. For example, the realities of research access required Cohen to exclude White House personnel from his study and to focus on precisely those officials—State Department bureaucrats—who are most sheltered from the effects of elections, and who thus might be somewhat freer to express and act upon cavalier attitudes toward "the man in the street." Nevertheless, the weight of the evidence cast significant doubt on the public's impact on policy. These findings should have assuaged those who shared Lippmann's (1955, 20) fears that mass public opinion "has shown itself to be a dangerous master of decision when the stakes are life and death."

Such results might also explain why interest in the topic, which had been so evident in the years immediately following the two world wars, had waned considerably. If the impact of public opinion on foreign policy ranges from little to none and from rarely to never, it robs the topic of significance and urgency. Students of voting behavior might continue to pursue research agendas directed at illuminating the sources, nature, representation, and impact of public opinion; these are, after all, some of the classic and enduring issues of democratic theory and governance. But there would be fewer compelling reasons for foreign policy analysts to invest much of their attention in these topics. It took another war, the longest, least successful, and ultimately least popular in American history, to rekindle interest in public opinion and foreign policy, while also stimulating a reexamination of the consensus about the volatility, lack of structure, and impotence of public opinion regarding foreign policy.

CHAPTER 3

Challenges to the Postwar Consensus

Just as World War II and fears of postwar isolationism among the mass public gave rise to concerns about public opinion and its impact on foreign policy, the war in Vietnam was the primary impetus for a renewed interest in the domestic sources of foreign policy. As the editor of a major symposium in 1965 on public opinion and foreign policy put it, "The intense controversy in the United States over the struggle in Vietnam has dramatized anew the fact that the foreign policy of governments is more than simply a series of responses to international stimuli, that forces at work within a society can also contribute to the quality and content of its external behavior" (Rosenau 1967, 2). That conflict was also a major catalyst in stimulating a reexamination of the consensus, described in chapter 2, that had emerged during the two decades after World War II. Most *broadly,* many of those who had believed that a stronger executive hand on the tiller of foreign policy, relatively free from the whims and vagaries of public moods, best serves both national interests and global stability came to reexamine their views in the light of the conflict in Southeast Asia. Indeed, the influential columnist Walter Lippmann, who only a little more than a decade earlier had despaired of the tyranny of a feckless public opinion and had called for a stronger executive to counteract the general public, became a leading critic of the Johnson administration's Vietnam policy. Eventually he even came to regard war protesters and draft card burners as more enlightened than the administration (Steel 1980, 571).

At a *narrower* level, some critics of U.S. policy became increasingly persuaded that the Gallup, Harris, and other commercial polls inadequately represented public attitudes toward the war by posing excessively restrictive and simplistic questions. For example, among the most widely asked questions was whether respondents supported or opposed current American policy in Vietnam. The critics complained that more probing questions that offered respondents an opportunity to express their views about policy options other than those favored by the Johnson administration were far less commonly employed by these polling organizations. Thus, in addition to generating secondary analyses of survey data relating to the war (Mueller 1973), the conflict in Southeast Asia also stimulated independent surveys designed specifically to assess foreign policy opinions in greater depth than the typical survey conducted by Gallup and other major polling firms.

The first of these studies, the Verba-Stanford surveys, focused on specific aspects of American policy in Vietnam, including some options other than support for or opposition to the Johnson administration's actions. Verba and his colleagues in fact found support for the administration's Vietnam policy, but they also unearthed approval for such alternative policies as negotiating an end to the conflict (Verba et al. 1967; Verba and Brody 1970). The period since the Verba-Stanford polls has witnessed a proliferation of public opinion surveys with a foreign affairs focus, including both the general public and opinion leaders.[1] As a consequence, we are no longer totally dependent on evidence generated by the major commercial polling organizations. Moreover, the independent surveys were often designed to deal with policy or theoretical concerns that can only imperfectly be probed by secondary analyses of the Gallup and other more general public opinion polls.

Thus, public opinion analysts, armed with growing central archives of data generated by major polling organizations as well as evidence produced by independent surveys, have begun to challenge important aspects of the consensus described in chapter 2.[2]

Is Public Opinion Really So Volatile?

The first systematic challenge to the Almond thesis that public opinion about international affairs is best characterized by volatile moods emerged from a study by William Caspary (1970). He took issue with Almond's (1950) heavy reliance on a single question in which respondents were asked to identify "the most important problem before the American people today." His own analysis of a broader set of foreign policy questions led Caspary to conclude that "American public opinion is characterized by a *strong* and *stable* permissive mood," rather than by mindless volatility, toward international involvement (Caspary 1970, 546). While differing from Almond on the nature of public opinion, he hardly characterized his findings as cause for celebration. Citing four years of combat in Vietnam as an example, Caspary concluded that the permissive public mood provides a blank check for foreign policy adventures rather than responsible support for international organizations, genuine foreign assistance, and basic defense measures.

A limitation of Caspary's analysis is that he included data for a period of only a little more than a decade, ending in 1953. A longer perspective would nevertheless appear to support his thesis, while assuaging the fears of those who forecast public disenchantment with and a retreat from an active U.S. role in world affairs. Since 1943, Gallup, the NORC, and several other organizations have asked the public whether it is better to take an active role or to stay out of international affairs. The first survey found that 76 percent favored the internationalist option whereas only 14 percent preferred withdrawal from world affairs. The subsequent half century of responses to forty-six surveys, summarized in figure 3.1, encompassed the end of World War II; the onset of the Cold War; two long costly wars in Asia and a short victorious one in the Persian Gulf region; crises in the Caribbean, the Taiwan Straits, Berlin, and the Middle East; several periods of warming relations between Moscow and Washington; and, finally the end of the Cold War and disintegration of the Soviet Union.

Despite the almost unprecedented turbulence of this fifty-year period and some variation in the precise wording used in the surveys, responses to these questions about the appropriate international stance of the United States have not been characterized by wild volatility. A modest decline in support for internationalism in 1947 coincided with worsening East-West relations, but at this low point approximately two-thirds of the public still favored an active American role, outnumbering the supporters of withdrawal by a margin of about five to two. Even in the wake of the costly failed war in Vietnam, not a single survey recorded more than 40 percent of the respondents stating that "it is better if we stay out of world affairs," and only two of them found that fewer than 60 percent felt that "it is better if we take an active part in world affairs." Because an "active role in world affairs" can encompass a wide array of international undertakings, it is important not to read too much into these data. Certainly they should not be counted as evidence of a broad consensus or sustained support for specific foreign policies. Nevertheless, they do suggest that at least the deepest concerns of some critics who feared an American return to isolationism after World War II, including those cited in chapters 1 and 2, may have been somewhat overdrawn.

The indictment of public caprice was also dismissed in an analysis that absolved it from blame for foreign policy shortcomings during the Korean War. While agreeing that erratic actions by a government may indeed threaten international stability and peace, Waltz attributed the "mixture of firmness and vacillation" in U.S. policy to leaders rather than to public pressures or fears of electoral retribution.

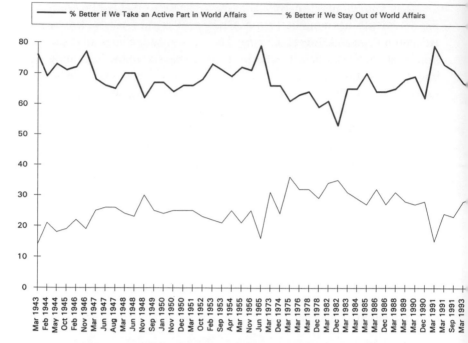

Fig 3.1. Should the United States play an active role in world affairs, or should it stay out? (1943–94). (Data from Gallup Poll, National Opinion Research Center, Chicago Council on Foreign Relations, *Fortune*, *Washington Post*. The exact wording of the questions and response options varied somewhat from survey to survey.)

Indeed, he concluded that, whatever shortcomings it may have exhibited in the past, "the mass of the American people have learned to live with danger, to tolerate ambiguity, to accept setbacks, and to understand that victory is sometimes impossible or that it can only be gained at a price the wise would refrain from paying" (Waltz 1967, 277, 279, 293; for an opposing view on the impact of public opinion, see Rosenburg 1967, 151).

A fuller and more systematic analysis of public opinion toward the wars in Korea and Vietnam posed another challenge to the thesis of irrational mood swings in public attitudes. To be sure, public support for the American war effort in both conflicts eventually declined but in ways that seemed explicable and rational rather than random and mindless. More specifically, Mueller (1973) found that increasing public opposition to both conflicts followed a pattern that matched a curve of rising battle deaths, suggesting that the public used an understandable, if simple, heuristic to assess American policy.

The most comprehensive challenge to the thesis that public opinion is volatile has emerged from a series of studies conducted by Benjamin Page and Robert Shapiro. Their evidence includes all questions that have been posed by major polling organizations, beginning with the inception of systematic surveys in the mid-1930s and extending through the 1980s. Of the more than six thousand questions included in these surveys, almost 20 percent have been asked at least twice, providing a substantial data set with which to assess the degree of stability or change in public attitudes. Employing a criterion of a difference of 6 percent from one survey to another to distinguish between continuity and change, Page and Shapiro found that public opinion in the aggregate is in fact characterized by a good deal of stability; moreover, this conclusion was equally valid for domestic and foreign policy issues (Shapiro and Page 1988; Page and Shapiro 1992). Most importantly, when attitude shifts took place, they seemed to be neither random nor completely removed from international realities. Rather, changes appeared to be "reasonable, events-driven" reactions to the real world, even if the factual information upon which they are based is marginally adequate at best. They concluded that,

> virtually all the rapid shifts [in public opinion] we found were related to political and economic circumstances or to significant events which sensible citizens would take into account. In particular, most abrupt foreign policy changes took place in connection with wars, confrontations, or crises in which major changes in the actions of the United States or other nations quite naturally affect preferences about what policies to pursue. (Page and Shapiro 1982, 34)[3]

A very similar conclusion about the importance of external events emerged from an analysis of opinion changes on both domestic and foreign policy during the period from the Kennedy through the Reagan administrations (Mayer 1992, 274).

It might be worth noting that the sudden shifts in public attitudes highlighted by Gabriel Almond and summarized in chapter 2 were also responses to wars, crises, and other dramatic international events, including Hitler's conquests during the spring of 1940, increasing Japanese-American tensions in the fall of 1941, the end of World War II, the Czech coup in 1948, and the like. Almond, however, chose to interpret the fluctuations as evidence of massive mood swings rooted in shallow opinions about the world rather than as reasonable responses to rapidly changing international conditions (Almond 1950, 70–80).

Because their analyses are based on aggregate responses rather than on panel studies in which the respondents in the sample are interviewed repeatedly, Page and Shapiro cannot address definitively one fundamental aspect of the debate about the volatility of public opinion: precisely what proportion of *individuals* in fact changed their minds on each question? For an issue on which the public divided evenly—50 percent in support of a particular policy and a like percentage in opposition—in each of two time periods, it is theoretically possible that all respondents switched positions. However, volatility approaching this magnitude seems highly unlikely because, as Page and Shapiro have shown, opinion changes tended to be in directions that "make sense" in terms of events.

The volatility thesis can be tested most directly and satisfactorily by individual-level rather than aggregate analyses of opinion data. Using alternative methods for correcting for measurement error, several studies have shown convincingly that at the individual level mass foreign policy attitudes are every bit as stable as those on domestic issues (Achen 1975). These studies revealed an impressive level of stability during times of constancy in the international environment. A panel study also found very substantial stability in policy attitudes and international images even during the late 1980s—a period that witnessed rapid and dramatic changes in Soviet-American relations and other important aspects of international affairs (Peffley and Hurwitz 1992).

Similar conclusions, supporting Page and Shapiro and casting doubt on the thesis of unstable and irrational public moods, also have emerged from other studies. During the post-Vietnam era, variations in public support for the use of force are best explained by differences between two quite distinct situations: when force is employed to coerce foreign policy restraint by others versus the use of force to influence or impose political changes within another state. The former goal consistently has received much stronger support than the latter (Jentleson 1992, 1996).

An interesting variant of the "rational public" thesis stipulated that the public attempted to moderate American behavior toward the USSR by expressing preferences for a conciliatory stance from a hawkish administration (Reagan) while supporting more assertive policies when a dovish leader (Carter) controlled the White House (Nincic 1988, 1992). The Nincic thesis gained additional support from Mayer's assessment of opinion changes. During the Ford and Carter years (1974–81), the preponderance of opinion changes, including foreign policy issues, was in a conservative direction. In contrast, during the eight Reagan years that followed, the public moved in a liberal direction on thirteen of nineteen issues, including all of those involving international affairs (Mayer 1992, 120–21). To the extent that one can generalize from these studies to other periods or other aspects of foreign policy, they further challenge the Almond-Lippmann thesis of volatility in public attitudes; indeed, they turn that proposition on its head for they identify the public as a source of *moderation* and *continuity* rather than instability and unpredictability.[4]

It is important to emphasize that none of these challenges to the Almond-Lippmann thesis is based on some newly found evidence that the public is in fact well informed about international affairs. Not only do surveys repeatedly reveal that the public has a very thin veneer of factual knowledge about politics, economics, and geography; they also indicate that most Americans are poorly informed about the specifics of conflicts, treaties, negotiations with other nations, characteristics of weapons systems, foreign leaders, and the like. Indeed, a seven-nation study in 1994 revealed that the American public trails well behind those in Germany, Italy, France, Great Britain, and Canada in levels of political information; only Spain was ranked behind the United States in this respect. The results were traced at least in part to the heavy dependence for information of Americans on television rather than newspapers (Dimock and Popkin 1995).

Because the modest factual basis upon which the mass public reacts to international affairs remains an unchallenged—and unchallengeable—fact, we are faced with a puzzle. If an often poorly informed general public does indeed react to international affairs in a stable and reasonable manner, and if opinion changes are driven by events rather than whimsy or emotion, what means permit it to do so? Have publics undergone a "skills revolution" that permits them to exercise sound political judgment despite low levels of factual knowledge (Rosenau 1990; Yankelovich 1991; Kay 1992a)? Do they make effective use of certain heuristics or rules of thumb to organize even the modest levels of information that they possess? Recall that a not insignificant body of research evidence, cited in chapter 2, indicated that mass public attitudes lack the kind of ideological underpinnings that would provide some structure and coherence across specific issues and stability through time.

Do Public Attitudes Lack Structure and Coherence?

Philip Converse's (1964) chapter on mass belief systems is one of the most widely cited studies in the literature of American political science. In recent years his research has also stimulated a plethora of studies that have, on the one hand, vigorously challenged his findings and, on the other, supported the main thrust of his conclusion that mass public attitudes lack ideological structure, whereas those of leaders are characterized by far greater coherence. Part of the debate is methodological, centering on the manner in which questions are framed, the clarity of questions, the degree to which the "unsure" respondents are prodded to state a position on issues, and similar aspects of research procedures. Did the evidentiary base include enough questions to support the conclusions? Did the analytical methods deal adequately with problems of measurement error? Did an analysis that examined correlations across specific public policy issues exhaust the possible structures that might be used to lend coherence to political thinking? These and other significant methodological questions about the Converse findings emerged from several studies (Achen 1975; Sullivan, Pierson, and Marcus 1978).

Another part of the controversy focuses on trends, specifically on the durability of findings that, to a large degree, drew from evidence generated during the 1950s. This was a period of American economic, political, and military dominance in foreign affairs—the shock of the pioneering Soviet space capsule Sputnik notwithstanding—and the 1956 and 1960 elections took place while the United States was at peace during the interim between the Korean War armistice and escalation of the Vietnam conflict. Domestically, the late 1950s and early 1960s were marked by relatively low inflation and unemployment, and, the Montgomery bus boycott and Greensboro sit-ins notwithstanding, the full impact of the Civil Rights movement had yet to be felt. According to the critics, this period, both celebrated and condemned for marking "the end of ideology," is insufficiently representative for assessing the degree of ideological consistency among the general public. In support of that view, a number of analysts found that, beginning with the Johnson-Goldwater election campaign of 1964, ideological consistency among the public did in fact increase (Nie and Anderson 1974; Nie, Verba, and Petrocik 1976). Some corroborating evidence also appeared to emerge from an assessment of public opinion polls on domestic and foreign policy issues from the late 1930s to 1967. Although there was generally a weak relationship between attitudes on domestic and international issues, the evidence also revealed a stronger correlation between them during the post-Eisenhower years (Hero 1969).

Those who claim to have found greater ideological consistency among the general public during the turbulent era of the late 1960s and 1970s have also encountered criticism. Are the claims of greater issue consistency really rooted in increasing ideological consciousness? Alternatively, do they merely result from the parroting of ideological rhetoric or from some methodological artifact? This is not the place to provide a blow-by-blow account of the many and varied answers to these and other questions on the issue, especially as excellent and detailed summaries of the vast literature are available elsewhere (Converse 1975; Kinder 1983; Kinder and Sears 1985; Sniderman and Tetlock 1986; Zaller 1992; Sniderman 1993). It will suffice to say that there appears to be an emerging consensus that public responses to political issues are not adequately captured by the most familiar bipolar dimensions: namely, liberal to conservative and internationalist to isolationist. If these dimensions constitute the standard by which to determine the existence of attitude structures, then mass public attitudes do indeed appear to lack coherence, although this may not be an insuperable barrier to making adequate sense of politics (Luttbeg and Gant 1985). Given that tentative conclusion, does the literature on international issues reveal anything else about organizing concepts that might lend some coherence to public attitudes on foreign affairs?

Although the more recent research has yet to create a consensus on all aspects of the question, there does appear to be a considerable convergence of findings on two general points relating to belief structures. First, even though the general public may be rather poorly informed about the factual aspects of international affairs, attitudes about foreign affairs are in fact structured in moderately coherent ways. Indeed, low information and an ambiguous international environment may actually motivate rather than preclude having some type of attitude structure. For example, the conception of humans as "cognitive misers" suggests that they may use a limited number of beliefs to make sense of a wide range of facts and events. Second, there is growing evidence that a single internationalist-to-isolationist dimension inadequately describes the structure of public opinion on international affairs.

A study based on the first of the quadrennial Chicago Council on Foreign Relations (CCFR) surveys of both the general public and elites employed factor analyses and other methods to uncover three foreign policy outlooks described as "liberal internationalism," "conservative internationalism," and "non-internationalism" (Mandelbaum and Schneider 1979). A comparable trichotomy labeled "the three headed eagle" emerged from early analyses of the data on opinion leaders generated by the Foreign Policy Leadership Project (FPLP) (Holsti 1979; Holsti and Rosenau 1979, 1984). These findings did not go unchallenged, however. Others questioned the division of foreign policy attitudes into three *types* rather than three *dimensions*, and they have offered useful evidence in support of their critiques. William Chittick and Keith Billingsley (1989) undertook both original and secondary analyses that supported the case for dimensions rather than types for the adequate description of the foreign policy beliefs of both leaders and the mass public, and their findings have also received other support (Chittick, Billingsley, and Travis 1990, 1995; Bardes and Oldendick 1978; Oldendick and Bardes 1982).

A major contribution to the debate about how best to describe foreign policy attitudes has come from Eugene Wittkopf's (1986, 1990) secondary analyses of the CCFR surveys of both leaders and the general public. His results, developed inductively from the CCFR surveys conducted in 1974, 1978, 1982, and 1986, revealed that with a single exception, two dimensions are necessary to describe foreign policy attitudes: "support-oppose militant internationalism" (MI), "support-oppose cooperative internationalism" (CI). Dichotomizing and crossing these dimensions yields four types of foreign policy belief systems, with the quadrants labeled as *hard-liners* (support MI, oppose CI), *internationalists* (support both MI and CI), *accommodationists* (oppose MI, support CI), and *isolationists* (oppose both MI and CI). The MI/CI scheme also proved useful for characterizing respondents to the first post–Cold War CCFR survey in 1994 (Wittkopf 1995).

At this point it is worth addressing a more general point about methods of classification such as the MI/CI scheme. What are the relative merits of discrete *types*—for example, liberal internationalists, conservative internationalists, and noninternationalists—versus categories defined by *dimensions*? If we think in terms of dimensions rather than types, we gain a good deal of conceptual freedom. For example, a critic might suggest that the fourfold MI/CI classification scheme is too simple or that it overemphasizes *between-type* differences, while obscuring those among persons who are classified *within* any of the four cells; the latter point is a common criticism of typologies based on fourfold tables. Focusing on the two dimensions rather than on the four types permits us to escape from the limits of a two-by-two matrix. Thus, the MI/CI scheme could be expanded into a three-by-three matrix by making somewhat finer distinctions along both dimensions (e.g., "strongly support," "neutral," "strongly oppose"). The types discussed here would then appear in the four corner cells, and additional descriptive labels would be developed for the other five types; for example, "indifferents" for those who are neutral on both dimensions. Moreover, when we think in terms of dimension rather than types, we are more likely to search for other dimensions that may enhance the analytical power of the scheme. The latter point is illustrated by Ronald Hinckley's (1992) classification scheme. It resembles Wittkopf's MI/CI, but it also adds an important third dimension: unilateralism-multilateralism. Hinckley demonstrates its utility not only for classifying respondents to Cold War surveys, but also for distinguishing adherents of competing schools of thought on the proper U.S. role and strategies during the interwar period. The importance of the unilateralism-multilateralism dimension also emerges from other studies, including Chittick, Billingsley, and Travis (1995).[5]

Strong support for Wittkopf's MI/CI scheme also has emerged from analyses of the FPLP data on American opinion leaders (Holsti and Rosenau 1990, 1993). Those studies put the MI/CI scheme to a demanding test because of three major differences between the CCFR and FPLP data sets. First, the CCFR surveys were undertaken at four-year intervals starting in 1974, whereas the five FPLP studies followed two years later in each case. Moreover, the two sets of surveys have only a few questionnaire items in common. Finally, the MI/CI scheme was developed largely from data on the mass public, whereas the FPLP surveys focused solely on opinion leaders.

It may be worth noting that although the origins of the MI/CI scheme are strictly inductive, the militant and cooperative internationalism dimensions correspond closely to the most venerable theoretical approaches to international relations: realism and liberalism. Realism views conflict between nations as a natural state of affairs, either because of human nature or owing to the anarchic structure of the system, rather than as an aberration that is subject to permanent amelioration. Such realist concepts as security dilemma, relative capabilities, and a zero-sum view of conflict are also basic to the militant internationalism dimension.

There are similar links between liberalism and the cooperative internationalism dimension. Liberalism denies that conflict is an immutable element of relations between nations. It defines security in terms that are broader than the geopolitical-military spheres, and it emphasizes the potential for cooperative relations among nations: institution-building to reduce uncertainty and fears of perfidy as well as information costs; improved international education and communication to ameliorate fears and antagonisms based on misinformation and misperception; and the positive-sum possibilities of such activities as trade are but a few of the ways, according to liberals, by which nations may jointly gain and thus mitigate, if not eliminate, the harshest features of international relations emphasized by the realists. In short, the CI dimension shares important elements with the liberal school of international relations theory. These MI and CI dimensions also seem clearly related to other conceptualizations of American thought on foreign affairs. For example, Thomas Hughes's (1980) distinction between the "security culture" and the "equity culture" in American foreign policy, and James Billington's (1987) categories of "realist-conservatives" and "idealist-liberals" appear to parallel, if not match exactly, the MI and CI dimensions. The MI/CI scheme has also been linked to broader American ideologies—cosmopolitan liberalism, nativism, and multiculturalism—in a study encompassing a period of six decades beginning in 1930 (Citrin, Haas, Muste, and Reingold 1994).

Although the empirical and theoretical cases for measuring attitudes about both militant and cooperative internationalism, rather than on a single isolationist-to-internationalist dimension, seems quite strong, there is also some evidence that these two dimensions may not be sufficient to describe all contours of contemporary international opinions. As noted earlier, a further distinction between *unilateralism* and *multilateralism* has been suggested in a number of studies (Wittkopf 1986; Hinckley 1988; Chittick and Billingsley 1989; Chittick, Billingsley, and Travis 1995; Russett 1990; for a somewhat different formulation, see Russett and Shye 1993). It is not reasonable, moreover, to expect that any belief structure could encompass all possible aspects of foreign affairs, and there is indeed rather persuasive evidence that attitudes toward some rather important issues cut across the main dimensions identified above. Trade and protectionism, issues that are likely to become more rather than less important during the coming decade—and perhaps more contentious as well—are one such example. Questions involving Israel and American policy toward that nation appear to form another cluster of attitudes that does not fit neatly into the MI/CI scheme. That is, the four types that emerge from that scheme—*hardliners, internationalists, isolationists*, and *accommodationists*—do not differ significantly on either trade issues or U.S. policy toward Israel.

A somewhat different approach to the question of attitude structures emerges from several studies of the general public conducted by Jon Hurwitz and Mark Peffley (1987). In contrast to Converse's search for a "horizontal" coherence that relies on correlations among attitudes toward various issues, Hurwitz and Peffley proposed and tested a hierarchically organized foreign policy belief structure in which specific policy preferences are derived from *postures*—militarism, anticommunism, and isolationism—that, in turn, are assumed to be constrained by a set of *core values* (morality of warfare, ethnocentrism) relating to the international community. They found that such structures did in fact exist among respondents to their surveys. Thus, a few rather general beliefs—attitudes toward militarism and a general preference for a "tough-minded" approach to international affairs—appear to have served as organizing devices that enabled subjects to respond in a reasonably coherent manner to a broad range of issues, including defense spending, nuclear arms policy, military involvement, policies toward the USSR, and international trade.

It is important to state once again that none of these studies challenges the overwhelming evidence that the American public is on balance poorly informed about international affairs. Indeed, even the Persian Gulf War, the first international conflict to be telecast in real time, increased the normally low level of information among the general public by only a very modest amount (Bennett 1992). Rather, the evidence appears to suggest that, even in the absence of much factual knowledge, members of the general public use some simple—perhaps even simplistic—cognitive shortcuts in order to make some sense of an increasingly complex world; a few salient criteria rather than complete information may serve as the bases of judgment. Perhaps it should be noted that even experts use such shortcuts to organize their attitudes. "Domino theory," "lessons of Munich," "lessons of Vietnam," and "my enemy's enemy is my friend" are among those that have served—for better or worse—to guide the thinking of more than a few policymakers and their expert advisers. Stated differently, although lacking a deep reservoir of factual information, members of the mass public may act as "cognitive misers," employing a few superordinate beliefs to guide their thinking on a broad spectrum of international issues. Thus, people may organize their political worlds in richer and more diverse ways than indicated by Converse and his colleagues (Conover and Feldman 1984).

Clearly, the recent research has yet to produce complete agreement on many important issues relating to the structure of foreign policy beliefs among the mass public. Nevertheless, it is also evident that the earlier consensus depicting public attitudes as lacking any real coherence has been challenged from many quarters and for many reasons. As a result of substantial empirical research, there is now a good deal of credible evidence suggesting that members of the mass public use various heuristics—although not necessarily the traditional liberal-to conservative or internationalist-to-isolationist blueprints—for organizing their political thinking.

Is the Public Really Impotent?

Among the most important questions about public opinion are these: To what extent, on what kinds of issues, under what circumstances, and in what types of political systems, if any, does it have an impact on public policy? If public opinion is indeed impotent, that would reduce the reasons for studying it; the topic might be of interest to cognitive psychologists, but it would be largely irrelevant to students of foreign policy. If it has an influence, what are the means by which public attitudes become known so that they can have an impact on decision-makers? These are also the most difficult questions to answer, for our ability to do so is not materially enhanced by the many technical improvements that have characterized public opinion research during the past half century: better sampling designs, greater attention to construction of questions, more sophisticated statistical models to analyze the data and, of course, the widespread availability of computers that make possible complex analyses rarely attempted even a few decades ago. Not surprisingly, then, we have a good deal more systematic evidence describing the state of, or trends in, public opinion than detailing how it has affected the actual conduct of foreign affairs.

As noted in chapter 2, much of the evidence through the 1960s pointed toward the conclusion of public impotence in the foreign policy-making process. Even when there appeared to be some correspondence between public sentiments and foreign policy, not all analysts were prepared to accept the inference that the former had any independent impact on the latter. According to some of them, for example, any evidence of a correlation between public opinion and foreign policy merely serves to underscore the effectiveness of efforts by policymakers, aided and abetted by pliant print and electronic media, to manipulate the mass public into acceptance of the ruling elites' political or class-based interests.

There is certainly no shortage of evidence that most post–World War II presidents have followed Theodore Roosevelt in thinking that the White House is a "bully pulpit," whether it was used by Harry Truman to "scare the hell out of them" in order to gain support for aid to Greece and Turkey in 1947; by Dwight Eisenhower to warn against the dangers of "unwarranted influence, whether sought or unsought, by the military-industrial complex" in 1961; by Jimmy Carter to generate approbation for the Panama Canal Treaties during the early months of his administration; by Ronald Reagan to drum up support for assistance to the "Contras" in Nicaragua during the 1980s; and by

Bill Clinton to gain passage of the NAFTA and GATT/World Trade Organization treaties. It is also evident that such presidential efforts to shape public opinion have not been equally successful. At least one noted public opinion analyst (Yankelovich 1978) has asserted that the relationship between leaders and the public has changed in the post-Vietnam era—"farewell to 'the President knows best.'" Although it remains to be demonstrated that the equation has been permanently altered, some recent evidence indicates that the public is both capable and willing to express views that do not necessarily follow those of policy makers or opinion leaders (Clough 1994; Isaacs 1994).

The more difficult question concerns influence in the other direction. How much did public impatience lead the Carter administration to embark on an ill-fated effort to free American hostages held in Teheran in 1980, or the Reagan administration to withdraw U.S. Marines from Lebanon after a terrorist bombing had killed more than 240 of them in 1983? Did President Kennedy genuinely believe that he would be impeached should he fail to force removal of Soviet missiles from Cuba, as he told his brother, or was he merely seeking to bolster decisions arrived at for reasons that had nothing to do with public opinion? Perhaps a more telling example from the Cuban missile crisis emerges from transcripts of a crucial White House meeting on October 27, 1962, the day before the crisis was resolved peacefully. It appears that Kennedy was prepared to accept a compromise solution that was strongly opposed by many of his top advisers— removal of American missiles in Turkey in exchange for withdrawal of the Soviet missiles in Cuba that had precipitated the Caribbean confrontation—rather than initiate a further escalation of the crisis, and that he would have done so in large part *because it would have been hard to explain to the public why such a seemingly symmetrical arrangement had been rejected* (Bundy and Blight 1987–88).

Some anecdotal evidence may also be suggestive, but it hardly offers irrefutable answers to these questions. Franklin D. Roosevelt was the first president to make extensive use of public opinion data, and he even specified to polling organizations exactly what questions he wanted to have posed to the public on a regular basis. Virtually all recent presidents have made extensive use of pollsters. John Kennedy's 1960 presidential campaign relied heavily on private polls conducted by Louis Harris, and after the election he made public opinion analysis a regular part of White House activities (Jacobs and Shapiro 1994, 1995). Lyndon Johnson, who often carried survey results to show critics that he had strong public support for his policies, expanded the use of public and private polls (Altschuler 1986). The process of institutionalizing and politicizing public opinion polling, not only for election purposes but also for making policy decisions, was even more fully advanced by the Nixon White House (Jacobs and Shapiro 1995). Moreover, whereas Nixon and his predecessors took considerable efforts to keep such polling activities secret, they have now become a well-known activity of every administration.

The Iraqi invasion of Kuwait in August 1990 stimulated an immense amount of public and private polling by a wide variety of sources, including almost nightly surveys commissioned by the government of Kuwait in order to determine, among other things, how the public reacted to various reasons for opposing Saddam Hussein's aggression: oil, restoration of Kuwait's preinvasion government, U.S. jobs, international norms, and Iraq's nuclear weapons aspirations. Although the Bush administration made less extensive use of polling than the Reagan White House, at least some observers believe that the government was not immune to the impact of public preferences. In recalling events of the period, General Schwarzkopf (1992, 468) wrote that "Washington was ready to overreact, as usual, to the slightest ripple in public opinion." (For results of the public polls, see Mueller 1994.)

We have relatively few detailed accounts from these opinion analysts within the government about how their expertise and survey results were used in the policy process, but those that exist suggest that the mass public is not viewed merely as an essentially shapeless lump that can readily be molded through public relations activities and compliant media to meet the immediate policy needs of the administration (Cantril 1967; Beal and Hinckley 1984; Hinckley 1992). Hadley Cantril, who undertook public opinion analyses for Presidents Roosevelt, Eisenhower, and Kennedy, summarized his experience in this manner: "I want to emphasize that no claim is made here that the [public opinion] data and suggestions that Lambert and I provided the President [Roosevelt] were crucial to his decisions. But actions taken were certainly very often completely consistent with our recommendations" (Cantril 1967, 42).

Although it bears repeating that the evidence *describing* public attitudes still far outstrips, both in quality and quantity, that on the *causal links* between mass opinions and foreign policy, research in recent years has begun to cast some doubt on the earlier thesis of public impotence. In addition to anecdotal evidence, two classes of studies have challenged the proposition that foreign policy-making processes are essentially impervious to public influence: quantitative-correlational analyses and intensive case studies.

Several recent quantitative studies have challenged some important foundations of the theory that, at least on foreign and defense
policy, the public is impotent. One element of that proposition is that
policymakers are relatively free agents on foreign policy questions
because these issues pose few dangers of electoral retribution by
voters. Elections are said to be decided by domestic questions, especially those sometimes described as "pocketbook" or "bread-and-
butter" issues because international affairs are so far removed from the
concerns and information of the average voter. For example, Dwight
Eisenhower's landslide victory at the height of the Korean War in
1952, giving Republicans control of the White House for the first time
in two decades, was described by Miller (1967, 229) in a way that
discounted the effects of foreign policy: "Coming up to 1956 and
1960, we can be sure of no more than that public opinion on foreign
policy matters constituted a thin veneer on the basic structure of the
vote decision."

That conclusion about the distinction between domestic and foreign policy in voting behavior has been challenged by Aldrich, Sullivan, and Borgida (1989, 125) on the grounds that "there has been no
theoretically plausible account of attitude formation and salience that
would explain why attitudes on domestic issues—as opposed to foreign policy issues—should be so accessible and so likely to affect
voting behavior." Their systematic study of presidential campaigns
between 1952 and 1984 revealed that in five of the nine elections
during that period (1952, 1964, 1972, 1980, and 1984), foreign policy
issues had "large effects." Or, as the authors put it, when presidential
candidates devote campaign time and other scarce resources to articu-
lating their positions and debating questions of external policy, they
are "acting reasonably, because voters do in fact respond to their
appeals. The candidates are waltzing before a reasonably alert audience that appreciates their grace. Also, given a choice, the public
votes for the candidate who waltzes best" (Aldrich, Sullivan, and
Borgida 1989, 136).

Recent research on voting behavior also has emphasized the importance of retrospective evaluations of performance on voter choices
among candidates, especially when one of them is an incumbent
(Fiorina 1981; Abramson, Aldrich, and Rhode 1990). Because voters
are perceived as punishing incumbent candidates or parties for foreign
policy failures (for example, the Iran hostage episode and the failed
rescue mission damaged President Carter's reelection campaign), or
rewarding them for successes (for example, victory over Iraq in the
Persian Gulf War brought President Bush's approval ratings to the

highest level—89 percent—ever recorded), decisions by foreign policy leaders may be made in anticipation of public reactions and the
probabilities of success or failure (Zaller 1992; Stimson, MacKuen,
and Erikson 1994, 1995).

The electoral retribution hypothesis received a different kind of
test in a study of American policy toward China during the three
decades following establishment of Mao Tse-tung's government in
1949. Kusnitz (1984) found that, with few exceptions, the correspondence between public preferences and U.S. policy toward China was
remarkably high. Sometimes policy led opinion and at other times
opinion led policy, but on the whole the two remained in harmony.
These findings are explained by issue visibility, partisan differences,
and the nonrandom changes of opinion, which combined to create the
belief among policymakers that the possibility of electoral retribution
required them to pay close attention to public opinion on the China
issue.

Two recent studies also seem to cast some doubt on the universal
validity of the classic Miller-Stokes (1963) finding that, compared to
domestic issues, public attitudes on foreign policy questions have far
less impact on members of Congress (Bartels 1991; Hartley and
Russett 1992). A careful analysis of voting on Pentagon appropria-
tions at the beginning of the Reagan administration's defense buildup
revealed that "public opinion was a powerful force for policy change
in the realm of defense spending in the first year of the Reagan
administration. Moreover, the impact of constituency opinion appears
to have been remarkably broad-based, influencing all sorts of representatives across a wide spectrum of specific defense spending issues"
(Bartels 1991, 467; see also Russett, Hartley, and Murray 1994).

Finally, two major studies have measured the congruence between
changes in public preferences and a broad range of policies over
extended periods. The first, an analysis of public opinion and policy
outcomes spanning the years 1960–74, revealed that in almost two-
thirds of 222 cases, policy outcomes corresponded to public preferences. The consistency was especially high (92 percent) on foreign
policy issues. The author offered three possible explanations for his
findings: Foreign policy issues permit more decision-making by the
executive, are likely to be the object of less attention and influence by
organized interest groups, and are especially susceptible to manipulation by elites (Monroe 1979). The second study of the opinion-policy
relationship covered an even longer time span—1935 to 1979—which
included 357 significant changes of public preferences. These data also
revealed a high degree of congruence between opinions and policy,

with little difference in this respect between domestic (70 percent) and foreign policy (62 percent) issues (Page and Shapiro 1983).

Although anecdotal and correlational analyses can make useful contributions toward understanding the public opinion-foreign policy relationship, they are not an entirely satisfactory substitute for intensive case studies that could shed more direct light on how, if at all, public opinion enters into and influences the policy-making process. It is not wholly sufficient to describe the state of or trends in public opinion on an issue immediately before or during foreign policy decisions because a finding that major decisions seemed to be correlated with public preferences does not establish, by itself, a causal link; "not even time-series analysis can provide a magic bullet that will kill all the demons of causal ambiguity" (Page, 1994). For example, policymakers might be responding solely to pressures and constraints from the international system, precisely as realist theorists insist that they should, without any significant attention to public sentiments on the issue, even if those attitudes are highly congruent with those of policy-making officials. If international events are sufficiently dramatic and unambiguous in their implications—for example, the Japanese attack on Pearl Harbor—both leaders and the general public may react similarly, but this would not demonstrate that the latter affected the former. Alternatively, the actual direction of causality might run from policymakers to the public, rather than vice versa, as depicted by critics who describe the public as the malleable targets of public relations efforts by American elites (Ginsberg 1988; Herman and Chomsky 1988; Margolis and Mauser 1989).

When opinion change precedes shifts in policy the latter interpretation loses potency. However, we could not rule out still another possibility: the administration manipulates events; the events, now a part of the information available to the public, result in changes of opinion about the issue in question, followed by policy changes that are congruent with public opinion. A somewhat related variant of this sequence is the "rally 'round the president" hypothesis, according to which the executive may manipulate the public indirectly by first undertaking external initiatives and then responding to the resulting events abroad in a manner calculated to increase his popularity with domestic constituents (Brody and Shapiro 1989; Marra, Ostrom, and Simon 1990; Hugick and Gallup 1991; Lian and Oneal 1993). But the "rally" effect is generally of moderate magnitude and it depends on whether elites are united on the issue. It is a dicey reelection strategy, as Jimmy Carter (who launched the effort to rescue American hostages in Teheran in 1980) and George Bush (who received only 37 percent of the popular vote a little more than a year after the Gulf War) might attest. Moreover, one of the understudied questions is whether adversaries abroad have initiated crises during election years on the belief that Washington's reactions might be constrained by the distractions of domestic politics. If and when Russian archives on the issues are opened, it would be interesting to determine the extent to which the Berlin blockade (1948) and the invasions of Hungary (1956), Czechoslovakia (1968), and Afghanistan (1979–80), for example, might have been affected by calculations in the Kremlin that presidential elections in the United States made the timing of aggressive action especially propitious.

Among the more difficult cases in which to assess causality are those dealing with public opinion as a possible constraint on action. During the 1980s, the Reagan administration undertook a massive public relations campaign of dubious legality to generate public support for assistance to contra rebels in Nicaragua, but careful analyses of surveys on the issue indicated that a majority of the public consistently opposed American military involvement in Central America (Parry and Kornbluh 1988; Sobel 1989; Hinckley 1992; Sobel 1993). Would the Reagan Administration have intervened more directly or massively in Nicaragua and El Salvador in the absence of such public attitudes? Unambiguous evidence about the causes of contemporary nonevents is, to understate the case, rather hard to come by. Intensive case studies involving archival research, elite interviews, or both, appear to be the only way to address such questions, although even this approach is not wholly free from potential problems of inference. Does an absence of documentary references to public opinion indicate a lack of interest by policymakers in public sentiments? Alternatively, was attention to public attitudes so deeply ingrained into their working habits that it was unnecessary to make explicit references to it? A participant in the deliberations that led to the bombing of Libya in 1986 recalled that public opinion was never discussed or brought up, but "it was clearly in the air," and "everyone knew what polls (their private ones) showed" about bombing a nation supporting terrorism. (Hinckley, private communication 1995). Even if there were frequent discussions and analyses of public views on the issue, the inference to be drawn from that fact may not always be wholly self-evident. Are we to conclude from these deliberations that public attitudes played a significant role in policy decisions, or does the evidence merely reveal a desire on the part of officials to be "on record" as seriously having taken public sentiments into account?

These examples do not imply that we are limited to simple, one-directional models of the links between the public and policymakers; a number of more complex alternatives have been put forward (Rosenau 1961; Graber 1968; Hughes 1978; Russett 1990; Hinckley 1992; Zaller 1992; Stimson, MacKuen, and Erikson 1995). Moreover, a full analysis of the opinion-policy links would often require explorations into many aspects of the domestic political process, including the role of parties and candidates in raising issues, the impact of interest groups, the role of the media, the manner in which opinions form and circulate in the body politic, and the level of elite competition, just to mention a few salient aspects of the process. The literature on each of these topics is enormous.[6]

V. O. Key's (1961, 14) definition of public opinion as "those opinions held by private persons which governments find it prudent to heed" provides an especially appropriate introduction to any causal analysis of the opinion-policy link. He also pointed to the central research task: "If one is to know what opinions governments heed, one must know the inner thoughts of presidents, congressmen, and other officials." Consequently, in order to develop and test competing hypotheses about opinion-policy linkages, there are no satisfactory alternatives to carefully crafted case studies employing interviews and, if possible, archival research, designed to uncover how, if at all, decision makers perceive public opinion; feel themselves motivated or constrained by it; factor it into their identification and assessment of policy options; and otherwise take it into account when selecting a course of action, including a decision not to take action.[7]

Although the literature systematically addressing these questions is dwarfed by the number of studies that describe the state of public opinion, several examples illustrate this type of research. The availability of substantial collections of documents relating to the 1914 European crisis enabled Richard Fagen (1960) to study the uses and assessments of public opinion by top German leaders during the weeks leading up to World War I. The Kaiser and other leaders in Berlin regarded public opinion as "hard goods" capable of being assessed in the same manner as military or economic capabilities. Although public opinion meant different things to different leaders, it was perceived as "an active, initiating, coercive, reified, and even personified force" (Fagen 1960, 457). For German decision makers, public opinion played four important roles during the six weeks prior to the outbreak of a general war: (1) adding a national dimension to governmental positions, (2) defining national limits of tolerance, (3) excusing actions of others, and (4) excusing one's own actions.

Doris Graber undertook an intensive study of four decisions during the early years of American history: John Adams's decision to renew negotiations with France in 1800, the Louisiana Purchase during the first Jefferson administration, James Madison's policies leading up to the War of 1812, and the enunciation of the Monroe Doctrine in 1823. Despite differences in personality, ideology, and other attributes among the four presidents, she found that in each case public opinion was "an important factor in decision making, but by no means the most important single factor" (Graber 1968, 318).

A study on foreign policymaking about a century later came to a rather different conclusion. Robert Hildebrand (1981) was unable to discover that public opinion had any significant impact on foreign policy during the quarter century (1897–1921) encompassing the McKinley, Roosevelt, Taft, and Wilson administrations. To the extent that public opinion entered into executive discussions, it was only after policy decisions had already been made. Other students of the Wilson presidency have come to somewhat different conclusions about his interest in and sensitivity to public opinion (Turner 1957; Cornwell 1959). Still different findings emerged from an analysis of public opinion and foreign policy from the period leading up to World War II through President Truman's March 1947 speech to Congress requesting aid to Greece and Turkey. Michael Leigh (1976) tested two approaches to the foreign policy process: the traditional democratic model that public opinion constrains American policymakers versus the radical model that manipulation of the public in favor of predetermined policy choices not only takes place but invariably succeeds. His findings validated neither the traditional nor the radical model.

Striking evidence that public opinion has a significant impact on policy emerged from a study of four cases of U.S. arms control policy—international control of atomic energy, the Limited Test Ban Treaty of 1963, the SALT I/Anti-Ballistic Missile Treaties, and the SALT II Treaty—spanning every administration between Presidents Truman and Reagan. Thomas Graham (1989) used a research design that included an analysis of more than five hundred public opinion surveys and an examination of primary source materials to determine whether correlations between public opinion and policy decisions were causal or spurious. The evidence indicated that public opinion had at least some impact on decisions at all stages of the policy process, including agenda setting, arms control negotiations, the treaty ratification process, and implementation of the agreement. Moreover, its impact varied directly with the level of public support for a policy; that is, whether it reached the level of *majority* (50 to 59 percent), *consensus* (60 to 69 percent), *preponderant* (70 to 79 percent), or *virtually unanimous* (80 percent or more).

Studies of the opinion-policy links are not limited to cases in which sufficient time has passed to permit full examination of the relevant archives. Philip Powlick's (forthcoming) analysis of the role of public opinion in U.S. decisions on the Lebanon intervention during the first Reagan administration relied almost entirely on interviews with policy officials. Whereas public opinion influenced many mid-level officials and a few higher ones—for example, Caspar Weinberger—it had little impact on others, including President Reagan, Robert McFarlane, and George Shultz.[8] Powlick concluded that public opinion formed the basis of several recommendations to pull the Marines out of Lebanon several months after a terrorist attack killed more than 240 of them; it also helped to ensure that the decision to withdraw would be warmly received by most officials and members of Congress. However, President Reagan's decision to withdraw apparently was less influenced by public opinion than by the kinds of external considerations to which realists would assign top priority in decision making. Public opinion was thus only one of several factors that came together to bring about the evacuation from Beirut in February 1984.

Powlick's conclusions regarding the Lebanon intervention may, however, have understated the impact of public opinion on those at the top levels of the government. According to another official in the administration, Ronald Hinckley, the president and McFarlane had constant public opinion information fed to them. Reagan received his from pollster Richard Wirthlin whereas McFarlane was briefed on public opinion by his crisis management center team. Hinckley concludes that the Lebanon episode (as well as the later decision to bomb Libya in response to suspected terrorist activities in 1986) illustrates the tendency of officials to discount public opinion when explaining their decisions "because it is not consciously on the table when the decision is made, but it has been in the mind of the decision maker for some time" (private communication 1995).

An analysis of the controversial issue of aid to the Nicaraguan contras during the 1980s also yielded somewhat mixed results. Although the public consistently opposed aid, the Congress was willing to provide assistance to the rebels, but in far more limited amounts and restricted form than requested by the Reagan administration. Several key members of Congress denied that their votes had been cast in direct response to public preferences within their districts, but under questioning they admitted sounding out their constituents' opinions and voting their own minds when they found evidence of public indifference. Administration officials also attempted to ignore public opposition. Nevertheless, public opinion did serve as a constraint against more aggressive intervention in Nicaragua, and, ultimately, it probably forced the Reagan administration to rely on the proceeds of illegal arms sales to Iran to fund the contras (Sobel 1993).

Lawrence Jacobs and Robert Shapiro (1995) engaged in perhaps the most ambitious analysis of the public opinion policy link in their study of the relationship between private presidential polling and presidential behavior in administrations since John Kennedy's. In addition to archival research, they interviewed top White House personnel as well as those engaged in conducting the surveys.

Taken as a whole, these studies clearly point to mixed conclusions about the impact of public opinion on foreign policy. They also seem to suggest that its effects may have intensified during recent decades. This tentative conclusion also receives some support from interview studies of foreign policy officials. Although the bureaucrats interviewed by Powlick (1991, 1995) were not notably more sanguine about the public and its ability to contribute constructively to foreign policy than were those interviewed in similar research by Bernard Cohen (1973) more than two decades earlier, they were more inclined to accept the legitimacy of a public contribution to the policy process. Consequently, these officials tended to avoid policy options that were perceived as likely to engender public opposition. In contrast, Graham's (1989) study of U.S. arms control policies found little change over time because his research revealed that public opinion has played an important role in such decisions in all administrations since President Truman's. This, then, is one of the many areas in which contradictory findings point to the need for further research.

Public Opinion on the Soviet Union and Russia

Some salient features of American public opinion on international affairs can be illustrated in more detail by examining responses to questions about the Soviet Union and Soviet-American relations.

On February 27, 1946, Arthur Vandenberg asked his colleagues in the Senate, "What is Russia up to now?" Few questions have so persistently engendered debate within the United States during the past half century as those concerning the Soviet Union, its foreign policies, and the appropriate American approaches for dealing with the USSR. In his famous "long telegram" of 1946 and in an essay on

"The Sources of Soviet Conduct" a year later, George F. Kennan wrote that Soviet foreign policy was driven largely by internal forces, including the need for real or imagined external enemies and, therefore, at least in the short run, American offers of friendship and cooperation were likely to prove fruitless. Kennan's (1947) diagnosis of Soviet international behavior and his prescription of a "long-term, patient but firm and vigilant containment of Russian expansive tendencies" were enormously influential in providing an intellectual framework for American policy toward Stalin's Russia, but they did not end the debate about Soviet foreign policy or the best means for dealing with the USSR.

The debate has often been stimulated by external events. The Berlin blockade; the invasion of South Korea; the death of Stalin; the invasions of Hungary, Czechoslovakia, and Afghanistan; Sputnik; the Cuban missile crisis; and the activities that constituted the high point of détente in 1972–73 are some of the more dramatic episodes that have intensified interest in the question. Almost as often the debate has been aroused by American domestic politics, especially presidential election campaigns. In 1952, the concept of containment came under attack from some Republicans, notably John Foster Dulles, as too "static." Later events demonstrated clearly that its putative replacement—"roll back"—was campaign rhetoric rather than policy. In order to disarm critics in the right wing of his own party in 1976, President Ford let it be known that détente was no longer a part of the White House working vocabulary. Four years later, the soon-to-be-nominated Ronald Reagan blamed the USSR for all international problems, and during the subsequent campaign he attacked arms control and détente as the causes of the "worst decade in American history" (House 1980, 1).

During recent years American interest in these questions has been enhanced by external and internal developments. After 1985, Mikhail Gorbachev provided the Soviet Union with a style of leadership that seemed light-years removed from that of his immediate predecessors; even those most skeptical about the significance or permanence of glasnost or perestroika agreed that Gorbachev possessed political and public relations skills unmatched in recent Soviet history. At the same time, the American president who excoriated the Soviet Union as an "evil empire" in 1983 was, within five years, meeting regularly with Gorbachev and describing him as "my friend." Relations between the superpowers continued to improve during the early 1990s, reaching a level of cooperation not witnessed since World War II; in 1990 and 1991 they joined forces at the United Nations Security Council to pass a series of resolutions aimed at compelling Iraq to reverse its invasion of Kuwait.

During the more than half century between the onset of World War II and the dissolution of the Soviet Union at the end of 1991, the Gallup and other polling organizations provided an immense amount of survey data on questions relating to superpower relations. Aside from the obvious importance of the Soviet Union for American foreign relations, there is also evidence that attitudes toward the USSR have played a central role in organizing public attitudes toward a wide array of international issues (Herrmann 1986; Holsti 1988; Hurwitz and Peffley 1990). Thus, the combination of ample data and the salience of these issues provides a good opportunity to assess several competing theories of public opinion.[9]

Two of the theories have been described earlier. The Almond-Lippmann thesis stipulates that public reactions to world affairs are characterized by volatility and little if any relationship to international realities. An alternative interpretation describes mass public reactions as "rational and events-driven." A third theory, developed largely to deal with the Cold War period, depicts the American public quite differently, although not necessarily in a more flattering light than the Almond-Lippmann thesis. Rather than focusing on volatility and mood cycles that have a random or negative correlation with the real world, this theory emphasizes certain continuities in public opinion, with special attention to a putative American propensity toward a Manichean worldview. The public is depicted as imbued with a frontier mentality for which the appropriate metaphor is the cowboy movie with its "white hats" and "black hats" and a concomitant absence of multidimensional characters, simplistic plots, violent shoot-outs as the characteristic mode of conflict resolution, and the inevitable triumph of the good guys over the villains. According to this thesis, Americans have regarded communism as the great evil and the Soviets as its black-hatted agents. To the extent that public opinion has been a factor in American foreign policy, it has buttressed and perhaps even cast into concrete the great constant in Washington's post–World War II diplomacy: a reflexive anti-Soviet policy that was allegedly so often out of touch with reality that it served neither the national interest nor the prospects for peace, stability, and justice.

There are at least two broad variants of this third theory. According to one, public opinion is the victim in that it was manipulated into a hard-line anti-Soviet position by the ruling class and its faithful handmaidens in the media and other key institutions. Because public opinion has little autonomous life of its own, it is also of limited relevance in any effort to understand American foreign and defense policies. This viewpoint may be found in several revisionist histories of the Cold War (for example, Kolko and Kolko 1972). A second version locates irrational anti-Soviet sentiments in certain widely shared values, beliefs, and attitudes about the world that are central features of American culture. For example, in analyzing the cultural bases of American foreign policy, Robert Dallek has written of an "unthinking anticommunism" that serves several nonrational needs, providing among other things, "a convenient excuse for not facing up to troubling domestic concerns" (Dallek 1983, xvii, xviii). The ample data on the Soviet Union provide an opportunity to assess, if not put to a definitive test, these quite distinctive depictions of American public opinion. Responses to questions about the Soviet Union and appropriate American policies for dealing with its Cold War rival provide the evidence for this purpose.

Soviet-American Cooperation

Almost from the moment that the United States entered World War II, various polling organizations started asking the public to appraise the prospects for relations between Washington and Moscow once the fighting ended. While the wording of the questions varied, all of them focused on the probability that the Soviets could be trusted to continue cooperation with the United States into the postwar period as envisaged, for example, by President Roosevelt's plan for collaboration among the "Four Policemen"—Britain, China, the USSR, and the United States—in order to maintain peace.

During World War II, the American public was offered a good deal of information that sustained hopes of good Soviet-American relations. Most public pronouncements by policymakers were optimistic on this score. One example will illustrate the extent to which the Roosevelt administration attempted to portray the USSR in favorable terms. During the summer and fall of 1941, survey evidence revealed a lack of public enthusiasm for aid to Russia, which had recently been invaded by its erstwhile German ally. Opposition was especially strong among American religious groups. Roosevelt mounted a strong campaign to disarm the critics by asserting that the Soviet constitution guaranteed freedom of conscience and worship (Dallek 1979). Such books as *Mission to Moscow* by former Ambassador Joseph Davies (1941) and *One World* by Wendell Willkie (1943), the Republican presidential nominee in 1940, depicted the Soviet Union in highly favorable terms. Many wartime movies, including the film version of *Mission to Moscow,* were similarly upbeat. To be sure, there were some skeptics, but the information available to the public stressed the important military role of the Soviets in defeating the Nazi regime and the wartime cooperation among the Allies, while deemphasizing the nature of Stalin's regime and the possibilities that there might be strong divergences of interests or competing and perhaps incompatible preferences about the nature of the postwar international order.

Of the many wartime surveys that touched upon the prospects for postwar collaboration between Washington and Moscow, not a single one yielded a plurality that answered the question in the negative (table 3.1). A peak in trust was reached in the wake of the 1945 Yalta Conference, which Roosevelt reported had resolved a number of outstanding issues between the United States, Britain, and USSR; at that time, the affirmative responses outnumbered the negative ones by a margin of almost two to one: 55 percent to 31 percent. Another Gallup poll revealed almost identical results immediately after the Soviet Union joined the war against Japan, as Stalin had promised to do at Yalta.

From these high points there was a steady if irregular erosion of public trust in Soviet cooperation that coincided with a potential crisis revolving around the laggard withdrawal of Soviet wartime occupation troops from northern Iran in 1946, as well as the failure of various foreign ministers' conferences to resolve such issues as peace treaties for Germany and Austria. Yet as late as December 1946, nineteen months after the German surrender, a Gallup survey revealed that a 43 percent plurality of the public remained optimistic on the question of Soviet cooperation with the United States. Within less than three years—a period that witnessed consolidation of the Soviets' hegemonic position in Eastern Europe, the coup that brought a communist government to power in Czechoslovakia, and the Berlin blockade—those who responded that the Soviets could be trusted to be cooperative had shrunk to a small minority.

The "cooperation" question was rarely used after 1950, but two decades later Harris surveys began regularly posing a somewhat similar question that asked Americans to assess the prospects for Soviet-American agreements "to help keep the peace." The results summarized in figure 3.2 trace a pattern that appears quite consistent with actual international developments. In July 1968, those who felt that agreements were possible outnumbered the naysayers by 12 percent, but following the Soviet invasion of Czechoslovakia in August, the number of optimists fell from 49 to 34 percent. The developing détente between the superpowers was also reflected in public opinion. Strong majorities, reaching a peak of 60 percent in 1973, answered that it was possible for the superpowers to reach such agreements. By

**TABLE 3.1. "Can Russia Be Trusted to Cooperate with the United States?"
1942–1949**

Dates		Number of Surveys	% Yes	% No	Key Events
1942:	Jan.–June	4	41	34	Moscow Conference: U.S., USSR,
	July–Dec.	6	49	26	U.K. (Aug.)
1943:	Jan.–June	3	46	30	Soviet victory at battle of Stalingrad (Jan.)
					Soviets dissolve Comintern (May)
	July–Dec.	3	49	25	Teheran Conference: U.S., USSR, U.K. (Nov.)
1944:	Jan.–June	2	45	30	Allied invasion of France (June)
	July–Dec.	2	47	36	Soviets allow Germany to crush Warsaw uprising (Aug.–Oct.)
1945:	Jan.–June	2	50	35	Yalta Conference: U.S., USSR, U.K. (Feb.)
					UN Conference at San Francisco (April)
					German surrender (May)
	July–Dec.	5	46	38	Potsdam Conference: U.S., USSR, U.K. (July)
					USSR declaration of war against Japan (Aug.)
					Japanese surrender (Aug.)
1946:	Jan.–June	6	36	48	Dispute over laggard Soviet withdrawal from Iran (Jan.)
					Stalin speech on "inevitability of war" (Feb.)
	July–Dec.	4	35	50	
1947:	Jan.–June	3	28	59	Truman Doctrine: Aid to Greece and Turkey (Mar.)
					Marshall Plan speech on aid to Europe (June)
	July–Dec.	2	19	70	
1948:	Jan.–June	1	25	63	Communist coup in Czechoslovakia (Feb.)
					Berlin blockade initiated (June)
	July–Dec.	2	18	73	
1949:	Jan.–June	4	21	67	Berlin blockade lifted (May)
	July–Dec.	3	21	68	First Soviet atomic bomb test announced (Sep.)

Sources: Survey data from National Opinion Research Center (NORC), Gallup Organization, and Office of Public Opinion Research (OPOR). Reported percentages are averages of the "yes" and "no" responses for each six-month period.

Note: Several NORC questions in 1947–49 asked: "Can the Russian be trusted to meet us halfway?"

the time Harris had stopped asking the question in 1975, détente had been subjected to a number of strains, including a major confrontation between Washington and Moscow during the Yom Kippur War of October 1973; concomitantly, positive responses concerning the prospects for U.S.-USSR agreements dropped to 45 percent.

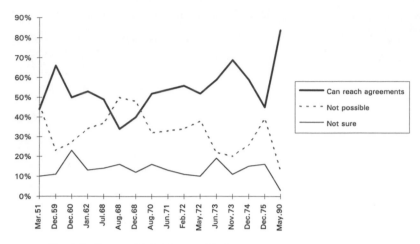

Fig. 3.2. Do you think it is possible for the United States and Russia to reach agreements to help keep the peace? (1951–90). (Data from Gallup polls (1951–62, 1990), Harris surveys (1968–75). The Gallup poll wording was "Do you, yourself, think it is possible or impossible for the United States to reach a peaceful agreement with Russia?")

Although strictly comparable data are more limited for the Gorbachev period, there were many indications of increasing optimism about cooperation between the superpowers. A 1988 survey found that only 19 percent of the respondents felt that improving relations between the two "will *not* lead to any lasting, fundamental changes." In contrast, 57 percent stated that the changes will be fundamental and lasting, "though the two countries will never be allies," and a surprisingly high 23 percent predicted that "one day" they would indeed be allies (Americans Talk Security 1988, No. 6: 64). By the end of 1989, when asked to look ahead to the end of the millennium, two-thirds of the respondents agreed with the statement that "The Soviet Union and West will be living peacefully together" (De Stefano 1990). Finally, when the "cooperation" question was posed again in 1990, after the pathbreaking Intermediate-range Nuclear Forces (INF) Treaty and other agreements between the superpowers, as well as well-publicized summit conferences between Soviet and American leaders, those events were reflected in the overwhelmingly optimistic responses to a Gallup survey on the question.

Soviet Foreign Policy Objectives

During the period since World War II polling organizations frequently have asked the public whether Soviet foreign policy goals are expansionist or defensive. The first period, 1946–53, witnessed a steady erosion of the cooperation that had marked wartime relations between Moscow and Washington, the start of the Cold War, the Korean War, and the death of Joseph Stalin. The second, since 1976, was marked by the collapse of détente, an accelerated arms race, rapid turnover in leadership of the Kremlin, the beginnings of dramatically better relations between the superpowers and, at the end of 1991, the disintegration of the USSR.

Survey data from the first period reveals a rather steady decline— from 29 to 12 percent between 1946 and 1949—in the proportion of Americans who believed that the Soviet Union was merely acting defensively by "building up protection against being attacked in another war." The invasion of South Korea in 1950, widely assumed to have had at least tacit Soviet support, further reduced to a minority of less than one in ten those who believed that the Kremlin was acting out of defensive motives.[10]

After a lapse of more than a quarter century a similar question was again posed regularly, but with a more diverse set of response options. As was the case during the earlier period, the results appear to have been at least moderately sensitive to the course of international events. Whereas in October 1979 only 18 percent of the respondents believed that the Soviet Union was willing to risk war in a quest for global domination, that figure more than doubled to 39 percent within four months—an interval highlighted by the Soviet invasion of Afghanistan. Conversely, the later 1980s saw a steady decline in the proportion of the public that believed that the USSR would use any means, not excluding war, to achieve essentially unlimited international goals. By January 1988 an Americans Talk Security survey revealed that a majority (54 percent) of Americans attributed defensive motives to the Kremlin, whereas a Roper poll at the same time indicated that fewer than half of them (44 percent) believed that global domination was "Russia's primary objective in world affairs." By the end of the year, almost two-thirds of the registered voters polled by the Americans Talk Security project attributed defensive motives to Soviet foreign policy. The trend toward a more benign view of Soviet foreign policy motives continued into the 1990s, with a steady increase in those who believed that self-defense was the driving motive behind the USSR's external policy.

General Assessments of the Soviet Union and Russia

When asked for general assessments of the Soviet Union, aggregate responses from the American public reveal considerable shifts in re-

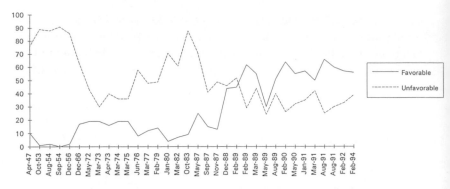

Fig. 3.3. General evaluations of the Soviet Union and Russia, 1947– 94 (in percentages). (1994: evaluation of Russia; 1992: evaluation of the Commonwealth of Independent States (C.I.S.) "Mixed," "neutral" and "no opinion" responses excluded. Data from Gallup poll, NORC, General Social Survey, *Los Angeles Times,* CBS-*New York Times,* Opinion Research Center, ABC-*Washington Post.*)

sponse to international developments rather than a consistently nega-tive image (fig. 3.3). During the 1950s, at the height of the Cold War, the ratings were overwhelmingly negative, but they tended to moder-ate somewhat thereafter. Not surprisingly, a survey undertaken in December 1956, immediately after the Soviet invasion crushed the Hungarian rebellion, found that only 2 percent of Americans had a favorable view of the USSR. Within the next ten years relations be-tween the superpowers had witnessed both crises, such as those in-volving American U-2 spy flights over Soviet territory and the intro-duction of Soviet offensive missiles into Cuba, and cooperation on arms control, including such agreements as the Limited Test Ban Treaty and the Nuclear Non-Proliferation Treaty. Concomitantly, American appraisals of the USSR, while still negative on balance, improved considerably. By the early 1970s, the peak of the Nixon-Kissinger period of détente that was characterized by agreements on arms (SALT I) and in other areas, as well as pronouncements from the White House that the Cold War was over, well under half of the public expressed unfavorable judgments of the Soviet Union; only 30 percent did so in response to a Gallup poll in March 1973. The erosion of détente during the remainder of the decade was similarly reflected in public assessments of the USSR.

After the invasion of Afghanistan at the end of 1979 and the destruction in 1983 of Korean Airlines Flight 007 as it strayed over Soviet territory, unfavorable ratings of the USSR increased sharply, reaching levels not seen since the 1950s. Another shift in sentiment began during the second Reagan Administration after Mikhail Gorbachev assumed leadership in Moscow. By 1987 two surveys reported that fewer than half of the respondents had an unfavorable opinion of the USSR. For the next four years public assessments continued to improve, although with some irregularity. President Gorbachev's crackdown on Lithuania and Latvia in 1991 resulted in some decline. More dramatically, a Gallup survey taken the day after hard-line communist coup plotters had deposed Gorbachev in August 1991 found that favorable appraisals dropped by 30 percent as compared to a poll taken a few days earlier, only to rebound after the failure of the coup. Despite the turbulent course of Russian politics and governance during the post-Soviet period, evaluations of that country remained favorable by a margin of three to two in early 1994.

Assessments of Soviet and Russian Leaders

Until the 1980s, polling organizations rarely asked the American public to evaluate individual Soviet leaders. Even Stalin's death in 1953 did not elicit probes about its implications for Soviet-American relations or for assessments of his successors. This apparent lack of interest on the part of polling organizations in specific Soviet leaders changed dramatically with Mikhail Gorbachev's accession to leadership in 1985. Indeed, the frequency with which pollsters asked the public to assess Gorbachev—the question was posed at least thirty-four times between 1985 and 1991—may have been a good indicator of his manifest public relations skills. Although the results reveal a considerable range of responses, in part from inconsistency in the wording or context of questions, one rather remarkable constant runs through the results for the entire six-year period: not a single survey found that as many as 40 percent of the public expressed a negative opinion of the Soviet leader. During his last three years in office, Gorbachev had an average favorable rating of more than 70 percent. By 1988, those with a favorable view of Gorbachev typically outnumbered his detractors by margins of two, three, or even four to one. A 1988 Harris survey found that the Soviet leader had a 76 percent positive rating, twenty points higher than that accorded to President Reagan during his final months in office. Just prior to Gorbachev's retirement upon the disintegration of the Soviet Union at the end of 1991, 80 percent of the public appraised the Soviet leader in favorable terms. These results confirmed that the Soviet leader enjoyed a higher degree of popularity in most Western nations, including the United States, than in his own country.

His manifest domestic political difficulties notwithstanding, the American public has continued to express support for beleaguered Russian President Boris Yeltsin. A remarkably small proportion of the public has not heard of him—in three Gallup surveys, those who failed to do so numbered fewer than 5 percent—and American support for Yeltsin has widespread public approval (Gallup 1993, 54; Gallup 1994, 15). Perhaps these figures also reflect a feeling that, whatever his shortcomings, Yeltsin is preferable to those who might replace him as Russian leader.

Arms Control

In addition to public attitudes about the Soviet Union, there are ample survey data on several aspects of U.S. policy toward the USSR. Support for arms control, both for general proposals and specific agreements, has been one of the constants in American public opinion since the 1950s. The SALT II agreement is the only exception to this generalization. A massive public relations campaign against the treaty, led by the conservative Committee on the Present Danger, sustained by the manufactured "Cuban brigade crisis," and brought to a climax by the Soviet invasion of Afghanistan, combined to erode early public support for the treaty. Even in the face of these events, a Gallup survey early in 1980, immediately after the invasion of Afghanistan, found that supporters of the agreement outnumbered its critics by a slim margin of 30 to 27 percent, but several Roper polls found declining support for the treaty during the remainder of that election year.

Except for SALT II, the public has strongly endorsed proposal for several kinds of agreements on nuclear weapons: to stop testing them, to place limits on their numbers, and to freeze nuclear arsenals. Even before President Reagan's proposal at the 1986 Reykjavik summit meeting with Gorbachev that all offensive strategic weapons be destroyed within a decade, a plan along these lines gained support from a plurality of respondents in a 1981 Gallup poll. The INF Treaty received overwhelming support, as have various START agreements to reduce offensive nuclear weapons. No doubt the latter measures gained some support because they were endorsed by a popular president—Ronald Reagan—whose harsh antiarms control rhetoric during the 1980 election campaign endowed him with the public image of a leader who would not rush into unfavorable agreements or otherwise be hoodwinked in superpower negotiations. But support of a popular president does not appear to explain fully the consistent public support for arms control; indeed, it does not even appear to be a necessary condition. Repeated polls and state-level referenda, only one of which failed, revealed widespread support for a "nuclear freeze" during the early 1980s even though President Reagan repeatedly denounced the proposals.

Confrontation or Accommodation?

During a five-year period (1948–53) encompassing the Truman administration and the first year of the Eisenhower administration, the NORC asked the public, "Do you think the United States should be more willing to compromise with Russia, or is our present policy about right, or should we be even firmer than we are today?" According to their responses, the proportion of Americans who felt that Washington should adopt a more accommodating stance toward the Soviet Union never exceeded one in ten. In contrast, a policy of greater firmness consistently garnered support from majorities ranging between 53 and 66 percent of the respondents. The inauguration of the Eisenhower administration in 1953, the death of Stalin six weeks later, and the Korean armistice that summer did not significantly affect responses to this question.

After a hiatus of more than a decade, a somewhat comparable question was included in a Free-Cantril survey in 1964. Although the latter poll took place in the aftermath of the Cuban missile crisis—a period that included the Limited Test Ban Treaty, the "Hot Line" agreement, and generally less confrontational relations between Moscow and Washington than had been the case during the turbulent years between the 1958 Berlin "deadline crisis" and the Caribbean confrontation in 1962—a substantial 61 percent of the respondents agreed that the United States should "take a firmer stand" in its dealings with the Kremlin. It should also be noted, however, that there were definite limits on what a "firmer stand" should entail; for example, the same survey found that only 20 percent favored "rolling back the Iron Curtain."

Sixteen years later, in the wake of the Soviet invasion of Afghanistan, two-thirds of those taking part in a CBS-*New York Times* poll also felt that the United States should "get tougher." During the Reagan years, however, every survey, save one taken immediately after Soviet destruction of Korean Airlines Flight 007, revealed that Americans preferred trying "harder to reduce tensions with the Russians" to a more confrontational policy. By 1987 the tension-reduction option had become the preferred choice by a margin of well over two to one. Even though there continued to be some support for a policy of "getting tougher," within a year the ratio in favor of reducing tensions increased to almost three to one. A year later, respondents who felt that President Bush should do more to help the Soviet Union "deal with social and political changes taking place there" outnumbered by more than four to one those who stated that he was already doing too much (Americans Talk Security 1988, No. 10, No. 8: 141).

The President's Handling of Relations with the USSR and Russia

Just before gaining the Republican presidential nomination in 1980, Ronald Reagan asserted in a long interview with the *Wall Street Journal* that the Soviets were the sole source of all international problems (House 1980, 1). Although he was elected in a landslide later that fall, some survey evidence from the Reagan era suggests that most Americans rejected such a Manichaean diagnosis of world problems. When asked three times during the 1980s to respond to the proposition that "The U.S. has to accept some of the blame for the tension that has plagued U.S.-Soviet relations in recent years," three-fourths or more of the public agreed each time. That three surveys undertaken by different organizations—*Time* magazine, the Public Affairs Foundation, and Americans Talk Security—over a span of more than five years yielded almost identical results lends greater credence to the data. Respondents to a 1988 survey also agreed by a margin of two to one that "The U.S. often blames the Soviet Union for troubles in other countries that are really caused by poverty, hunger, political corruption and repression" (Americans Talk Security 1988, No. 7: 57). These figures would also seem to cast some doubt on the thesis that a moralistic and hypocritical American public is incapable of transcending a simplistic "black/white" assessment of world affairs.

Questions about presidential performance have long been a staple item in opinion surveys but, before the Reagan era, only the Harris poll regularly asked the public to assess the president's handling of relations with the USSR. Evidence from the Nixon years reveals that respondents were generally divided on the question until the blossoming of détente (fig. 3.4). In mid-1972 the public gave Nixon a positive rating by a margin of 68 to 25 percent, and six months later the margin of approval had swelled to an even more favorable 70 to 22 percent. The Yom Kippur War, which raised such questions as, "what did the

Soviets know about the impending Egyptian attack on Israel, and when did they know it?", saw a sharp decline in the approval ratings to 55 percent, but they remained favorable, on balance, until 1975. The first survey of the Carter years, during his "honeymoon period" and at a time of highly visible White House support for human rights in the USSR, revealed that a plurality approved of his Soviet policies, but his rating fell steadily, if irregularly, from that point on. A low point was reached late in 1979, when only 22 percent supported his handling of relations with the Kremlin, and that figure had scarcely improved on the eve of the presidential election thirteen months later.

Although many Americans apparently disagreed with Reagan's 1980 diagnosis that the Russians were behind all international problems, they nevertheless gave him relatively good marks for his policies toward the USSR. The data also offer a valuable lesson in caution about using survey data. In this case the lesson centers on systematic differences between results produced by various polling organizations. For this reason, figure 3.4 reports data from the Harris and Gallup surveys separately. In some cases differences between them are quite dramatic. For example, whereas in 1984 (a presidential election year) nine Harris polls found an average net rating for Reagan's Soviet policies of minus 18 percent, the comparable figure from five Gallup surveys was a positive 6 percent. Three other polls by ABC, the *Washington Post*, and CBS-*New York Times* yielded results almost identical to those from the Gallup organization. These differences notwithstanding, it appears clear that Reagan generally received public approbation for his policies toward the USSR. Indeed, aside from the consistently negative ratings that emerged from Harris surveys, only four others out of more than one hundred found a plurality or majority that disapproved of Reagan's Soviet policies.

The data also indicate that after the honeymoon period in 1981, Reagan's strongest approval ratings on Soviet policy tended to come during his second term, years that were marked by regular meetings with Mikhail Gorbachev, progress on arms control, and a general easing of tensions between the superpowers. Because this was also a period when Reagan's overall performance rating scores tended to suffer—for example, he experienced the sharpest drop on record when it was revealed that his administration had been selling arms to the fundamentalist Islamic regime in Iran—the evidence is especially revealing. By mid-1988, a Harris survey found that the president's high approval ratings on Soviet policy (67 percent) and his performance at the Moscow Summit meeting far outstripped his overall

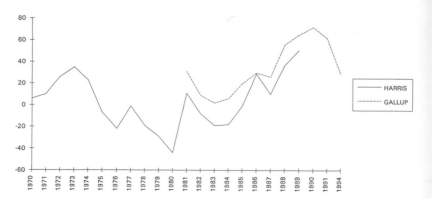

Fig. 3.4. Assessments of presidential handling of relations with the USSR and Russia, 1970–94 (net assessments: percentage "Approve" minus percentage "Disapprove").

popularity (54 percent). This suggests at least two interpretations linking public opinion to foreign policy that are not mutually exclusive.

> Reagan was driven to seek a rapprochement with the Soviets in part to bolster his popularity ratings and, perhaps, his standing in history.
> Whether or not "bear baiting" was good domestic politics in 1980, by 1985, the year Gorbachev assumed Soviet leadership, the domestic climate of opinion had shifted sufficiently to make dancing with "the bear" a more attractive option.[11]

The strong public approval for Reagan's Soviet policies extended into and swelled during the Bush years; for example, Bush's performance rating increased sharply after he announced that he would meet with Gorbachev at Malta. Bill Clinton's overall performance ratings have generally been rather lukewarm, but his dealings with Russia have received greater public approval; in October 1993 those supporting his policies outnumbered the critics by a margin of 54 to 25 percent, with the remainder expressing no opinion (Gallup 1993, 175).

Goals for American Foreign Policy

Although much of the data cited to this point suggests significant changes in public opinion relating to the USSR, especially during the Gorbachev era, there are also some significant continuities. Since 1974 the CCFR surveys have included a cluster of items asking re-

TABLE 3.2.   The Importance of American Foreign Policy Goals: Assessments
in Chicago Council on Foreign Relations (CCFR) Surveys, 1974–94
(percent "Very important" ratings)

"For each [foreign policy goal], please say whether you think that it should be a very important
foreign policy goal of the United States, a somewhat important foreign policy goal, or not an
important goal at all."

	1974	1978	1982	1986	1990	1994
Protecting the jobs of American workers	74%	78%	77%	78%	65%	83%
Protecting the interests of American business abroad	39	45	44	43	63	52
Securing adequate supplies of energy	75	78	70	69	61	62
Defending our allies' security	33	50	50	56	61	41
Preventing the spread of nuclear weapons	—	—	—	—	59	82
Promoting and defending human rights in other countries	—	39	43	42	58	34
Improving the global environment	—	—	—	—	58	58
Protecting weaker nations against aggression	28	34	34	32	57	24
Reducing our trade deficit with foreign countries	—	—	—	62	56	59
Matching Soviet military power	—	—	49	53	56	—
Containing communism	54	60	59	57	56	—
Worldwide arms control	64	64	64	69	53	—
Strengthening the United Nations	46	47	48	46	44	51
Helping to improve the standard of living of less developed nations	39	35	35	37	41	22
Helping to bring a democratic form of government to other nations	28	26	29	30	28	25
Stopping the flow of illegal drugs into the U.S.	—	—	—	—	—	85
Controlling and reducing illegal immigration	—	—	—	—	—	72
Combatting world hunger	61	59	58	63	—	41
Maintaining superior military power worldwide	—	—	—	—	—	50

Source: John E. Reilly, editor, *American Public Opinion and U.S. Foreign Policy 1975.* Chicago: Chicago
Council on Foreign Relations, 1975. Also, similar monographs edited by Reilly in 1979, 1983, 1987, 1991,
and 1995.

spondents to rate the importance of various U.S. foreign policy goals.
"Containing communism" was among the goals in each of the polls
through 1990, and the 1982, 1986, and 1990 surveys also asked
respondents to rate the importance of "matching Soviet military
power." Substantial proportions of Americans rated both of these as
"very important," and very few considered them to be "not important"
(table 3.2). However, it should also be noted that neither of these
quintessential Cold War goals ranked within the four most important
in any of the five surveys undertaken prior to disintegration of the

USSR.[12] More specifically, "matching Soviet military power" ranked only eighth among the fourteen possible goals in both 1982 and 1986, and it fell to a tie for ninth four years later. In *each* of the first five CCFR surveys, two economic goals received more "very important" ratings than those relating directly to the USSR: "protecting the jobs of American workers" and "securing adequate supplies of energy." These continued to be important goals, ranking second (behind only stopping the flow of illegal drugs) and fifth, respectively, among the sixteen goals in the 1994 survey.

Conclusion

It would clearly be overstating the results summarized here to conclude that the public was generally correct in its opinions about the Soviet Union and Russia, if only because with respect to such critical questions as Stalin's intentions—or indeed those of his successors—it is often impossible to identify the "correct" answer. Nevertheless, it is possible to draw some tentative conclusions that would appear to shed light on the three theories identified earlier.

Despite considerable volatility in responses to those questions, the first major conclusion is that aggregate opinions tend to reflect events and trends in the real world. When shifts take place, they appear to be neither random nor systematically out of touch with international realities, as suggested by Almond (1950) and Lippmann (1955) four decades ago. Second, the findings do not appear to offer a great deal of support for the thesis that the public has been wedded to a reflexive and unyielding hostility toward the USSR. To the contrary, substantial numbers of Americans appear to have yearned for good relations between the superpowers and, when given reasonable pretexts for doing so, they expressed opinions to that effect. This is evident not only in data from the World War II period, when the common war effort against Nazi Germany provided a clear mutuality of interests; it is also apparent in evidence from the détente of the early 1970s, as well as the "détente II" that began in the mid-1980s. In short, the survey data summarized here would seem to offer greater support for theories that depict the public as "rational and events-driven" than for the competing theses.

Finally, the evidence that the public reacted to what the Soviets *did* rather than who they *were* during the Cold War suggests how it is likely to assess Russia during the post–Cold War era. Further steps toward democratization and economic liberalization, as well as agreements on control of nuclear weapons and arms sales, will almost surely ensure that appraisals of Russia will remain favorable. Although relatively few Americans have much knowledge of politics, personalities, and parties within the republics of the former USSR, wariness borne in part of an appreciation of the difficulties of creating democratic institutions in these countries is likely to persist. Moreover, support for any major U.S. aid program is likely to remain lukewarm, but that is part of a general skepticism about foreign aid— the public would also reduce assistance to such allies as Israel and Egypt—rather than an expression of displeasure targeted against Moscow.

Conversely, any campaign by Moscow to reconstitute the Russian empire by force, especially should such efforts be directed against the newly independent countries on Russia's western frontier—most notably Latvia, Lithuania, Estonia, Belarus, and Ukraine—would almost surely give rise to a sharp reversal of the more favorable public attitudes that have developed since the mid-1980s. Even repeated use of force against internal groups, as in Chechnya during 1995–96, is likely to demonstrate that the reservoir of public good will toward the former Soviet Union is not inexhaustible. Just as the public often reacted favorably to signs of easing superpower tensions during the Cold War, it is likely to register its disapproval should Russian behavior revert to an imperialist mode.

CHAPTER 4

Opinion Leaders

Until recently, one of the glaring gaps in public opinion research has been the neglect of opinion leaders. Indeed, most analysts have assumed that opinion leaders serve as a critical link between policymakers and the general public; that is, the public receives its cues about politics through opinion leaders (see, for example, Katz and Lazarsfeld 1955; Katz 1957; Neuman 1986). Although this premise has recently been challenged on the grounds that the public can and does get its information directly from the media, only in a pure "bottom-up" model of direct democracy would the distinction between the general public and opinion leaders appear to be superfluous. All other approaches to government—from theories that view the United States as a pluralist democracy to those that depict it as a pseudodemocracy ruled by self-perpetuating elites who seek to use foreign policy as an instrument of narrow class-based interests—recognize the disproportionate influence of some citizens (Devine 1970). Moreover, at least since Almond's (1950) seminal study, *The American People and Foreign Policy,* it has been customary to distinguish between various strata of the public. With a few exceptions, the polity has been depicted as a pyramid with decision makers at the apex. Typically, a further distinction has been drawn between a small coterie of opinion leaders, a somewhat larger group comprising the informed public, and a large base of the general or uninformed public, although the precise terms and shape of the distribution among strata may vary from study to study (compare Kriesberg 1949; Almond 1950; Rosenau 1961; Genco 1984; Neuman 1986). Despite a general consensus on a stratified conception of the American polity, with a few exceptions (Rosenau 1963) there has been a paucity of systematic evidence about the political beliefs of opinion leaders. On occasion the Gallup Organization has surveyed samples of biographees in *Who's Who in America*— for example, in a 1941 poll on whether the United States should join a general international organization after the war or in a 1953 survey on tariffs—but these have typically been one-shot studies that are of limited value, especially for purposes of assessing trends.

Three reasons may explain the puzzling neglect of opinion leaders in survey research. The realist perspective on international affairs places primary emphasis on the imperative arising from the international system and on the manner with which decision makers cope with these systemic threats and opportunities. Other domestic political actors, including opinion leaders, rarely enter into the analysis except, perhaps, as residual categories to explain the nation's deviations from rational choices in international affairs. From this perspective, there are rarely sufficient reasons to undertake leadership surveys.

The prior question of identifying "opinion leaders" is also among the possible barriers to this type of research. There is, of course, an extensive debate on the precise definition of who the leaders are in the United States; if a consensus on that question were a prerequisite for elite surveys, they would never be undertaken. Those designing leadership studies have typically bypassed the broader question and selected subjects in one of two ways: (1) by identifying key roles and then surveying a sample of the persons filling them or (2) by identifying groups thought to be logical sources of opinion leaders and then drawing samples from directories of such persons. The first method might survey a sample of persons holding key offices in business, governmental, media, or other organizations. The latter approach might draw samples from biographies in *Who's Who in America, Who's Who in American Politics,* and similar directories; subscribers to the journals *International Security* or *Foreign Affairs;* or students at the National War College. Some studies have combined these sampling designs.

Still another area of disagreement that might have constrained leadership surveys centers on the ability to use a selected stratum of the data from national probability samples for studying elites; if one can do so validly, there is little reason to endure the very substantial costs of separate surveys. To oversimplify somewhat, the contending views can be reduced to two positions on the adequacy of respondents' education levels as a surrogate measure of leadership status. Certainly there is considerable evidence that international attitudes are strongly related to levels of education. The affirmative view on this issue was presented in a prognosis of how public opinion research is likely to develop during the next half century.

The mathematics and economics of surveys make them most cost-effective for assessing large, undifferentiated populations, i.e., mass publics. And until you get to a handful of individuals at the very top, you don't learn much from studying "elites"—

they seem to be just like better educated people in the general population. These two generalizations suggest no major shift in our attention. The same is true in totalitarian countries (and, I suspect, poor countries). (Davis 1987, S178–S179)

Although the question is far from settled, at this point the proponents of the opposite viewpoint would appear to have at least an equally plausible case. A number of studies have found that, by itself, the level of educational attainment is an inadequate yardstick for identifying opinion leaders (Neuman 1986). Extensive analyses of the 1968, 1980, and 1984 National Election Studies and the first three CCFR surveys by Krosnick and Carnot (1988) indicate that education is an insufficient indicator of the attentive foreign policy public, much less of foreign policy opinion leadership. Their findings reveal little support for the hypothesis that the "foreign policy attentive public" is composed simply of highly educated persons who are concerned with all aspects of public policy. An earlier study also cast doubt on the sufficiency of education as a measure of leadership (Rogers, Stuhler, and Koenig 1967).

Despite these possible impediments to survey research on leaders, the past two decades have seen a substantial number of projects directed specifically at the foreign policy beliefs of this group. As I noted in chapter 3, the Vietnam War was a catalyst in provoking challenges to the Almond-Lippmann consensus about public opinion. In the same way, it is not purely coincidental that systematic surveys on the views of opinion leaders followed upon the heels of the controversial conflict in Southeast Asia. There was a widespread sense that the Vietnam War was a major watershed in American foreign policy because the bitter debates on that conflict had fractured, if not permanently shattered, the post–World War II consensus on the fundamental axioms underlying U.S. policy for a quarter century.

Indeed, the two most extensive elite surveys originated in the mid-1970s as a direct consequence of the post-Vietnam debates on the proper future course of American foreign relations. As a result of these concerns, Secretary of State Henry Kissinger is reported to have asked the CCFR to undertake the first of its surveys, including samples of both the general public and leaders, in 1974. The CCFR subsequently has conducted similar surveys at four-year intervals (Rielly 1975, 1979, 1983, 1987, 1991, 1995). The FPLP, which focuses on opinion leaders, was initiated in 1976 to explore in depth the ways in which leaders interpreted the Vietnam experience, including diagnoses of the causes of American failure in that costly undertaking, prescriptions about "lessons" that should be learned from the conflict, and predictions about the domestic and international consequences of the war. FPLP surveys also have been undertaken at four-year intervals (Holsti and Rosenau 1984, 1990, 1993).

In addition to the series of CCFR and FPLP surveys, there have been a number of onetime studies of American elites. Some of them have included leaders in a broad spectrum of occupations. Others have focused on more specific groups, including business and military leaders and general officers.[1] Several features of the samples in these studies are summarized in table 4.1.[2]

The General Public and Leaders: The Content of Foreign Policy Beliefs

Interest in opinion leaders arises from the hypothesis that in at least some respects they may differ systematically from the general public. If they do not, then there is indeed no reason to go to the very considerable effort and expense that is required to undertake surveys on their foreign policy views. The remainder of this chapter will explore this question by comparing the general public and opinion leaders with respect to, first, the *content* of their foreign policy beliefs and, subsequently, to the ways in which those beliefs are organized or *structured*. The analyses that follow will compare the content of foreign policy beliefs among leaders and the general public at the aggregate level. This approach does not assume, however, that either leaders or the public constitute a homogeneous group. Chapter 5 will undertake analyses that disaggregate data for both groups with a view to identifying some of the background correlates of views on foreign policy.

U.S. Role in the World

Data presented earlier revealed that for more than five decades—more specifically, since less than two years after the attack on Pearl Harbor that brought the United States into World War II—a majority of the general public has favored an "active role" for the United States in world affairs; not a single survey during that period has shown a ratio of less than three to two in favor of internationalism (refer to fig. 3.1). By the late 1980s, a period marked by dramatically improving relations between Washington and Moscow, that margin had increased to more than two to one. The end of the Cold War did not bring about a

TABLE 4.1. A Description of Samples in Some Surveys of Leaders on Foreign Policy and Defense Issues

Survey Name	Year	Sample Size	Sample designed to include these groups									
			POL	MIL	BUS	MED	FPX	STD	LAB	CLE	ED	WOM
CCFR	1974	328	+	0	+	+	+	+	+	+	+	0
CCFR	1978	366	+	0	+	+	+	+	+	+	+	0
CCFR	1982	341	+	0	+	+	+	+	+	+	+	0
CCFR	1986	343	+	0	+	+	+	+	+	+	+	0
CCFR	1990	377	+	0	+	+	+	+	+	+	+	0
FPLP	1976	2,282	+	+	+	+	+	+	+	+	+	+
FPLP	1980	2,502	+	+	+	+	+	+	+	+	+	+
FPLP	1984	2,515	+	+	+	+	+	+	+	+	+	+
FPLP	1988	2,226	+	+	+	+	+	+	+	+	+	+
FPLP	1992	2,312	+	+	+	+	+	+	+	+	+	+
Barton	1971/72	593	+	0	+	+	0	0	+	0	0	0
Russett and Hanson	1973	1,188	+	+	0	0	0	0	0	0	0	0
Kinnard	1974	173	0	+	0	0	0	0	0	0	0	0
Sussman	1976	2,469*	+	0	+	+	0	0	0	0	+	+
Chittick et al.	1984/85	506**	+	0	0	0	0	+	0	0	0	0
Koopman et al.	1986	604	0	+	0	+	+	+	0	0	+	0
Times-Mirror	1993	649	0	0	+	+	+	0	0	+	+	0

Key: POL [political leaders], MIL [military], BUS [business], MED [media], FPX [foreign policy experts], STD [State Department/Foreign Service], LAB [labor], CLE [clergy], ED [education], WOM [women]

+ = group targeted in sampling design

0 = group not targeted in sampling design (but persons in these groups may appear in the sample by virtue of other affiliations. For example, women are included in the CCFR and several other surveys because of their membership in one or more occupational groups).

*Also included farm leaders, black leaders, youth at elite universities

**"Foreign policy elites": government officials and those in nongovernmental organizations

dramatic reorientation of public attitudes in this respect. A 1991 NORC survey revealed that almost three-fourths of the public favored an active American role in the world. Two years later, when it had become clear that the disintegration of the Soviet Union did not necessarily mean an end to troubling conflicts abroad, support for an internationalist American role remained quite high; 67 percent favored that position as against only 28 percent who preferred to "stay out of world affairs." Even continuing controversies over the appropriate American role in peacekeeping operations, such as those in Somalia, Haiti, Bosnia, and elsewhere, had little impact on the strong majority (65 to 27 percent) favoring "an active part in world affairs" during the weeks leading up to the 1994 congressional elections (Rielly 1995, 6).[3]

Although comparable evidence about leaders' preferences is less extensive and is heavily concentrated in the post-Vietnam era, most of it indicates that elites outstrip the general public in their support for active involvement in international affairs. The CCFR surveys, conducted every four years since 1974, have posed the question directly to the general public and to a smaller sample of elites starting in 1978. Because the surveys of the two groups were conducted at the same time by the same polling organization and using identically worded questions, the results provide an excellent basis for comparing leaders and the general public with respect to preferred roles for the United States.

The results of these CCFR surveys reveal strong and consistent differences between leaders and the general public. During the twenty years covered by the six CCFR surveys, the general public preferred an active American international role rather than withdrawal from world affairs by margins ranging from a high of 66 to 24 percent (1974) to a low of 53 to 35 percent (1982). The latter figures constitute the smallest margin in favor of internationalism in any of the more than forty surveys since 1943 in which some variant of that question has been posed.

In contrast, leaders taking part in the CCFR studies have been virtually unanimous in judging that it is better for the United States to "take an active part in world affairs"; that option never failed to gain the support of fewer than 97 percent of them. Indeed, it is hard to find any other significant question about foreign policy that has yielded such one-sided results. However, because it reduces international involvement to only two broad options, this question is too general to provide much insight into how the two groups appraise U.S. policies on specific issues and undertakings abroad. Nor does it reveal how they might react when confronted with trade-offs or with the costs of active involvement in world affairs, especially when the costs are measured in terms of casualties. Thus, in order to get a more precise understanding of how leaders and the general public may differ, if at all, it is useful to examine in more detail the evidence about their attitudes toward specific policies and programs.

Trade and Protectionism

The Vietnam era coincided with a fading U.S. hegemony in international economic matters; the most visible symptoms included worsening trade balances and eroding confidence in the dollar. The "Nixon economic shock" of August 1971, effectively ending the Bretton Woods monetary regime established at the end of World War II, symbolized the declining U.S. international economic position. During the preceding quarter century, polling organizations only infrequently posed questions about trade and protectionism. Several points emerge from a half-dozen Gallup surveys taken between 1947 and 1962 that asked about trade issues. Only one-third to one-half of the respondents were familiar with such issues as the 1947 Geneva agreement to lower tariffs and the Reciprocal Trade Agreement. Among those who knew of these agreements, proponents of reducing tariffs outnumbered the protectionists by substantial margins. For example, of those who were familiar with President Kennedy's trade program, 58 percent supported lower tariffs whereas only 9 percent wanted to raise them. The comparable figures among all respondents were 38 percent and 15 percent, respectively. The lone Gallup survey of opinion leaders, conducted in 1953, revealed that supporters of the Reciprocal Trade Agreement outnumbered opponents by a margin of 67 to 11 percent; moreover, at least three-fifths of the leaders in every occupational category favored that agreement (Gallup 1972, 505, 695, 1151, 1155, 1760).

As trade and other international economic issues became more contentious, survey evidence about public and elite attitudes toward them mounted. The five most recent CCFR surveys have asked both the general public and leaders whether they "sympathize more with those who want to eliminate tariffs or those who think such tariffs are necessary." The results indicate a wide gap between the two groups, with a steady majority of the general public supporting tariffs through 1990. Four years later, in the midst of energetic efforts by the White House and many congressional leaders in both political parties to gain approval of the treaty incorporating the Uruguay Round of the GATT agreement and establishment of the World Trade Organization, those favoring tariffs had fallen below 50 percent; however, proponents of such trade barriers still outnumbered those who would eliminate them by a margin of 48 to 32 percent. Contrary to the widespread belief that protectionism is largely confined to union members and blue-collar workers, retention of tariffs actually received higher than average approval from the college-educated (51 percent) and those with annual incomes above $50,000 (53 percent) (Rielly 1995, 29–30).

In contrast, although there had been some increase in support of protectionism among leaders during the dozen years ending in 1990, that position was espoused by no more than one-third of those polled in any of the CCFR surveys. By 1994 only one leader in five wanted to retain tariffs, whereas more than three-fourths of them favored their elimination (table 4.2). It should be noted, however, that the wording of the questions may have affected the results. Respondents were not offered an opportunity to assess such options as "maintain tariffs at their current levels" or "reduce but do not eliminate tariffs."

Leadership opposition to protectionism also emerges from a question posed three times between 1984 and 1992 to larger samples of leaders in the FPLP surveys. Even though the question was phrased in a manner that explicitly incorporates the most widely used argument for protectionism—"erecting trade barriers against foreign goods to protect American industries and jobs"—fewer than one leader in four expressed either strong or moderate agreement with such a policy in any of the three surveys.

Finally, assessments of the North American Free Trade Agreement (NAFTA), a controversial pact bringing Mexico, Canada, and the United States into a free-trade zone that narrowly passed through Congress in December 1993, provide a further means of comparing public and leadership attitudes on trade. The evidence in table 4.2 reveals that leaders were overwhelmingly in favor of NAFTA, whereas the public was much more evenly divided on the agreement, with the opponents slightly outnumbering the supporters until 1994; the CCFR poll in that year found that NAFTA was judged as "mostly a good thing for the U.S. economy," but that survey was undertaken just before the financial crisis triggered by devaluation of the Mexican peso. Thus, the wide gap between the general public and leaders on trade spans general attitudes toward tariffs as well as such specific undertakings as NAFTA.

Economic and Technical Aid

Strong majorities among the general public favored such early post–World War II foreign aid undertakings as the European Recovery Program; a November 1948 Gallup survey found that the public sup-

TABLE 4.2.   Opinions on Trade, Protectionism and the North American Free Trade Agreement (NAFTA): The General Public and Leaders, 1978–94

"Generally, would you say you sympathize more with those who want to *eliminate* tariffs or those who think such tariffs are *necessary?*"

	Date	Survey	Tariffs are necessary (%) General public	Leaders
	1978	CCFR	57	23
	1982	CCFR	57	28
	1986	CCFR	53	29
	1990	CCFR	54	33
	1994	CCFR	48	20

"Please indicate how strongly you agree or disagree with:"			Agree strongly or agree somewhat (%)	
Erecting trade barriers against	1984	FPLP	—	24
foreign goods to protect	1988	FPLP	—	16
American industries and jobs	1992	FPLP	—	21
Opening negotiations for a free-				
trade zone with Mexico	1992	FPLP	—	84
Creating a free-trade zone with				
Canada	1992	FPLP	—	95

			Favor NAFTA (%)	
Favor or oppose the North American	1993	T-M	46	89
Free Trade Agreement	1993	Gallup*	38	—
	1994	CCFR**	50	86

Note: CCFR = Chicago Council on Foreign Relations surveys; FPLP = Foreign Policy Leadership Project Surveys; T-M = Times-Mirror survey, "America's Place in the World."

*Average of "favor" NAFTA responses in four surveys conducted in August, September, early November, and mid-November. The average "oppose" and "no opinion" responses in these surveys were 43 and 19 percent, respectively.

**Respondents who rated NAFTA as "mostly good" for the U.S. economy.

ported the Marshall Plan, as the ERP was widely known, by a margin of 65 to 13 percent. During the past two decades, however, international economic and technical assistance programs have fallen into public disfavor. They often rank as the most popular candidates for reduced budget allocations, although there is also evidence that this negative view of foreign aid is grounded in widespread misconceptions about the actual level of U.S. spending for assistance abroad. According to the results emerging from a survey conducted in 1995, "A strong majority says that the United States is spending too much on foreign aid. But this attitude is based on the assumption that the United States is spending vastly more than it is in fact. Asked what an 'appropriate' amount would be, the median level proposed is five times the present spending level" (Kull 1995b, 3; see also Kull 1995–96).

The six CCFR surveys conducted between 1974 and 1994 again provide directly comparable evidence about support for such programs among leaders and the general public. When asked, "On the whole, do you favor or oppose our giving economic aid to other nations for purposes of economic development and technical assistance," the general public was generally quite evenly divided on the question, with support for such programs ranging between 45 percent (1990 and 1994) and 53 percent (1986). These figures actually reveal a surprisingly high degree of support for foreign assistance in that most other surveys have shown considerably less enthusiasm. Respondents favored reduction of assistance to all major recipients, most notably Israel and Egypt, the countries receiving the largest amounts of U.S. aid. College graduates, liberals, travelers abroad, and those with higher incomes were the strongest supporters of foreign aid.

Nevertheless, the contrast with elite opinions is quite dramatic insofar as leaders have consistently stated their strong approval of economic and technical assistance. In none of the CCFR surveys through 1990 did fewer than 90 percent of the leaders express support for foreign assistance when asked the identical question; in 1994, the comparable figure—86 percent support for foreign aid—was still double that of the general public. Leaders expressing the strongest opposition were those in business (24 percent) and Congress (19 percent) (Rielly 1995, 31).

A related question asked opinion leaders taking part in the five FPLP surveys whether they would support economic aid to poorer countries "even if it means higher prices at home." After an equal division between supporters and opponents on the question in 1976, moderate majorities of respondents in the subsequent four surveys have favored such assistance.

Military Assistance

Since the outbreak of the Korean War, a very substantial part of American foreign aid programs has consisted of various forms of military assistance. Of the $390 billion devoted to various U.S. foreign assistance programs between 1946 and 1991, about $146 billion consisted of military aid (U.S. Department of Commerce 1994, 816). In comparison to the level of support for economic development and technical aid, neither leaders nor the general public have expressed as much enthusiasm for military assistance programs. The CCFR surveys asked leaders and the general public whether they support or oppose foreign military aid, providing an opportunity to compare the sentiments of the two groups. Even though the question explicitly stated that "by military aid I mean arms and equipment but not troops," support among the general public for such assistance was never especially strong. After reaching a peak in 1986, when one-third of the respondents expressed approval, support fell to less than one-fourth of the public four years later. By 1994, military aid ranked as the favorite target of budgetary cutbacks.

In contrast, strong majorities among leaders supported military aid through 1986; the gap between the general public and leaders on this issue exceeded 30 percent in each of the CCFR surveys to that point. Between 1986 and 1990, support for these programs also fell sharply among leaders, no doubt reflecting such dramatic events as the demolition of the Berlin Wall and, more generally, the end of the Cold War. By 1994 leaders and the general public were in complete agreement on military aid; those favoring a cutback outnumbered proponents of expanded military aid by 64 percent among both groups (Rielly 1995, 12). The five FPLP surveys posed a related question, asking leaders to assess one of the arguments used by opponents of military aid programs—that they "will eventually draw the United States into unnecessary wars." That critique of military assistance has never gained the support of a majority among opinion leaders. Forty-two percent agreed with it in 1984, but by 1992 the level of support had dropped to 36 percent.

U.S. Troops Abroad

The deployment of troops abroad has been among the most controversial aspects of American foreign policy almost since the beginning of the Republic. A public controversy was sparked during the War of 1812 when militia units refused to invade Canada on the grounds that fighting for "the common defense" could only be done on American soil.[4] Even before World War II there were also numerous deployments of U.S. troops abroad without declarations of war—for example, to quell the Philippine insurrection after the Spanish-American War and to pursue Pancho Villa in Mexico during the Wilson administration. The issue became even more visible with the expanded American international role after 1945. During one of his wartime meetings with Winston Churchill, Franklin Roosevelt told the British prime minister that the public would force him to withdraw all troops from Europe within two years after the end of the conflict. Roosevelt's prognosis, which did not take into account the deterioration of East-West relations over such issues as the fate of Poland and other Eastern European countries, the status of Berlin, and the other events that contributed to the Cold War, proved to be wrong. Nevertheless, the overseas deployment of troops rarely has been free of controversy. Symbolizing the controversy were the contentious debates over the obligations entailed in the NATO Treaty and the constitutionality and wisdom of the War Powers Resolution of 1973, a congressional effort to restrict the president's ability unilaterally to send troops into combat or into situations that might entail combat. The expansion of United Nations peacekeeping activities during the past decade has added new and controversial dimensions to the issue: under what circumstances should U.S. forces be included in such international forces and under whose command should they be permitted to serve? Senator Robert Dole's proposed "Peace Powers Resolution" would restrict the president's ability to deploy American forces in the context of international peacekeeping efforts. In this political climate, proposals to send troops to Bosnia stimulated vigorous debates about the feasibility and desirability of American intervention, the proper role of public opinion in policymaking, and the meaning of survey data on the Bosnia issue (see, for example, Kull 1995–96; Rosner 1995–96; Newport 1995; Saad 1995; Saad and Newport 1995; and Sobel 1995b).

Proponents of intervention acknowledged the lack of public enthusiasm for deploying troops but asserted that it was imperative for the United States to assume a leadership role in maintaining a tolerable world order (Schlesinger 1995). Emphasizing that American interests rather than values should govern foreign policy decisions, opponents of intervention attacked President Clinton for "applying the standards of Mother Teresa to U.S. foreign policy" (Mandelbaum 1996). Survey data revealed persisting and stable opinions on several points: a solid majority believed that solution of the Bosnia problem was a very important or somewhat important foreign policy goal; an equally large proportion of the public asserted that Congress must approve any military involvement; and, although a few Americans believed that unilateral American intervention in Bosnia was either a moral obligation or in the national interest, there was moderately strong support for deploying troops as part of a United Nations peacekeeping force. These opinions remained relatively stable after President Clinton's decision to send American forces into Bosnia as part of a multinational effort to enforce the 1995 Dayton peace accord.

Whether public support for the Bosnia peacekeeping undertaking would collapse if it were to result in even moderate casualties—a proposition that, fortunately, had not been put to a test by early 1996—is not clear. Survey evidence on this point depends on the manner in which the question is posed (compare Saad 1995 with Kull 1995c).

Each of the CCFR surveys asked leaders and the general public to indicate whether they favored or opposed the use of U.S. troops in various hypothetical situations, including four that involved an enemy invasion of American friends or allies: Western Europe, South Korea, Israel, and Saudi Arabia. A very similar question was included in a 1993 Times-Mirror survey on "America's Place in the World." At the time of these surveys, the results of which are presented in table 4.3, U.S. troops were already stationed in Western Europe and South Korea.[5] The only case in which majorities among the general public consistently approved of such action by Washington concerned a hypothetical Soviet or Russian invasion of Western Europe. Presumably much of the public was aware that U.S. troops were already stationed in Germany and thus would almost surely be involved if Western Europe were attacked.

In 1990, while American forces were being deployed in the Persian Gulf area after Iraq's invasion of Kuwait, a slight majority also approved using U.S. troops if Iraq also invaded Saudi Arabia; this attitude remained little changed in 1993 and 1994, long after the troops that had been engaged in Operations Desert Storm and Desert Shield had been withdrawn. In contrast, questions in 1982 and 1986 about protecting Saudi Arabia from a revolutionary Islamic regime in Iran yielded minimal support, even though few Americans had a great deal of affection for the Teheran government. Although Israel has never asked for aid in the form of American manpower, Saddam Hussein's frequent and vocal threats, combined with Scud missile attacks against that country during the Persian Gulf crisis also appear to have resulted in a sharp increase among those favoring assistance to Israel. That support persisted into 1994.

Compared to the general public, leaders have consistently been more willing to use American troops in the hypothetical situations described above, with one notable exception; whereas only 18 percent of leaders would send American troops to Cuba if people on that island attempted to overthrow the Castro dictatorship, more than twice as many among the general public would approve a deployment of U.S. forces in such circumstances. Differences between the two groups

TABLE 4.3. Opinions on Use and Stationing of U.S. Troops Abroad: The General Public and Leaders, 1976–94

"Would you favor or oppose the use of U.S. troops if:"

	Date	Survey	General public	Leaders
			Percent who favor	
Soviet troops invaded Western Europe	1978	CCFR	54	92
	1982	CCFR	65	92
	1986	CCFR	68	93
	1990	CCFR	58	87
Russia invaded Western Europe	1994	CCFR	54	91
North Korea invaded South Korea	1978	CCFR	21	45
	1982	CCFR	22	50
	1986	CCFR	24	64
	1990	CCFR	44	57
	1993	T-M	31	69
	1994	CCFR	39	82
Arab forces invaded Israel	1978	CCFR	22	31
	1982	CCFR	30	47
	1986	CCFR	33	57
	1990	CCFR	43	70
	1993	T-M	45	67
	1994	CCFR	42	72
Iran invaded Saudi Arabia	1982	CCFR	25	54
	1986	CCFR	26	—
Iraq invaded Saudi Arabia	1990	CCFR	52	89
	1993	T-M	53	74
	1994	CCFR	52	84
People in Cuba attempted to overthrow the Castro dictatorship	1994	CCFR	44	18

"Please indicate how strongly you agree or disagree with:"			Agree strongly or agree somewhat (%)	
Stationing American troops abroad encourages other countries to let us do their fighting for them	1976	FPLP	—	60
	1980	FPLP	—	54
	1984	FPLP	—	63
	1988	FPLP	—	66
	1992	FPLP	—	65

Note: CCFR = Chicago Council on Foreign Relations surveys; FPLP = Foreign Policy Leadership Project surveys; T-M = Times-Mirror survey.

on the uses of troops abroad were typically quite large, ranging from 9 percent to more than 40 percent.

An FPLP survey item posed the issue of troops abroad in a somewhat different and more general way. Instead of focusing on reactions to using U.S. troops in specific hypothetical conflicts, it asked leaders to appraise the general critique that, "Stationing American troops abroad encourages other countries to let us do their fighting for them." Consistent majorities of those taking part in these five leadership surveys expressed agreement with this proposition. Thus, it appears that while leaders are generally predisposed to come to the aid of key friends and allies under siege, they are also wary of more general commitments, especially to countries that may be willing to turn the conflict over to the United States because they are unable or unwilling to make a full commitment to self-defense. No doubt these views are at least in part a lingering residue of the war in Vietnam.

The data summarized here reveal a consistent pattern of substantially higher support by leaders for various aspects of internationalism, not only in the form of stronger approval for an "active part in world affairs," but also in greater support for liberal trade policies, economic and military assistance, and deployment or use of American troops abroad. The evidence also indicates that both leaders and the general public make distinctions between various types of international policies and undertakings, and these distinctions appear to reflect events and developments in the international arena.

Foreign Policy Goals

Results from the CCFR surveys presented in chapter 3 indicated that the general public has tended to give top priority to goals that promote American economic interests (table 3.2). Protecting the jobs of American workers ranked as the number one goal in all but two of the CCFR surveys of the general public, and it just barely missed doing so in 1974 as well; in the most recent study (1994) it ranked second to stopping the flow of illegal drugs into the United States. Energy security also has consistently been accorded a high ranking, and the survey in 1990 saw a sharp increase in the number of respondents who rated "protecting the interests of American business abroad" as a "very important" foreign policy goal. In contrast, despite occasional charges that the American public has been obsessed with Cold War concerns, such goals as "containing communism" and "matching Soviet military power" have ranked at the top of the foreign policy agenda in none of the CCFR surveys. A more general post–Cold War goal—"maintaining superior military power worldwide"—ranked only tenth among respondents to the 1994 CCFR survey; moreover, another Cold War goal, "defending our allies' security," did not appear among the top three until *after* the Cold War had ended. No doubt its high ranking in 1990 reflected the events surrounding the invasion of Kuwait by Iraq and, perhaps, the fact that the United States and Soviet Union were on the same side rather than adversaries in that episode, thereby eliminating the risks of a confrontation between the superpowers. Four years later, the goal of protecting allies received its lowest rating since 1978 as fewer than half of the respondents rated it as "very important."

The "goals" questions also were posed to leaders in the six CCFR studies, although at times there were some variations in the specific items presented to the two groups. Many of the same questions appeared in the five FPLP questionnaires as well. These two studies thus provide assessments of a wide range of possible foreign policy goals in eleven surveys of leaders conducted over the 1974–94 period. Aside from a shared judgment that energy security is "very important," other goals accorded the highest rating by leaders revealed a somewhat different and broader set of priorities than those similarly rated by the general public. The differences are generally consistent with the proposition that leaders are more internationally oriented. Thus, their most highly ranked goals usually included such world order issues as arms control, "fostering international cooperation to solve common problems, such as food, inflation and energy," "improving the global environment," and "combatting world hunger." The latter goal also was accorded a high priority by the general public in surveys prior to 1990, when the question was dropped. By 1994 it ranked only eighth among the sixteen foreign policy goals in the judgment of the general public.[6] In contrast to the views of the general public, "Defending our allies' security" was accorded a high priority by leaders in three of the CCFR surveys (1978, 1982, 1986); after declining in importance in 1990, it rebounded in the judgment of leaders to rank as the third most important goal (behind only preventing nuclear proliferation and energy) in 1994.

On the other hand, compared to leaders, the CCFR surveys found that the general public consistently appraised the goals of "strengthening the United Nations" as more important. What might at first glance appear to be an anomaly is perhaps actually consistent with the rest of the data. Although the evidence does not permit the proposition to be tested, it is possible that many among the general public view a stronger United Nations as an *alternative* to American interventions and other international undertakings or at least a way of sharing the burdens of such activities. That hypothesis suggests that a pro-United Nations attitude may in fact be consistent with a public yearning for a somewhat less active international role for the United States. It might be noted that support for the UN among leaders increased sharply in the 1990 CCFR and 1992 FPLP surveys, probably as a result of Security Council activities in the wake of Iraq's invasion of Kuwait in August 1990, before dropping in 1994, when only one-third of the leaders taking part in the CCFR survey rated "strengthening the United Nations" as a "very important" foreign policy goal.

There are, finally, some broad similarities in the less highly rated goal priorities of the general public and leaders. Such Cold War goals as containment or "matching Soviet military power" dominated the rankings of neither group. Nor did either leaders or the general public exhibit a great deal of fervor for promoting U.S. values and institutions abroad. "Promoting and defending human rights in other countries" as a foreign policy goal only once received a "very important" rating from even one half of either group; the exception was the public appraisal of that goal in 1990. Even in the wake of the collapse of many communist and other authoritarian regimes in the late 1980s and early 1990s, few respondents, whether among the elite or the general public, expressed much interest in "helping to bring a democratic form of government to other nations." Indeed, that goal consistently ranked among the lowest in the priorities of both leaders and the public. The difficulties of achieving success in such undertakings, especially in countries lacking any tradition of democratic institutions, probably contributed to these ratings. Perhaps abuse of the term *democracy* by American officials when referring to friendly tyrants— for example, when President Reagan compared the Nicaraguan contras to the American founding fathers or when other presidents toasted the Shah of Iran or Ferdinand Marcos of the Philippines in glowing terms as friends of democracy—has also made both opinion leaders and the general public somewhat cynical about America's ability to export democracy.

In summary, the generalization that leaders outstrip the general public in their support for a broad range of internationalist policies and undertaking seems well supported by the evidence. However, an important limitation of the findings bears repeating. Survey data on leadership attitudes before the 1970s are at best very sketchy and certainly not sufficient to permit the types of comparisons that have been possible for the period since the end of the Vietnam War.

The General Public and Leaders: The Structure of Foreign Policy Beliefs

As shown in the previous chapter, the earlier consensus that public attitudes lack coherence and structure has been challenged from a variety of perspectives. A growing body of evidence suggests that some organizing concepts and heuristics enable even a poorly in-formed general public to make some sense of the "blooming, buzzing confusion" that characterizes twentieth-century foreign affairs.

Debates on the structure—or lack thereof—of political attitudes among the general public continue. However, there is somewhat greater consensus on the proposition that elite political beliefs are in fact more highly structured than those of the general public. Whereas evidence from studies of the general public on this point is mixed, elite studies have rarely failed to uncover some coherence and struc-ture; the debates tend to focus on the best ways of describing the structures rather than on their existence (compare Mandelbaum and Schneider 1979; Wittkopf 1990; Hinckley 1992; Chittick and Billingsley 1989; Chittick, Billingsley, and Travis 1995).

Perhaps more importantly, comparative studies generally have found a higher degree of belief structure among leaders. Converse's (1964) widely cited study found that the political beliefs of congres-sional candidates had a much higher degree of coherence or "con-straint" than those of the general public. A more recent parallel anal-ysis of panelists in the National Election Studies and National Convention Delegate Studies provided additional strong evidence on this score.

> Overall, political party elites have a vastly more constrained and stable set of political preferences—in terms of the traditional liberal-conservative dimension—than does the mass public, a conclusion that applies whether the test is a demanding one based on opinions about policy issues or a less stringent one based on appraisals of socio-political groups and prominent political ac-tors. (Jennings 1992)

This section addresses two related questions about the structure of elite foreign policy beliefs. First, to what extent do they resemble those of the general public? More specifically, a scheme based on a distinction between *militant internationalism* and *cooperative internationalism* was found to have provided a powerful means of describing the structure of public attitudes (Wittkopf 1990, 1995). Are the attitudes of leaders similarly organized?

The dramatic events since the late 1980s, marking the end of the Cold War, have given rise to a second and related question to be addressed here. Inasmuch as a preponderance of the evidence on public opinion and international affairs was generated by research during the period between the end of World War II and the demolition of the Berlin Wall—that is, the Cold War era—how can we be sure that our findings are not severely time- and context-bound? For example, is it possible that the salience, intensity, and endurance of the Cold War gave rise to only temporary organizing devices or heuristics for structuring beliefs about international affairs? Were the threats posed by the Soviet Union and the possibility of a Soviet-American nuclear war of such significance that they provided a powerful but evanescent degree of coherence and structure to attitudes on foreign affairs? Stated differently, are research findings that drew almost exclusively on more than four decades of the Cold War sufficiently robust to survive a period of unprecedented international change? Because attitudes toward the Soviet Union and the possibility of nuclear war with that nation played a central role in structuring foreign policy beliefs during the Cold War, what are the consequences of Soviet disintegration and a dramatic transformation of relations between the United States and the successor states of the former USSR?[7]

According to one line of reasoning, the end of the Cold War should result in fundamental changes in the structure of foreign policy belief systems. Evidence summarized in the first three chapters indicates that major events, notably World War I, World War II, and the Vietnam War, have not only had a significant impact on public opinion, but they have even affected the ways in which public opinion analysts have approached the subject of public opinion and foreign policy. One can make a reasonable argument that, taken together, the monumental events of the past decade—including but not limited to the liberalization within, followed by the disintegration of, the USSR; vast political change in Eastern Europe; the Persian Gulf War; the continuing erosion in the international economic position of the United States; and steps toward the economic unification in Western Europe—represent international changes of a magnitude that could be expected to effect fundamental changes in ways of thinking about international affairs.

An alternative line of reasoning suggests that the end of the Cold War may have changed opinions about specific countries and issues, but that the fundamental structure of opinions has remained intact. This view is grounded in the assumption that basic orientations toward international affairs, reflected for example in the persisting debates between "realists" and "liberals," preceded the Cold War, transcended the specific issues of that era, and will survive its demise. Hence, although it would scarcely be surprising to find that opinions about one-time adversaries or specific issues may have changed, it does not automatically follow that more fundamental ways of thinking about the nature of international politics have also done so.

These questions will be addressed by analyzing data from a series of nationwide surveys of American opinion leaders. The FPLP has conducted such surveys by means of a mailed questionnaire in March of every fourth year since 1976. The sample for each survey, representing leaders in a wide range of occupations—including politics, business, the military, the media, the State Department and Foreign Service, labor unions, churches, academia, law and health care—was drawn in part from such standard sources as *Who's Who in America, Who's Who of American Women, Who's Who in American Politics,* and the *State Department Directory.* Others were included by virtue of their positions in specific institutions; for example, membership in the current class at the National War College, chief editorial writers of newspapers with a circulation of 100,000 or more, and labor union officers. (For a more precise description of the FPLP samples, see table 4.1 above). Each of the five surveys brought forth completed questionnaires from more than 2,200 opinion leaders. The most recent survey, undertaken in March 1992, yielded responses to a sixteen-page questionnaire on domestic and foreign policy issues from 2,312 opinion leaders for a return rate of 58 percent. The analyses that follow will focus on the 1992 data because they are the first generated since the end of the Cold War.

A series of studies of public opinion on foreign affairs by Witt-kopf (1990), described briefly in chapter 3, has demonstrated that attitudes toward two dimensions—support or oppose *militant internationalism* (MI) and *cooperative internationalism* (CI)—provide an effective way of describing the belief structures of both elites and the mass publics. Dichotomizing and crossing these two dimensions yields four types, with quadrants labeled as *hard-liners* (support MI, oppose CI), *accommodationists* (oppose MI, support CI), *internationalists* (support both MI and CI), and *isolationists* (oppose both MI and CI). Analyses of the 1976, 1980, 1984, and 1988 FPLP surveys revealed that the MI/CI scheme effectively describes core elements of leaders' beliefs about international affairs. Knowing respondents' placement in the four quadrants defined by the MI and CI dimensions provided a powerful predictor of attitudes toward a broad array of international issues (Holsti and Rosenau 1990, 1993).

In the first four FPLP surveys, the militant internationalism scale focused on two core elements: attitudes toward the USSR or communism and the use of force. Responses to seven questions from the 1976–88 FPLP surveys represent various dimensions of an MI orientation, with an emphasis on a conflictual world in which the USSR and its expansionist policies represent a major threat to the United States; the necessity of being prepared to use force, including by the CIA, to cope with the threats; the dangerous consequences, as postulated by the "domino theory," of failing to meet international challenges; and a zero-sum view of the Cold War conflict.

Although the validity of longitudinal analyses is materially enhanced by using precisely the same wording each time a question is posed, altered global realities made it necessary to make four changes in the 1992 version of the Militant Internationalism scale. "Russia" replaced "Soviet Union" in one question. The wording in two questions on the domino theory and on U.S. obligations to cope with aggression was altered by using the terms *aggressor nations* and *expansionist power* in lieu of *communism*. Finally, a proposition that seems quite central to an MI perspective—"Rather than simply countering our opponent's thrusts, it is necessary to strike at the heart of the opponent's power" (Schlesinger 1975, 25)—replaced an item opposing better relations with the USSR. Owing to these changes, any direct comparison of overall support for an MI perspective in 1992 relative to the four previous FPLP surveys may be somewhat problematical. The specific questionnaire items that constituted the militant internationalism scale are these:

There is considerable validity in the "domino theory" that when one nation falls to communism, others nearby will soon follow a similar path. (1976–88 surveys)

There is considerable validity in the "domino theory" that when one nation falls to aggressor nations, others nearby will soon follow a similar path. (1992 survey)

Any communist victory is a defeat for America's national interest. (All surveys)

The Soviet Union is generally expansionist rather than defensive in its foreign policy goals. (1976–88 surveys)

Russia is generally expansionist rather than defensive in its foreign policy goals. (1992 survey)

There is nothing wrong with using the CIA to try to undermine
hostile governments. (All surveys)

The United States should take all steps including the use of force
to prevent the spread of communism. (1976–88 surveys)

The United States should take all steps including the use of force to
prevent aggression by any expansionist power. (1992 survey)

Containing communism (as a foreign policy goal). (All surveys)

It is not in our interest to have better relations with the Soviet
Union because we are getting less than we are giving to them.
(1976–88 surveys)

Rather than simply countering our opponent's thrusts, it is necessary to strike at the heart of the opponent's power. (1992
survey)

Leaders taking part in the five FPLP leadership studies generally
have been almost evenly divided in their support for militant internationalism, although there have been some sharp changes in responses to
specific items. Not surprisingly, varying majorities attributed expansionist motives to Soviet foreign policy in the 1976, 1980, 1984, and
1988 surveys whereas, by 1992, 68 percent of the leaders denied that
Russian foreign policy goals were thus motivated. Another notable
shift took place in response to the proposition that "The U.S. should
take all steps including the use of force to prevent the spread of
communism." A majority of leaders taking part in the first four surveys
(1976–88) expressed their disagreement with that policy prescription.
However, when the item was reworded in 1992 to reflect the end of the
Cold War—"The U.S. should take all steps including the use of force to
prevent *aggression by any expansionist power*"—support increased
sharply, as over 70 percent of the respondents agreed. Thus, their
willingness to accept international security undertakings rose when
such commitments were broader than containing communism. This
evidence would appear to provide another challenge to the thesis,
discussed in chapter 3, that Americans have been imbued with an
unalterable anticommunism that borders on the obsessive.

The seven items on the cooperative internationalism (CI) scale
emphasize international cooperation and institutions; world order and
"North-South" issues, including hunger and the standard of living in
less developed nations; arms control; and foreign aid. The specific
questions that constituted the cooperative internationalism scale in all
five FPLP surveys are these:

It is vital to enlist the cooperation of the UN in settling international disputes.

The United States should give economic aid to poorer countries
even if it means higher prices at home.

Helping to improve the standard of living in less developed countries (as a foreign policy goal).

Worldwide arms control (as a foreign policy goal).

Combatting world hunger (as a foreign policy goal).

Fostering international cooperation to solve common problems,
such as food, inflation, and energy (as a foreign policy goal).

Whereas changed international realities seemed to mandate alterations
in the wording of some MI items, this was not true of those in the CI
scale; the items and their wording has remained precisely the same in
all five FPLP surveys. Responses to these items have shown a very
modest trend toward greater support of cooperative internationalism
during the twelve-year period covered by the first four FPLP surveys
and a somewhat sharper increase in this respect in 1992. The latter
change was entirely the consequence of a striking shift toward more
favorable attitudes regarding the United Nations. No doubt the direction and magnitude of these opinion changes reflect the events surrounding the Persian Gulf War and the ability of the United States,
with the cooperation of the Soviet Union and the acquiescence of
China, to lead the Security Council toward action to force Iraq out of
Kuwait. Responses to questions on the United Nations offset moderately declining support, sometimes labeled "compassion fatigue," for
three items that have a significant Third World focus: global hunger,
foreign aid, and the standard of living in LDCs.

Despite the changes described above, correlations among responses to the seven questions on the 1992 MI scale are uniformly
positive, as they have been in all of the leadership surveys. The
correlation coefficients across the five FPLP surveys averaged .40 and
ranged from a low of .10 to a high of .66. Although the average
interitem correlation declined in 1992, Cronbach's *alpha,* a measure
of the reliability of a scale, remained above the conventional requirement that it reach the .70 level. The interitem correlations for the CI
scale have also been uniformly positive, ranging from .12 to .67, and
they have scaled well. In the five FPLP surveys, Cronbach's *alpha*
coefficients have never fallen below .77. The premise that the two
scales are measuring different dimensions of internationalism is supported by the fact that correlations of responses to the items on the MI
scale versus those on the CI scale were uniformly negative.

TABLE 4.4.   The Distribution of Hard-Liners, Internationalists, Isolationists, and Accommodationists in the 1976–92 FPLP Surveys

Militant Internationalism	Cooperative Internationalism			
	Oppose (%)		Support (%)	
	Hard-liners		Internationalists	
Support	1976	20	1976	30
	1980	20	1980	33
	1984	17	1984	25
	1988	16	1988	25
	1992	9	1992	33
	Isolationists		Accommodationists	
Oppose	1976	8	1976	42
	1980	7	1980	41
	1984	7	1984	51
	1988	8	1988	52
	1992	5	1992	53

In order to classify respondents into four groups, a score of 0.00 was used as the cutting point on both scales for each of the five surveys.[8] Whereas those opposing militant internationalism have slightly outnumbered the supporters since 1984, there has been a moderate but steady trend toward increasing support for cooperative internationalism. Table 4.4, depicting the distribution of *hard-liners, isolationists, internationalists,* and *accommodationists,* confirms that the latter two groups—leaders with a favorable stance toward cooperative internationalism—outnumber the other two. As in the 1984 and 1988 surveys, *accommodationists* constituted a slight majority of the entire sample in the most recent survey. The most discernible change in 1992 is the increased number of *internationalists,* mostly at the expense of the *hardliners* and, to a lesser degree, the *isolationists.* It bears repeating, however, that changes in the items constituting the 1992 MI scale also may have affected these results. In any case, neither the distribution of leaders in the MI/CI classification scheme for 1992 nor a comparison of that distribution with those of earlier surveys will suffice to establish its adequacy for depicting the structure of attitudes toward international affairs. Although analyses of earlier FPLP surveys revealed that leaders in the four groups consistently and systematically varied in their responses to other issues, for reasons discussed previously it remains to be demonstrated that patterns and relationships that existed during the Cold War era have survived its demise.

In order to answer that question, the durability of the MI/CI classification scheme can be tested by exploring how leaders taking part in the 1992 survey responded to a broad range of questions about international affairs, including beliefs about the current structure of the international system, approaches to peace, future threats to U.S. national security, U.S. roles and interests; the Persian Gulf War; and perceived sources of change in the USSR and Eastern Europe.[9]

The Structure of the Post–Cold War International System

The military preponderance of American- and Soviet-led blocs—that is, a bipolar international system at the strategic level—was a dominating feature of the Cold War era. When asked to describe the contemporary international system, almost 90 percent of respondents to the 1992 leadership survey agreed that it was multipolar. A 10 percent range of responses across the four groups defined by the MI/CI classification scheme is statistically significant, but that difference pales in comparison to the striking convergence of views on the structure of the system. Although Russia remains a highly armed nuclear power, the sea change in attitudes is reflected in the fact that fewer than 3 percent of the opinion leaders viewed the system as bipolar. Nor did the thesis that the disintegration of the USSR has created a "unipolar moment" in which only the United States has the means, and therefore the responsibility, to create and maintain international stability gain much support among leaders taking part in the 1992 survey (Krauthammer 1990–91); only 8 percent of the respondents asserted that "unipolar" best describes the post–Cold War international system.

Approaches to Peace

Opinion leaders were asked to evaluate the effectiveness of a broad array of approaches to peace (table 4.5). Responses to these questions reveal striking and consistent differences among leaders in the four groups. More importantly, the differences offer very substantial support for the MI/CI classification scheme. "Military superiority of the United States" was the only approach to peace that generated strong support from the *hard-liners*, and leaders in this group offered very negative assessments of three approaches strongly identified with their opposites (*accommodationists*): arms control, narrowing the gap between rich and poor nations, and strengthening the United Nations and other international organizations. The *internationalists* favored prescriptions that are consistent with a group defined as supporting both militant and cooperative internationalism. Specifically, they awarded

TABLE 4.5. Assessments of Approaches to Peace by Opinion Leaders in 1992: Isolationists, Hard-Liners, Accommodationists, and Internationalists

How effective do you consider each of the following as an approach to world peace? Please indicate your assessment.

			Very effective (%)			
	All Respondents (N = 2,312)	Isolationists (N = 120)	Hard-Liners (N = 216)	Accommodationists (N = 1,222)	Internationalists (N = 754)
Trade, technical cooperation, and economic interdependence	50	31	29	56	48
Better communication and understanding among peoples and nations	45	22	24	49	49
Collective security through alliances	41	18	31	37	53
Arms control	33	18	10	38	33
Military superiority of the U.S.	32	39	67	12	53
Narrowing the gap between rich and poor nations	30	8	6	42	22
Strengthening the United Nations and other international organizations	30	1	3	39	28
Political efforts to achieve a balance of power within regions and between great powers	20	10	11	22	22

Note: Differences among groups significant at the .001 level for all items.

the highest effectiveness ratings to two approaches that fit well with militant internationalism: U.S. military superiority and collective security through alliances. They were also inclined to support approaches to peace that are associated with cooperative internationalism: trade, technical cooperation, and economic interdependence and better international communication and understanding.

The *isolationists,* defined as opposing both militant and cooperative internationalism, would not be expected to express a great deal of support for any of the prescriptions listed in table 4.5. The data are fully consistent with that expectation. None of the four varied approaches favored by their opposites—the *internationalists*—elicited much enthusiasm among the *isolationists,* and they were even more skeptical of the other four prescriptions. Finally, the MI/CI classification scheme suggests that the *accommodationists'* responses should be the mirror image of those elicited from the *hard-liners.* That is precisely the case. The latter emphasized the effectiveness of military superiority, while scorning the value of arms control, a narrowing of the rich nation/poor nation gap, and international organizations. In contrast, the *accommodationists* were by far the least enthusiastic about the efficacy of military superiority, and by a very substantial margin they accorded the highest rating to four approaches to peace that incorporate a strong element of international cooperation: economic interdependence, arms control, narrowing the economic gap between nations, and international organization. A fifth cooperative approach, better international communication, drew equally high ratings from the *internationalists* and *accommodationists.* In summary, the pattern of favored prescriptions for peace reveals striking differences that are wholly consistent with the scales used to define the four groups.

Future Threats to U.S. National Security

Evidence from a number of surveys has shown that even before the disintegration of the Soviet Union, much of the American public was inclined to focus on threats to national security other than those arising from the Soviet Union or traditional Cold War issues. For example, a 1988 Americans Talk Security survey revealed that Soviet policies ranked seventh in a list of such threats, tied with the greenhouse effect (Americans Talk Security 1988, No. 9: 51–54). The 1992 FPLP questionnaire asked respondents to assess the seriousness of thirteen potential threats to American national security during the remaining years of the century. The threats are not limited to traditional security concerns, as they include military, economic, social, environmental, demographic, and domestic issues.

Of the thirteen potential future threats, the nine deemed to be the most serious by the entire leadership sample are listed in table 4.6. The four additional dangers that appeared in the 1992 survey, none of which was rated as "extremely serious" by as many as 20 percent of the leaders, were: "armed conflict in the Middle East" (16 percent "extremely serious" responses), "economic competition from Japan and Europe" (14 percent), "American interventions in conflicts that are none of our business" (13 percent), and "mass migrations" (10 percent). Assessments by the MI/CI groups of these four items differed significantly in each case and in ways that generally fit the expected pattern; for example, 22 percent of the *hard-liners* rated economic competition as an extremely serious threat, whereas only 10 percent of the *accommodationists* did so. But perhaps the more important conclusion is that relatively few respondents judged these prospective developments to be a major concern. In contrast, three threats were deemed to be extremely serious by more than half of the entire leadership sample: nuclear proliferation, an inability to deal with various domestic problems, and the federal budget deficit.

Responses of the four groups reveal that differences among them are significant on all threats save one; a majority of leaders in all groups except the *isolationists* rated the dangers of the federal budget deficit as "extremely serious." They also indicate that most of the intergroup differences sustain the potency of the MI/CI scheme. The two nuclear weapons issues and international drug trafficking (defined by some as an issue for which there can be an effective military solution) elicited the highest concern from the *hard-liners* and *internationalists;* responses to another military issue, relating to unwise U.S. interventions abroad, fit the expected pattern less clearly.

Assessments of four economic-social issues that can only be resolved by international cooperation—the rich nation/poor nation gap, population growth, the environment, and the greenhouse effect—also sustained the MI/CI scheme. Strongest concern in each case was expressed by the *accommodationists* and *internationalists*. Finally, as would be expected, except for nuclear proliferation, the *isolationists* focused largely on domestic threats, and they typically registered the lowest level of concern with the potential external threats, be they environmental, social, or military.

Thus, the pattern of threat assessments generally supports the MI/CI scheme. However, the perceived threats arising from trade competition and the Middle East conflict do not fit this pattern very

TABLE 4.6. Predictions of Future National Security Threats by Opinion Leaders in 1992: Isolationists, Hard-Liners, Accommodationists, and Internationalists

This question asks you to evaluate the seriousness of the following issues as threats to American national security during the remaining years of this century. Please indicate how serious you regard each possible threat.

		Extremely serious (%)			
	All Respondents (N = 2,312)	Isolationists (N = 120)	Hard-Liners (N = 216)	Accommodationists (N = 1,222)	Internationalists (N = 754)
The possession of nuclear weapons by Third World countries and terrorists	62	51	68	54	75
An inability to solve such domestic problems as the decay of cities, homelessness, unemployment, racial conflict, and crime	60	47	31	68	57
The federal budget deficit	54	43	54	51	60
International drug trafficking	41	24	40	33	56
Environmental problems like air pollution and water contamination	40	14	15	47	37
Uncontrolled growth of the world's population	37	20	23	44	34
A growing gap between rich nations and poor nations	27	7	6	36	21
The greenhouse effect and other changes in the global climate induced by human activities	27	8	8	33	24
Nuclear weapons in republics that seceded from the former Soviet Union	25	15	30	19	34

Note: Differences among groups significant at the .001 level for all but the third item ("federal budget deficit").

well. Earlier studies, predating the end of the Cold War, have also shown that questions relating to trade and protectionism and Israel-Middle East conflicts typically yield patterns of responses that are largely independent of partisan, ideological, or other classifications of respondents, including the MI/CI scheme (Holsti and Rosenau 1990).

U.S. International Interests and Roles

Much of the foreign policy debate of the past few years has focused on the proper role for the United States in a world transformed. When asked to assess American interests and roles in the post–Cold War international system, there is little evidence of support among opinion leaders for an indiscriminate retrenchment into isolationism. Four propositions in the 1992 survey that probe for various aspects of isolationism received rather limited support. Only about a third of the respondents agreed that the United States should "concentrate more on our own national problems," and an even smaller proportion supported the view that its vital interests are limited to the industrial democracies and nations in this hemisphere. Propositions indicating that U.S. international interests are limited to questions of peace and stability, and that Third World conflict cannot jeopardize those interests, gained the agreement of fewer than one respondent in six. Although the *isolationists* were generally most supportive of retrenchment, the differences across the four groups are rather muted, as they were on another item related to the Third World—that the United States can best promote democratic development by solving its own problems. Finally, at least 80 percent of the leaders in all groups supported an element of the "Weinberger Doctrine": "Before the U.S. commits combat forces abroad, there must be reasonable assurance of support by the American people."

Two other questions focus on the *type* of international role that the United States should play. A slight majority (57 percent) agreed that "America's conception of its leadership role must be scaled down," but differences among the four MI/CI groups were very large and, as expected, the strongest support came from the *accommodationists* (73 percent) and *isolationists* (57 percent) whereas there was far less agreement among the *internationalists* (38 percent) and *hardliners* (30 percent). A related item—"Although its power is greater relative to other countries, the United States is no superpower and it ought not to act as if it is"—yielded a very similar pattern of responses. Fewer than two-fifths of the leaders agreed with this assessment, but about half of the *accommodationists* did so, far outstripping the *internationalists* (26 percent) and *hard-liners* (18 percent) in this respect.

Finally, two questions with strong realpolitik overtones addressed the appropriate goals for the projection of American power abroad. The leadership sample divided almost evenly in its preferences if faced with a trade-off between supporting international stability and self-determination movements, but fewer than one leader in five favored intervention into the domestic affairs of other countries in support of a more democratic world order. As one would expect, the *hard-liners* and *internationalists* expressed significantly stronger support for both propositions than did leaders in the other two groups.

The Persian Gulf War

Two clusters of questions permitted those taking part in the 1992 leadership survey to record their policy preferences during and after Operation Desert Storm and to assess the consequences of the most significant U.S. military intervention abroad since the end of the Cold War or, indeed, since the war in Vietnam.

Much of the policy debate ignited by the Iraqi invasion of Kuwait centered on the relative merits of initiating military operations against the Baghdad regime versus relying on economic sanctions to force Iraq out of Kuwait; relatively fewer participants in those debates questioned whether the United States should even have become involved in the issue. When asked which of these options they had preferred prior to the start of "Desert Storm" in mid-January 1991, those favoring the immediate use of force outnumbered the advocates of giving economic sanctions a longer time to work by a margin of about three to two, and only 5 percent opposed getting involved at all (table 4.7). Respondents were also asked about their policy preferences after the war. Despite the overwhelming defeat of Iraqi armed forces and the relatively light U.S. casualties, the overall increase in support for the use of force was a rather modest 5 percent, and there was an almost equal increase in the number of those who opposed any U.S. involvement.

Responses to the Persian Gulf War should provide an especially salient test of the MI/CI scheme because the two primary policy options are closely linked to militant internationalism (use force) and cooperative internationalism (rely on the effectiveness of economic sanctions imposed by a substantial part of the world community). Differences across the four groups are very substantial, and they are consistent with expectations based on the MI/CI scheme. The *hard-*

TABLE 4.7. Policy Preferences before and after the Persian Gulf War among Opinion Leaders in 1992: Isolationists, Hard-Liners, Accommodationists, and Internationalists

People differed over President Bush's decision to start the war against Iraq. Some felt he was right to use military force right away. Others felt he should have given economic sanctions a longer time to work. Still others opposed getting involved at all. Please indicate which position comes closest to your own feelings—both just before the U.S. launched military operations on January 16, 1991, and retrospectively after the war ended.

	All Respondents (N = 2,312)	Isolationists (N = 120)	Hard-Liners (N = 216)	Accommodationists (N = 1,222)	Internationalists (N = 754)
				Checking each option (%) (Before the start of the Gulf War)	
I tended to favor using force right away	56	67	86	37	75
I tended to favor giving sanctions a longer time to work	38	23	10	54	22
I tended to oppose getting involved at all	5	10	4	7	2
Not sure	1	1	*	2	1
			(Retrospectively after the war)		
I tended to favor using force right away	61	66	89	44	83
I tended to favor giving sanctions a longer time to work	27	17	5	40	13
I tended to oppose getting involved at all	8	13	4	12	2
Not sure	4	4	2	5	3

*Less than 0.5 percent.
Note: Differences both before and after the war significant at the .001 level.

liners and *internationalists* are defined as supporting militant internationalism, and in fact they overwhelmingly favored the use of force; the former did so in somewhat greater proportions than the latter. *Accommodationists* favor cooperative internationalism, and they were by a substantial margin the strongest advocates of giving sanctions more time to effect an Iraqi withdrawal from Kuwait. *Isolationists* support neither militant nor cooperative internationalism. In this instance they preferred the use of force to economic sanctions, but they were also the strongest advocates of not getting involved at all.

The opinion leaders were also asked to express agreement or disagreement with ten judgments—five favorable and five unfavorable—of the Persian Gulf War (table 4.8). Each of the five positive judgments received agreement from a majority of the respondents. Four out of five leaders agreed that the war increased U.S. influence and that cooperation with the Soviet Union during the war would enhance the prospects for creating a new world order. Smaller majorities supported assessments that the war was a great U.S. victory, provided leverage for a settlement of other Middle Eastern issues, and "put the Vietnam war behind us." Support for the five unfavorable consequences ranged from 39 percent who felt that the funds spent in the war should have been spent at home to 21 percent who feared that the war would breed overconfidence in the U.S. ability to cope with future foreign threats.

Responses to the Gulf War items by leaders in the four groups provide another example of strong support for the MI/CI scheme. Four of the five favorable consequences received significantly stronger support from *hard-liners* and *internationalists;* the item on Soviet-American cooperation yielded a more ambiguous pattern of responses. Conversely, four of the five unfavorable consequences elicited the strongest support from *accommodationists* and *isolationists;* as one would expect, the fifth, concerning fears of unwarranted U.S. overconfidence in dealing with future threats, received the strongest support from *hard-liners* and *internationalists.*

Sources of Change in the USSR and Eastern Europe

Referring to developments in Eastern Europe and the Soviet Union that culminated in destruction of the Berlin Wall, columnist George Will described 1989 as the "most startling, interesting, promising and consequential year, *ever*" (*Newsweek,* November 20, 1989, 90). No doubt that judgment could be challenged, if only because events of the next several years were hardly less intriguing—or less widely pre-

TABLE 4.8. Assessments of the Persian Gulf War by Opinion Leaders in 1992: Isolationists, Hard-Liners, Accommodationists, and Internationalists

Here are some assessments of the Persian Gulf War. Please indicate how strongly you agree or disagree with each statement.

	All Respondents (N = 2,312)	Isolationists (N = 120)	Hard-Liners (N = 216)	Accommodationists (N = 1,222)	Internationalists (N = 754)
			Agree strongly + Agree somewhat (%)		
It increased the influence of the United States with other nations	80	79	89	72	90
Soviet-American cooperation before and during the war helped to establish firmer foundations for a new world order	80	73	75	77	86
It was a great victory for the United States	60	57	83	45	78
It has given the United States the leverage needed to gain settlement of other Middle Eastern issues such as the Arab-Israeli conflict	58	44	62	52	70
It put the Vietnam War behind us	55	47	69	44	68
The U.S. spent money abroad that needed to be spent at home	39	31	17	55	22
Too many Iraqis were killed	38	24	10	56	19
The U.S. will be too ready to use military force and go to war again	36	32	13	50	22
It increased frustration and hatred in the Middle East and will bring more violence and terrorism	33	30	20	42	22
The U.S. will be too confident and drop its guard against foreign threats	21	14	37	14	29

Note: Differences among groups significant at the .001 level for all items.

dicted by either practitioners or scholarly specialists on Eastern Europe and the Soviet Union.[10]

The 1992 leadership survey, which followed the disintegration of the USSR by only three months, asked respondents to evaluate eight possible explanations for the monumental changes in the Soviet Union and Eastern Europe. The results reveal a pattern of very strong agreement on internal causes and much greater disagreement on external explanations for change. Virtually all respondents, irrespective of their placement in the MI/CI classification scheme, agreed that Soviet internal weakness (97 percent), the failures of communism to provide a satisfactory standard of living (95 percent), and Mikhail Gorbachev's reformist policies (92 percent) contributed importantly to the unprecedented changes. A somewhat smaller proportion (69 percent) of opinion leaders agreed that "The desire on the part of the people in the Soviet Union and Eastern Europe to get rid of governments that rule by force" was an important reason for change.

Questions relating to the impact on the Soviet Union and Eastern Europe of external forces gave rise to much sharper intergroup differences. The defining characteristics of the four MI/CI groups would suggest that, compared to the *isolationists* and *accommodationists*— the two groups opposing militant internationalism—the *hard-liners* and *internationalists* should be more inclined to credit external sources for transformation of the USSR and Eastern Europe. That expectation is supported amply by the data. A preponderance of leaders (74 percent) in all four groups agreed that the Western media contributed importantly to change, with modestly stronger support from the two groups supporting militant internationalism. The same pattern, although with much stronger intergroup differences, emerged on the role of Western defense policies in general and, more specifically, on "the military build-up by the U.S. during the Reagan years." The latter question divided the leadership almost evenly as 48 percent expressed their agreement with it. However, intergroup differences were huge and in the direction predicted by the MI/CI scheme. Whereas three-fourths of the *hard-liners* and two-thirds of the *internationalists* agreed that the American military buildup had contributed to changes in the Soviet Union and Eastern Europe, only about one-half of the *isolationists* and one-third of the *accommodationists* expressed the same judgment. Finally, the proposition that the election of a Polish Pope in 1978 could have stimulated change received relatively little support (20 percent), but differences among groups were significant and in the predicted direction in that *hard-liners* and *internationalists* were most inclined to agree.

Two competing lines of reasoning presented at the outset of this section hinged on the extent to which the end of the Cold War has altered the structure of beliefs about international affairs. The first predicted that the dramatic events culminating in the disintegration of the USSR would affect the structure of foreign policy beliefs, whereas the second emphasized the likelihood of continuity in belief structures. On balance, evidence from the 1992 leadership survey indicates that positions on militant and cooperative internationalism, yielding four distinct types, continue to provide an effective way of depicting opinion leaders' attitude structures on a broad range of issues. From one perspective this may seem an anomaly in the light of the unprecedented international changes in recent years. From another viewpoint this finding is less surprising. The militant and cooperative internationalism dimensions correspond closely to the most venerable theories of international relations: *realism* and *liberalism*. Inasmuch as the debates between these schools of thought predate the Cold War, it is perhaps not so surprising that, in the main, the MI/CI scheme has continued to identify important elements in the structure of thinking about international affairs.

It must also be acknowledged, however, that the MI/CI scheme is not sufficient to encompass all important aspects of foreign relations. The most notable example of this failure concerns trade-related issues. Recall that only a small proportion of leaders rated "economic competition from Japan and Europe" as a major future threat to American security. Several other questions reveal that the pattern of responses is poorly predicted by placement in the four quadrants of the MI/CI scheme. Only one-fifth of the opinion leaders agreed with a proposal to erect "trade barriers against foreign goods to protect American industries and jobs," and only among those in one group, the *hard-liners,* did support reach as high as 30 percent. And when asked to choose between two economic growth scenarios—Japan grows at a 6.5 percent annual rate and the United States at 2.5 percent or Japan grows at 1.1 percent per year and the United States at 1 percent—57 percent of the entire sample preferred the former option even though the latter scenario would ensure that the Japanese could never catch up with the United States. This is interesting evidence for the debate among proponents of "relative gains" versus "absolute gains" as the driving force in foreign affairs. For present purposes, the more important point is that leaders in all four groups favored the high-growth scenario and differences between them were rather narrow and not statistically significant. Although the MI/CI scheme does not adequately predict responses to trade and protectionism, this does *not* represent a post–Cold War change in the structure of foreign policy beliefs. Evidence from earlier FPLP surveys revealed that neither the MI/CI scheme nor such otherwise powerful variables as party and ideology effectively predicted positions on international trade (Holsti and Rosenau 1990).

Thirdly, the 1992 survey evidence demonstrates that a high level of agreement on structural aspects of the international system does not necessarily predicate responses to other issues, whether broad ones such as the most effective approaches to peace or narrower questions such as how best to cope with Iraq's invasion of Kuwait. A central axiom of realist theories is that systemic structures severely constrain, if not dictate, foreign policy choices. However true this may be at the most abstract level—not even superpowers can be totally oblivious to the international environment—this is also a fundamental weakness of structural realism. Realism appropriately points to survival and security as core goals, but beyond this it does not tell us about the other values and preferences that can affect the selection of goals, strategies, and tactics. An overwhelming majority of American leaders believes that the contemporary international system is multipolar but, by itself, multipolarity does not dictate that major powers must or must not adopt specific international roles, rank foreign policy goals (beyond survival) in a certain order, or pursue or abstain from specific undertakings. It was shown that *hard-liners* usually placed the greatest emphasis on the military dimensions of security, whereas *accommodationists* were most inclined to focus on international organizations and Third World development issues. These represent quite different policy stances, but it is not possible to derive either approach directly and unambiguously from perceptions about the structure of the international system or to judge their relative merits merely by references to the logic of multipolarity.

A fourth point that emerges from this analysis is that the most contentious and divisive issues revolve around militant rather than cooperative internationalism. Several reasons come to mind. Recall that more than three-fourths of the entire leadership sample support cooperative internationalism; that is, they are classified as either *accommodationists* or *internationalists* (table 4.4). On the other hand, the *hard-liners* and *internationalists*—those who support militant internationalism—constitute a minority. To the extent that one can draw broader conclusions from these figures, they suggest that it may be easier to build domestic coalitions for undertakings abroad that have a tenor of cooperative rather than militant internationalism. The probability of high casualties is also greater in the latter than the former case. This reasoning may offer at least a partial explanation for the broad support behind the 1992 Operation Restore Hope in Somalia (at least until broadening the initial scope of the humanitarian mission into an exercise in "nation-building" led to American casualties), in contrast to the decidedly more lukewarm enthusiasm for military intervention to restore peace in Bosnia.

The Structure of Leaders' Beliefs: Domestic and Foreign Policy

Still another question about belief structures is the relationship between attitudes on domestic and foreign policy issues. Are preferences on domestic issues systematically linked to those international ones, or are they largely independent of each other? As on many questions relating to public opinion, the evidence is mixed. Much of it is derived from analyses generated either by panel studies of the electorate or Gallup and other surveys of the general public. Comparable data about opinion leaders are in much shorter supply.

At first glance it appears that virtually all the findings point toward the conclusion that attitudes about issues in the domestic and international arenas are independent rather than systematically linked. In their study of the 1948 election, Berelson and his colleagues (1954) found a limited correlation between domestic "position (economic) issues" and either civil rights or foreign policy "style issues." "The dilemma is that the two contemporary axes of liberalism-conservatism, the one economic-class and the other ethnic-international, vary independently of each other. . . . To know, for example, that someone supported the New Deal on economic issues provided no indication of his international or civil rights opinions" (Berelson, Lazarsfeld, and McPhee 1954, 197–98). Similar findings emerged from several other studies of the electorate. Campbell and his colleagues reported, "Across our sample as a whole in 1956 there was no relationship between scale positions of individuals on the domestic and foreign attitudinal dimensions" (Campbell, Converse, Miller, and Stokes 1964, 113). Partisanship characterized responses to domestic issues but not to foreign policy issues. V. O. Key uncovered a similar pattern. Assessing the relationship between internationalism—a willingness to tolerate international involvement—and domestic liberalism, he concluded, "The lines of cleavage in the two policy areas did not coincide" (Key 1961, 158). Converse's (1964) previously cited analysis of belief systems among elites and the general public reported correlations among responses by both groups to domestic and foreign policy issues. He came to the same conclusion. Among the general public, the degree of policy consistency, whether on domestic issues, foreign policy issues, or across the two issue areas, was quite low.

For my present purposes, the more directly relevant question concerns the degree of consistency of views across domestic and foreign policy issues among persons in leadership positions. Compared to data for the general public, evidence about elite attitudes is much scantier. Many findings point toward greater ideological consistency among leaders, and the usual explanations are located in different levels of education and awareness of the issue content associated with such terms as *liberal* and *conservative*. Almond's (1950, 150) pioneering study *The American People and Foreign Policy* asserted the existence of a broad consensus among elites that cut across the two issue areas.

> More basically, this foreign policy consensus is founded upon a consensus of fundamental attitudes and ideologies that may be described in two dimensions—values and means. The advocates of the American foreign consensus are, in general, agreed that the primary aims of American policy, both domestic and foreign, should turn on a reconciliation of individual freedom and mass welfare of a primarily material kind.

Although Almond did not present systematic survey evidence to buttress his findings on this score, most analysts have tended to agree at least with the point that, compared to the general public, elites are more likely to hold policy positions that are consistent—that is, that their beliefs are held together by some underlying ideological principles. Russett and Hanson (1975) surveyed military officers and business leaders, and they also had access to Barton's (1974–75) data from a broader spectrum of elites. They found "dovish (international) and liberal (domestic) attitudes consistently together on the one hand, and conservative (domestic) and hawkish (international) attitudes regularly together on the other" (Russett and Hanson 1975, 138). Similar results emerged from an analysis of a 1984 survey of American opinion leaders, as well as from a panel study of American elites (Holsti and Rosenau 1988; Murray 1996).

Despite the indications of a greater propensity toward consistency among elites than among the general public, conclusions on this score should be drawn with some caution because contradictory evidence also exists. For example, Luttbeg (1968) found no substantial difference between elites and the general public with respect to the structure of their beliefs, a conclusion supported by Wittkopf's (1990) reanalysis of the CCFR surveys. Also, it bears repeating that the base of evidence from which tentative conclusions about leadership beliefs may be adduced is rather limited, especially when compared to the mountains of data on the opinions of the general public. Finally, not all elite studies deal with both domestic and foreign policy issues. For example, the CCFR surveys and the first two FPLP surveys are devoid of questions on domestic policy.

The analysis that follows is based on data from the three most recent FPLP surveys; unfortunately, the 1976 and 1980 studies did not include enough domestic issue items to be included in this analysis. It is perhaps worth noting that the 1984-92 studies encompass three strikingly different international settings, especially in the range of relations between Washington and Moscow. The 1984 survey took place at the height of "Cold War II" when vitriolic rhetoric and arms racing had long since overtaken any manifestations of détente. Only four years later, President Reagan and Chairman Gorbachev were meeting regularly, had signed an unprecedented arms control agreement eliminating an entire class of weapons, and referred to each other as friends rather than as leaders of "evil empires." Startling as the changes between 1984 and 1988 were, they paled in comparison with those of the next four years, which witnessed not only the end of the Cold War but also of the Soviet Union. To summarize very briefly, then, the three surveys spanned the Cold War, the transition from confrontation to cooperation, and the early post–Cold War era. Any findings that persist through such dramatic changes would appear to be very robust indeed.

Domestic Issue Scales

As a first step toward classifying respondents, scales were created for economic and social issues. The six items for each scale had to meet two criteria: (1) the questions had to appear in each of the three surveys since 1984, and (2) they had to meet several standards for forming a reliable scale. The first criterion excluded several questions that appeared in the later surveys but not in 1984. These included items about AIDS testing, the balanced budget amendment, and term limitations for elected officials, all of which scaled well.

Table 4.9 summarizes responses for each of the twelve issues in 1984, 1988, and 1992. The economic issues scale includes items on taxation, tuition tax credits, regulation, defense spending, and income redistribution; those in the social issues scale focus on several of the most controversial and emotion-laden issues of recent years: school

TABLE 4.9. Economic and Social Issues Scales: Surveys of U.S. Opinion Leaders, 1984–92

This question asks you to indicate your position on certain domestic issues. Please indicate how strongly you agree or disagree with each statement.

	Agree strongly + Agree somewhat (%)		
	1984 (N = 2,515)	1988 (N = 2,226)	1992 (N = 2,312)
Economic Issues Scale			
Reducing the federal budget deficit by raising taxes	67	67	66
Relaxing environmental regulation to stimulate economic growth*	28	16	21
Providing tuition tax credits to parents who send children to private or parochial schools*	37	35	40
Reducing the defense budget in order to increase the federal education budget	58	61	75
Easing restrictions on the construction of nuclear power plants*	39	37	46
Redistributing income from the wealthy to the poor through taxation and subsidies	43	42	45
Social Issues Scale			
Busing children in order to achieve school integration	37	39	37
Leaving abortion decisions to women and their doctors	81	81	79
Reviving the Equal Rights Amendment	55	54	52
Permitting prayer in public schools*	38	40	44
Barring homosexuals from teaching in public schools*	37	33	28
Banning the death penalty	33	35	33

Note: For items without an asterisk [*], "agree" responses scored as "liberal" and "disagree" response scored as "conservative." Reverse scoring used for items with an asterisk.

busing, abortion, the Equal Rights Amendment (ERA), school prayer, gay rights, and the death penalty. Virtually all of these issues appear to have played a prominent role in the 1992 and 1994 elections.

Aggregate responses to these dozen questions reveal a greater degree of stability than change over the eight-year period in question. Support for reducing the defense budget increased from 58 percent in 1984 to 77 percent eight years later, a change that no doubt reflects the end of the Cold War. Two other economic issues, relating to environmental regulation, gave rise to 7 percent changes but in offsetting directions; relaxing environmental regulations drew even less support in 1992 and 1984, but there was a corresponding increase of those who approved easing regulations on construction of nuclear plants. Responses to the six social issues were even more stable. For four issues—school busing, abortion, ERA, and the death penalty—the changes were negligible. Support for school prayer increased by 7 percent and there was a 9 percent decline among those who favored banning homosexual teachers from public schools.

Correlations among the six items on the economic issues scale were uniformly positive for all three surveys, averaging .30, and those for the social issues scale were also positive in all instances, with a somewhat higher average correlation coefficient of .36. For both scales Cronbach's *alpha* ranged between .70 and .78 in the three surveys, thus meeting or exceeding the conventional criterion of acceptable scale reliability.

The classification scheme for domestic issues assumes that respondents may have policy preferences on economic issues that do not necessarily correspond ideologically to those on social issues and, therefore, that it is useful to distinguish between them. The terms *liberal* and *conservative* have varied sufficiently in meaning so that their contemporary content cannot be considered self-evident. The present analysis incorporates the following defining premises. With respect to *economic issues, liberals* were assumed to *favor:*

> an active role for government in regulating the economy.
> an active role for government in regulating activities that may threaten the environment.
> taxation for purposes of income redistribution, while opposing tax policies that provide benefits primarily to the more affluent.

On *social issues* it was assumed that *liberals* were in *favor* of the following:

> an active role for government in promoting the interests of those who have traditionally been at a disadvantage owing to race, class, gender, or other attributes.
> a ban on the death penalty, at least in part because it has been inflicted disproportionately upon some traditionally disadvantaged groups.

Conservatives were assumed to *favor* the following positions on *economic issues:*

> removing or reducing governmental restrictions on economic activity.
> reducing taxes.
> a large defense budget to ensure a strong national defense.

On *social issues, conservatives* were assumed to *oppose:*

> an active role for government in attempting to legislate equality
> between classes, sexes, races, and other groups.
> an active role for government in support of those who challenge
> "traditional values."

These premises are incorporated into scoring responses to the
twelve items that constitute the domestic issue scales. Agreement with
seven of them was scored as "liberal," whereas agreement with the
other five (identified by an asterisk in table 4.9) was rated as a "conservative" answer. Each respondent was then given two scores, the first
based on summed responses to the six economic issues, and the second
derived from preferences on the six social issues. A cutting point of
0.00 was used for each of the scales.[11] Respondents who scored on the
"liberal" side of both the economic and social scales are classified as
liberals, and those who were on the "conservative" side with respect to
both economic and social issues are designated as *conservatives.* Respondents with a liberal position on economic issues and conservative
preferences on social issues are labeled *populists.* The final group—
those who favored a conservative position on economic issues and a
liberal stance on social issues—are the *libertarians.*[12]

According to these criteria, leaders taking part in these three
surveys were distributed in the following manner.

> *Liberals* (leaders who were liberal on both the social and eco-
> nomic and issue scales) constituted 45 percent of those taking
> part in the 1984 survey. The comparable figures for the next
> two surveys were 48 and 47 percent, respectively.
> *Conservatives* (conservative on both scales) accounted for 33
> percent of the 1984 leadership sample. Their numbers fell to
> 28 percent in 1988 and to 27 percent four years later.
> *Populists* (conservative on the social issues scale and liberal on
> the economic issues scale) made up 15 percent of leaders in the
> 1984 study. That group increased to 17 percent four years later
> and by a similar amount to 19 percent in 1992.
> *Libertarians* (liberals on social issues and conservatives on eco-
> nomic issues) constituted 7 percent of the entire leadership
> sample in each of the three surveys.

Several points emerge from the distribution of respondents. First,
of the two underlying dimensions, the social issues appear to be more

divisive than the economic ones. Second, although the *liberals* and *conservatives*—those whose positions on both scales correspond to the premises just defined—constitute a strong majority of the entire leadership sample, there are enough *populists* and *libertarians* to support the premise that a single ideological scale is not sufficient to capture preferences on both economic and social issues. Indeed, whereas *liberals* and *conservatives* combined to account for 78 percent of the total in 1984, the figure had declined to 76 percent in 1988 and still further to 74 percent in the most recent survey. The *populist* group increased between 1984 and 1992, mostly at the expense of the *conservatives*.

Domestic and Foreign Policy Beliefs: 1984–92

We can get a summary assessment of the extent to which positions on domestic and foreign policy are related by combining the classification schemes for the two types of issues in the three leadership surveys under consideration (table 4.10). The distributions indicate that there is a rather strong correspondence, a conclusion supported by the summary statistic, *phi*, which ranges from .56 to .61. A strong and consistent majority of domestic *liberals* are also foreign policy *accommodationists*—that is, they support CI and oppose MI. On the other hand, approximately equal proportions of the domestic *conservatives* are either foreign policy *hard-liners* or *internationalists*—the two groups that favor militant internationalism. With respect to foreign policy issues, the *populists* and *libertarians* are quite similar; both are predominantly *accommodationists* and *internationalists*. These are the two groups that favor cooperative internationalism. One possible interpretation is that although both *populists* and *libertarians* favor CI, their reasons for doing so differ. The former (economic liberals) may support CI because they prefer government spending for domestic rather than defense purposes, and perhaps the latter (economic conservatives) do so because they oppose the type of "big government" that almost invariably attends wars, crises, confrontations, and extensive commitments abroad.[13]

An obvious question that emerges from these findings is whether there are some more fundamental overarching beliefs that link one's views on domestic and foreign policy beliefs. If there are, these might be somewhat comparable to but broader than the "core values" that Hurwitz and Peffley (1987) identified on their hierarchical model of foreign policy attitudes. At best, the FPLP data lend themselves to speculation rather than any definitive answers. One candidate might

TABLE 4.10.   Relationship between Militant and Cooperative Internationalism [Accommodationists, Internationalists, Hard-Liners, Isolationists] and the Domestic Issue Typology [Liberals, Conservatives, Populists, Libertarians] among U.S. Opinion Leaders, 1984–92

Militant Inter- nationalism	Cooperative Internationalism							
	Oppose				Support			
	Hard-Liners	1984	1988	1992	Internationalists	1984	1988	1992
Support	Liberals	7%	8%	8%	Liberals	21%	23%	23%
	Conservatives	74	70	71	Conservatives	51	42	42
	Populists	13	16	13	Populists	20	27	26
	Libertarians	6	6	7	Libertarians	8	8	9
	Isolationists				Accommodationists			
Oppose	Liberals	40%	41%	31%	Liberals	71%	73%	70%
	Conservatives	33	34	41	Conservatives	10	8	8
	Populists	17	17	17	Populists	13	13	16
	Libertarians	10	8	11	Libertarians	6	6	6

Note: Phi for 1984 = .60; 1988 = .61; 1992 = .56.

be the degree to which one believes in carrots (incentives) or sticks (penalties) as the most effective means of influence and social control. Does this simple proposition explain, at least in part, the link between hard-line attitudes toward foreign affairs (the primacy of military force, deterrent threats, etc.), conservatism on social issues (belief in the efficacy of capital punishment, support for the use of state power to enforce certain standards of conduct, etc.), and conservatism on economic issues (support for high defense budgets, reliance on markets to mete out penalties and rewards, etc.)?

Conversely, are there comparable links between an accommodationist view on foreign affairs (support for foreign aid and other forms of rewards, emphasis on issues that lend themselves to bargaining and negotiation), liberalism on social issues (support for state incentives to reduce or eliminate differences in opportunities and perhaps outcomes as well), and economic liberalism (preferences for redistributive policies, restrictions on the penalties arising from market forces, etc.)? Obviously this is at best highly speculative.

Conclusion

Despite fears expressed during the past half century by presidents and other top leaders, the evidence presented in chapter 3 indicated that, even in the wake of the disastrous Vietnam War, the American public has not retreated into an indiscriminate isolationism. A more specific question, for which the evidence presented here is certainly not conclusive, is whether Americans have adopted a stance that will accept international undertakings only as long as they involve no casualties (for example, Luttwak 1994; Schlesinger 1995; Friedman 1995; for a more detailed analysis, see Larson 1995). Proponents of this thesis point to the decision in 1993 to withdraw U.S. forces from Somalia almost immediately after eighteen troops were killed in a firefight as well as to the decision not to land forces in Haiti after a dockside demonstration suggested that there might be some resistance to the landing. Opponents point to the Persian Gulf War to buttress their argument that casualties will be accepted for undertakings that have clear goals. The distinction drawn by Jentleson (1992) between the use of force to restrain aggressor states, as in the Gulf War, and to impose internal political changes within another state, as in Somalia and Haiti, seems relevant to this debate. He found that the public support is higher in the former than the latter cases. Evidence from another series of surveys suggests that the public is not unequivocally set against the use of force, even in such civil wars as Somalia, Bosnia, and Haiti (Kull and Ramsay, 1993a, 1994a, 1994b).

However, the data summarized in this chapter provide additional support for the proposition that, in comparison to the general public, leaders have been consistently more inclined to support an active international role for the United States. This conclusion appears to be valid both at the most general level and across a wide variety of more specific issues.

The policy implications of these divergences between leaders and the general public depend in substantial part on one's conception of the American polity and the role that public opinion plays in that political system. I will explore this question further in the concluding chapter (chap. 6). Suffice it to say for now that if one assumes that top officials and opinion leaders will have an overwhelming influence in shaping the primary features of American foreign policy, whereas the general public will have little or none and will play a role only as the target of elite manipulation, then the evidence suggests that the United States will continue to pursue an internationalist foreign policy, broadly defined. In that case, the debates are likely to center on *how* the United States participates in global affairs; the *hard-liners* and *accommodationists* will put forward quite different blueprints in answer to that question. They will also express sharply different preferences about the appropriate *means* to be employed. If, on the other hand, public preferences play a significant role in shaping at least the broad contours of American foreign policy, the policy debates are likely to focus on *whether* the United States should play an active international role or focus more on issues that have a direct domestic impact. In that eventuality, the differences between the *internationalists* and *isolationists* will take center stage.

Although the evidence on the structural features of foreign policy attitudes is somewhat less conclusive, there appears to be some convergence in the ways leaders and the general public think about international affairs. The data summarized previously suggests that two dimensions of internationalism—the militant and cooperative versions—capture a good deal, although surely not all, of the variance. The convergence of attitudes on domestic and foreign policy issues also suggests at least a moderate degree of ideological coherence in the political beliefs of leaders. This will be welcome news for critics on both the right and left who lament what they believe to be an excessive pragmatism and disregard for ideological principles in American politics. Others may be less certain that the erosion of crosscutting cleavages augurs well for the tenor and content of political debates.

Finally, these findings bring up questions about the sources and correlates of foreign policy attitudes among both the general public and opinion leaders. These are the questions to which I will turn in chapter 5.

CHAPTER 5

Sources of Foreign Policy Attitudes

During the middle 1980s three perceptive analysts of American foreign policy, one of whom currently serves as National Security Adviser to President Clinton, asserted: "For two decades, the making of American foreign policy has been growing far more political—or more precisely, far more partisan and ideological" (Destler, Gelb, and Lake 1984, 13). Although their observation was not specifically focused on or limited to public opinion, it brings up a number of interesting questions related to the sources of public attitudes. First, in pointing to partisanship and ideology, did they properly locate the main fault lines on the American political landscape? More specifically, do party and ideology reinforce each other as sources of foreign policy attitudes or are they, as in some earlier periods of American history, essentially independent of each other? Is it even possible that they create crosscutting cleavages? Second, are there other sources of foreign policy attitudes that compete with, or perhaps even supersede, the impact of partisanship and ideology? Extensive post-Vietnam debates have identified some other prominent candidates, most notably generation and gender, as potent sources of foreign policy attitudes.

Third, are the demographic sources of foreign policy attitudes stable across issues? Across time? These questions are essentially variants of a broader one encountered in the first three chapters. Those who hold that an ill-informed public possesses little more than "non-attitudes" about politics—and especially about world affairs—would expect the demographic correlates of attitudes to be weak and unstable. If much of the public responds to foreign affairs in an almost random manner and if their reactions to such issues are anchored in little more than the mood of the moment, then one would not expect to find powerful and enduring correlations between demographic attributes and foreign policy attitudes. The alternative view is that the public may effectively use simple, or even simplistic, guidelines to help them make some sense of the complex and remote actors, issues, and events that constitute foreign affairs. Do such permanent or relatively stable background characteristics as gender, generation, or occupation play any significant role in that process? Other attributes, including party and ideological preferences, are more easily subject to change but, if Destler, Gelb, and Lake are correct, their impact has increased. Which, if any of these, has been consistently related to ways of thinking about foreign policy?

The final question concerns how the end of the Cold War may have affected the sources of foreign policy attitudes. The era of systematic public opinion polling was scarcely a decade old when an era of confrontation, punctuated by periodic crises, superseded the wartime cooperation between Washington and Moscow. The vast bulk of the data, theories, hypotheses, and analyses of public opinion derive from the more than four decades of the Cold War. Given the central role of Soviet-American relations, not only in global affairs but also in shaping foreign policy attitudes, how can we be sure that the theories and findings generated during the decades prior to the disintegration of the Soviet Union are sufficiently robust to survive into the post–Cold War era? For example, even if Destler, Gelb, and Lake were correct in identifying partisanship and ideology as the primary sources of cleavages of foreign policy during the early years of the Reagan administration, is it possible that their diagnosis is no longer valid for the post–Cold War era? After all, Ronald Reagan, a highly partisan and ideological president, underwent an almost complete reversal in attitudes about the USSR during the period of his presidency, as did the general public.[1] Could these changes have also brought about a significant erosion of partisan and ideological stances on foreign affairs?

This chapter will explore these questions and examine some relevant evidence from both the general public and opinion leaders. In addition to reviewing findings that emerged from research during the Cold War, we will examine at least some evidence from the period since the end of that conflict. Reactions to one event will receive special attention. The Persian Gulf War, the culmination of events precipitated by Iraq's invasion of Kuwait on August 2, 1990, has been described as "the mother of all polling events" (Mueller 1994, xiv). It may well have been the subject of more public opinion surveys than any prior episode of comparable duration.[2] Because it was a *victorious* undertaking that took place over a relatively *short* period and resulted in relatively *light U.S. casualties,* the Gulf War avoided at least three of the characteristics that ultimately ignited widespread public opposition to the conflict in Vietnam. These reasons, combined with the nature of Iraq's action and the character of its leaders, suggest that the war against Iraq should be a strong candidate for the "rally 'round the flag" phenomenon. If in fact vast numbers of Americans, irrespective of party, ideology, and other attributes, rallied behind the administration, the impact of background characteristics would be suppressed rather than heightened.[3] Conversely, any demographic correlates of foreign policy attitudes that persisted in these circumstances would be especially significant.

The pages that follow will begin with the impact of party, followed by ideology, generation, gender, education, region, and race. Surveys have not always probed for each of these respondent attributes and thus the evidence is not equally plentiful for each of them.

Political Party

The General Public

Two generalizations about American politics, if valid, would lead to the expectation that party affiliation is at best weakly linked to foreign policy attitudes. The first is that the two major parties are broad coalitions that cut across rather than between ideological orientations or other major sources of beliefs. The second stipulates that, however divided Americans may be on domestic questions, bipartisanship rather than partisanship is the rule on foreign policy issues. "Politics stops at the water's edge" has been a favorite slogan of countless orators on the hustings.

Whether these generalizations were ever an even moderately accurate depiction of the foreign policy process over any period is open to question. It would be hard to deny that partisan differences colored debates on issues as diverse as responses to the wars arising from the French Revolution, the tariff issue at various times during the nineteenth and early twentieth centuries, and the question of American participation in the League of Nations. On the other hand, deliberate efforts by the Roosevelt administration to develop a bipartisan coalition in support of American membership in the United Nations were highly successful, and the Hull-Dulles agreement assured that the UN would not become a partisan issue in the 1944 presidential election. As a result of these efforts, the UN Treaty won Senate approval by an overwhelming 89 to 2 margin. During the early post–World War II years, bipartisan cooperation between the White House and Congress on many issues related to Europe made possible such initiatives as aid to Greece and Turkey (the Truman Doctrine), the Marshall Plan, and the North Atlantic Treaty Organization.[4] Each of these striking departures from traditional American foreign policies had rather solid public support. Agreement among prominent leaders of the two major parties no doubt contributed to the fact that, among the general public,

TABLE 5.1.   Partisanship on Selected Foreign and Defense Policy Issues: The General Public, 1946–63

Date/Poll	Issue*	Response	Responses by Party Affiliation (%)**		
			Republican	Democrat	Independent
February 1946	Role U.S. should play	Active	72	72	NR
Gallup	in world affairs	Stay out	23	22	NR
March 1947	Aid to Greece (Truman	Approve	56	56	NR
Gallup	Doctrine)	Disapprove	31	32	NR
April 1948	Should U.S. and all				
Gallup	European Marshall				
	Plan nations join in				
	a permanent military	Yes	66	68	57
	alliance?	No	22	16	29
July 1948	Evaluation of U.S.	Too soft	73	70	NR
Gallup	policy toward Soviet	Too tough	3	4	NR
	Union	About right	14	14	NR
February 1950	Defense budget	Too much	16	12	18
Gallup		Too little	22	25	24
		About right	46	46	40
July 1950	Send military supplies				
Gallup	to Chiang Kai-shek				
	government on	Should	48	50	NR
	Taiwan	Should not	39	32	NR
July 1951	Send U.S. troops to				
Gallup	Europe or keep them				
	at home to defend	Europe	53	61	49
	the Americas	At home	39	30	38
May 1954	Send U.S. troops to	Approve	18	22	17
Gallup	Indochina	Disapprove	76	70	72
June 1955	Should the U.S. and				
Gallup	Russia work out a	Should	55	57	54
	trade arrangement?	Should not	33	27	29
December 1956	Approve foreign aid to				
Gallup	help stop	Yes	59	58	58
	communism	No	28	28	28
January 1963	Foreign aid	For	54	59	61
Gallup		Against	35	28	28

*Summary statement of the issue rather than the exact wording of the question asked.
**Excludes "no opinion," "not sure," and "don't know" responses.
NR = Not reported.

Democrats and Republicans differed little with respect to these and other major internationalist foreign policy undertakings. For example, a 1946 Gallup survey revealed that 72 percent of respondents in both political parties favored an "active" international role for the United States, and the 1947 program of aid to Greece and Turkey also received identical levels of approval from Democrats and Republicans (see table 5.1).

Issues relating to the Far East tended to be more contentious and placed greater strains on bipartisan cooperation, especially after the Truman-MacArthur confrontation during the first year of the Korean War. The president's decision to dismiss MacArthur, culminating a dispute that reflected some fundamental differences about civil-military relations as well as the appropriate conduct of the Korean War, was not popular among Democrats (opposed 53 to 30 percent), independents (51 to 30 percent), or (especially) Republicans (72 to 17 percent).[5] But even on most issues related to Asia, survey data revealed limited partisan differences. For example, the decision to resist aggression in Korea, the move to aid the Chinese government in Taiwan, and a proposal to send American forces to Indochina as the French effort there was collapsing, found Republicans and Democrats about equally supportive or critical.

To be sure, by 1952 American participation in the Korean War—"Harry Truman's War" as it often was called by critics—had lost far more support among Republicans than among Democrats, but sharp partisan divisions on foreign and defense policy did not persist into the Eisenhower years. Even though the defense budget had become a controversial issue in 1960, with charges from Senator John F. Kennedy and other prominent Democrats that a complacent Eisenhower administration had permitted a dangerous "missile gap" to develop, a Gallup poll revealed that differences attributable to party loyalties were relatively modest. Although more Democrats (24 percent) than Republicans (15 percent) asserted that the Pentagon was receiving "too little" in the Eisenhower budget, far more respondents in both political parties judged defense spending to be "about right." Even foreign aid programs received approximately similar levels of support from adherents of the major political parties. Republican nominee Barry Goldwater's 1964 attacks on the "eastern establishment" that had provided an important base for bipartisanship in foreign and defense policy issues, and his campaign theme that the GOP should offer voters a "choice, not an echo," proved to be insufficiently persuasive to avert a landslide electoral loss. The absence of strong partisan cleavages extended into the early years of the Vietnam War, as majorities within both parties expressed strong support for the policies of the Johnson administration.[6]

For two decades spanning the Truman, Eisenhower, Kennedy, and early Johnson administrations, then, whatever differences divided the American public on foreign policy issues rarely fell along a cleavage defined by partisan loyalties. Writing in the 1970s, Barry Hughes (1978, 128) concluded that the "evidence points overwhelmingly to

insignificant party differences in the general population" on most foreign policy issues. Indeed, during the pre-Vietnam period the distribution of attitudes among supporters of the two major parties was
sufficiently similar that the self-identified "independents" usually
stood on one side or another of the Democrats and Republicans, rather
than in between them.

The period since the end of the Vietnam War has witnessed the
emergence of striking partisan differences on a broad range of issues
relating to foreign and defense policy. The very concept of bipartisanship came under increased attacks from several quarters; by 1979 a
leading Republican senator called for its termination and for a return
to a frankly partisan foreign policy. At the same time, efforts by
several administrations to create a foreign policy consensus fell short
of enduring success. The Nixon-Kissinger campaign to create a post-
Vietnam foreign policy consensus grounded in détente with the Soviet
Union ultimately failed. Attempts by the Carter administration to
achieve the same goal through an emphasis on human rights, and by
the first Reagan administration to create a consensus around a more
assertive and confrontational stance toward the Soviet Union, were
equally unavailing in the longer run.

During the years immediately following the 1975 evacuation of
the last Americans from Saigon, pollsters generally concentrated on
such domestic issues as inflation, unemployment, and crime because
these seemed to be of the most immediate concern to much of the
public. Even the controversial question of how the United States
should respond to the civil war in Angola did not elicit a probe by the
Gallup organization. Data on foreign policy attitudes became more
plentiful during the 1980s, however, and they reveal clearly that sharp
and persistent partisan differences characterized most issues related to
the Cold War (table 5.2). Defense budget increases initiated by President Carter and escalated by President Reagan, the intervention in
Lebanon, the Strategic Defense Initiative ("Star Wars"), the proper
role for the United States in the civil wars in Central America, and
proposals to place economic sanctions on South Africa were among
the controversial issues that gave rise to very substantial differences
between Republicans and Democrats. The bifurcation along partisan
lines was sufficiently great that, unlike during the pre-Vietnam period,
responses of political independents typically fell between those of
Democrats and Republicans.

Toward the end of the 1980s, however, the evidence also reveals
some diminution of partisan differences on questions linked most
closely to Soviet-American relations. A sense of diminishing threat

TABLE 5.2. Partisanship on Selected Foreign and Defense Policy Issues: The General Public, 1977–93

			Responses by Party Affiliation (%)**		
Date/Poll	Issue*	Response	Republicans	Democrats	Independents
June 1977 Gallup	Withdrawal of U.S. troops from South Korea	Favor Oppose	32 51	47 30	36 41
March 1982 Gallup	Defense budget	Too much Too little About right	18 27 46	43 16 32	39 18 36
October 1983 Gallup	A mistake to send Marines to Lebanon?	Yes, mistake No	36 53	61 29	50 36
January 1985 Gallup	Defense budget	Too much Too little About right	29 15 49	60 7 27	49 10 35
May 1985 Gallup	Trade embargo against Nicaragua	Approve Disapprove	65 16	26 58	45 38
March 1986 Gallup	Should the U.S. provide an aid package to the contras in Nicaragua?	Should Should not	44 44	29 60	34 51
June 1988 ATS-6	Star Wars [SDI] programs	Approve Disapprove	65 24	36 53	53 38
July 1991 Gallup	Decision to remove economic sanctions against South Africa	Approve Disapprove	56 22	35 39	45 31
April 1992 Gallup	Plan to join other nations in providing various types of aid to former Soviet Union	Favor Oppose	64 33	46 50	50 45
February 1993 CNN/USA Today/Gallup	The level of U.S. involvement in Bosnia	Too much Too little About right	31 17 49	28 12 53	31 15 45
August 1993 CNN/USA Today/Gallup	North American Free Agreement [NAFTA]	Favor Oppose	49 47	37 62	33 64

*Summary statement of the issue rather than the exact wording of the question asked.
**Excludes "no opinion," "not sure," and "don't know" responses.
ATS = Americans Talk Security surveys.

from the USSR, shared by members of both major parties, no doubt reflected the emergence of "détente II" during the period following Mikhail Gorbachev's accession to power in the Kremlin and coinciding with Ronald Reagan's second presidential term. By the time Reagan left the White House in 1989, almost half of the Republicans assessed the Soviet Union as no more than a "minor threat," and fully 60 percent of the Democrats responded in a like manner. In light of a rather strong tendency by Republicans to have been more skeptical of the Kremlin during the Reagan years, it is perhaps more than a little ironic that, four months after disintegration of the USSR, Republicans outstripped Democrats by a margin of 64 to 46 percent in their support for assistance to the former Soviet Union. Indeed, the proposed aid package received the highest approval from various groups often more closely associated with the GOP than the Democrats: white, male, higher-income college graduates (Gallup 1992, 71–72).

Finally, two post–Cold War nonmilitary issues yielded evidence in 1993 of both partisan differences and bipartisan convergence. The NAFTA gained the support of Republicans by the slimmest of margins, but it was opposed by more than 60 percent of Democrats. In contrast, when asked, "Should immigration be kept at the present level, increased or decreased?" substantial majorities in both parties preferred the latter option. The overwhelming approval one year later of Proposition 187 by California voters, although it was supported by Republican candidates for the governorship and the U.S. Senate and opposed by their Democratic counterparts, also suggests the emergence of a bipartisan agreement on a restrictive immigration policy. Further evidence on this point emerged from the 1994 CCFR survey. "Controlling and reducing illegal immigration" ranked among the general public as the fourth most important foreign policy goal, with almost three-fourths of the respondents rating it as "very important" (Rielly 1995, 15).

For reasons cited earlier, the Persian Gulf War in 1991 provides a good opportunity to determine the extent to which partisan foreign policy differences among the general public have persisted or dissolved in the post–Cold War period. The naked Iraqi aggression against Kuwait, Saddam Hussein's well-deserved reputation for exceptional brutality, and the absence of a risk that the crisis would turn into a dangerous confrontation between Washington and Moscow would be expected to increase the prospects for bipartisan support of American policies. Table 5.3 reports the results from a very small sample of the many Gallup surveys on the situation in the Persian Gulf area undertaken before the initiation of the American air war on Iraq, during the conflict, and in its aftermath. Excluded are all the many questions that mentioned President Bush by name; for example, "Do you approve of the way George Bush is handling the current situation in the Middle East involving Kuwait?" (January 6, 1991; see Gallup 1991). Such questions could be expected to inflate partisan divisions among the public; in fact, they did do so by about 10 per-

TABLE 5.3.   **Attitudes on Selected Issues Relating to the Persian Gulf Conflict, Before, During, and After the War: The Impact of Party**

Date	Question	All	Republicans	Democrats	Independents
Prewar surveys					
Jan. 13	Do you think the United States made a mistake in sending troops to Saudi Arabia, or not? [% yes]	29	18	39	30
Jan. 13	Which of the following comes closest to your opinion? Favor: withdraw; sanctions; war. [% initiate a war]	50	62	40	52
Wartime surveys					
Jan. 20	Do you approve or disapprove of the U.S. decision to go to war in order to drive the Iraqis out of Kuwait? [% approve]	80	91	70	80
Jan. 26	Do you favor or oppose using tactical nuclear weapons against Iraq if it might save the lives of U.S. troops? [% favor]	45	46	45	46
Jan. 26	Would you favor or oppose a law to ban peace demonstrations while U.S. troops are fighting overseas? [% favor]	31	31	37	26
Feb. 17	Do you favor or oppose the U.S. use of tactical nuclear weapons in the Persian Gulf War? [% favor]	28	31	30	25
Postwar surveys					
July 14	All in all, was the current situation in the Mideast involving Iraq and Kuwait worth going to war over, or not? [% yes]	66	80	54	64
July 21	Looking back, do you approve or disapprove of the U.S. decision last January to go to war with Iraq in order to drive the Iraqis out of Kuwait? [% approve]	78	91	67	74

Source: Gallup surveys. The typical survey was spread out over a 3–4-day period. The left hand column reports the final date of the survey.

cent compared to similar questions in which the president was not named.

The evidence indicates that, although the Bush administration enjoyed a high degree of overall public support for its Persian Gulf policies—notably with respect to the decision to initiate a war within hours after the January 15, 1991, deadline for Iraqi withdrawal from Kuwait had expired—rather substantial partisan differences may nevertheless be found in survey responses before, during, and after the conflict.[7] Only three of the questions in table 5.3, two of them dealing with the possible use of nuclear weapons, failed to yield significant differences. Strong majorities within both parties opposed the use of tactical nuclear weapons against Iraq, although nearly half of both Democrats and Republicans were willing to do so "if it might save the lives of U.S. troops." A proposition to ban peace demonstrations during the conflict found favor from only about one-third of the respondents, with only a moderate gap between members of the two major parties. Each of the remaining questions gave rise to substantial differences that ranged from 21 to 26 percent. Moreover, these cleavages were not bridged as a consequence of the successful military campaign to drive Iraqi forces out of Kuwait.

Although some degree of disenchantment with the war effort emerged later in the year—apparently as the result of Saddam Hussein's ability to stay in power and to attack with impunity the Shiite and Kurdish minorities within Iraq—public assessments several months after the ceasefire found that the overall approval of American actions was distributed very unevenly across parties. Stated differently, the longer-term consequences of the Persian Gulf conflict do not appear to have included a lasting, bipartisan post–Cold War foreign policy consensus among the general public. It remains to be seen whether comparable cleavages have divided opinion leaders.

Opinion Leaders

As I noted earlier, compared to the vast collections of systematic data on the general public, information on opinion leaders for the decades prior to the Vietnam War is in relatively short supply. The available evidence, some of it including indirect indicators, would seem to point to two conclusions.

First, partisan differences among leaders probably exceeded those found among the general public. To be sure, debates and votes on some of the most important foreign policy issues in Congress, including but not limited to the United Nations Treaty, Truman Doctrine, Marshall Plan, NATO, tended not to follow strictly partisan lines. The Truman and Eisenhower administrations were able to work fairly effectively on many foreign policy issues with Congresses dominated by the opposition party during periods of divided government in 1947–49 and 1955–61. Indeed, Eisenhower faced more consistent and vocal opposition from rightwing members of the GOP—for example, from Senators William Knowland, Joseph McCarthy, William Jenner, and John Bricker—during the years of Republican control of Congress (1953–55) than from Democrats. A classic study of executive-legislative relations during this period found that the president was typically better able to get congressional support on foreign policy than on domestic issues (Wildavsky, 1966). Even debates during the election campaigns that gave rise to changes in control of the White House in 1953 and 1961 focused more on implementation and administration of American foreign and defense policies than on the principles underlying such basic policies as containment, deterrence, alliance membership, economic and military assistance programs, and the like.

On the other hand, evidence of partisan differences among leaders is also available. A study of party leaders and followers during the 1950s revealed that partisan gaps on several international questions were greater among the former than the latter (McCloskey, Hoffmann, and O'Hara 1960). Similarly, an analysis of congressional voting on *all* foreign policy issues, rather than just the most consequential ones cited earlier, also found evidence of partisanship, especially after the Korean War (Wittkopf 1990). Finally, the occasional Gallup special surveys of *Who's Who in America* biographees suggest some partisan differences on such issues as the Bricker Amendment to restrict executive treaty-making powers and on the admission of communist China to the United Nations. The latter issue gave rise to an especially wide partisan gap, as half of the Democrats favored bringing the Beijing regime into the world organizations, whereas only 20 percent of Republicans did so.[8]

The second major conclusion is that partisan cleavages among leaders widened considerably during the 1970s and 1980s. Since the end of the Vietnam War, systematic data about the foreign policy attitudes of opinion leaders have become much more plentiful. Most of the evidence provides considerable support for the Destler, Gelb, and Lake (1984) observation, cited at the beginning of this chapter, about the growing partisan chasm on foreign policy issues during the post-Vietnam era. This point emerges clearly, for example, from studies of business and military leaders as well as secondary analyses of the small elite samples in the quadrennial CCFR surveys (Russett and Hanson 1975; Wittkopf 1990).

The FPLP surveys, extending from 1976 through 1992, also found quite striking differences among Republicans, Democrats, and independents. When respondents to each of the surveys are classified as *hard-liners, isolationists, internationalists,* or *accommodationists,* a clear and consistent pattern of partisan differences emerges (see table 5.4). In each survey, two-thirds to three-fourths of Republicans are either *hard-liners* or *internationalists,* the two groups that expressed support for militant internationalism. In contrast, even more substantial majorities among the Democrats were *accommodationists,* a group defined as opposing militant internationalism, while supporting cooperative internationalism. The end of the Cold War has wit-

TABLE 5.4. The Relationship between Party and Foreign Policy Orientations among American Opinion Leaders, 1976–92

Of the leaders who identify themselves as . . .	Year	the percentage whose foreign policy attitudes classify them as . . .			
		Hard-liners	Isola-tionists	Inter-nationalists	Accommo-dationists
Republicans	1976	34	7	39	21
	1980	34	7	43	17
	1984	34	6	40	20
	1988	34	7	40	20
	1992	17	6	52	25
Democrats	1976	9	7	22	62
	1980	9	7	25	60
	1984	6	6	14	74
	1988	4	7	13	76
	1992	3	3	19	75
Independents	1976	21	8	33	38
	1980	20	6	34	40
	1984	12	8	25	54
	1988	13	8	24	55
	1992	9	7	29	55

Note: Phi for 1976 = .55; 1980 = .61; 1984 = .60; 1988 = .63; 1992 = .54.

nessed some movement among Republicans away from a *hard-line* position and toward an *internationalist* one. In contrast, the positions of Democrats have remained relatively stable over the sixteen-year period in question, although the number of *isolationists* fell with the end of the Cold War. Perhaps the only point of strong agreement among these leaders is that few of them, whether Republicans or Democrats, are *isolationists*. The correlation between party and foreign policy orientation has remained quite high, never falling below .50 in any of the surveys.

We can gain a more detailed view of how the end of the Cold War has affected the impact of political party by examining the pattern of responses to several clusters of questions, including some about the Gulf War, in the 1992 FPLP survey. I noted in chapter 4 that almost 90 percent of opinion leaders believed that the post–Cold War international system is multipolar rather than bipolar or unipolar. The very slight two percentage point difference between Republicans and Democrats on this issue pales in comparison to the striking convergence of views across party lines.

The End of the Cold War

Predictions about the consequences arising from the end of the Cold War provide further insight into leadership views of the international system.[9] Four major themes emerge from the data. The first is a rather widespread agreement that many fundamental features of international relations will persist into the post–Cold War era. An overwhelming majority of opinion leaders (93 percent), irrespective of party identification, believed that greater international cooperation rather than unilateral action will be necessary to deter and resist aggression. Because international cooperation in the form of alliance systems was a crucial feature of the Cold War period, this judgment does not necessarily represent a perception of fundamental systemic change.

Responses to other items reinforce the point that a majority of opinion leaders anticipated continuity rather than revolutionary change in international relations. For example, more than two-thirds agreed that nations will continue to adhere to traditional definitions of their national interests; barely over one-third of them believed that any sort of world government is likely to be established, even within the next half century; and a comparable minority predicted that loyalty to nation-states will decline because they are decreasingly able to meet the demands of their citizens. The leadership group as a whole was almost evenly divided on the proposition that "The collapse of the Soviet Union and the unwillingness of the U.S. to deal with its budget deficit are likely to accord ever greater influence of the United Nations and other international organizations." Democrats were somewhat more likely than Republicans to foresee changes on each of these questions but the differences, although statistically significant in several cases, were generally rather moderate—in the range of 5 to 11 percent.

A second theme, on the prospects for international stability, is addressed by two items. The questions ask whether we are entering a period of fragmentation and disorder arising from, first, weakening support for governments and, second, exploding nationalist sentiments. Both questions gave rise to sharp divisions within the entire leadership sample, although not necessarily along partisan lines. Compared to Republicans, Democrats were somewhat more pessimistic on both questions, but once again the differences are of a very modest magnitude.

A third pair of questions focuses on the agenda of critical international issues. Very strong majorities of Democrats (73 percent) and Republicans (69 percent), without significant partisan differences, agreed that "Non-strategic issues such as pollution, the drug trade, migrations, and AIDS are likely to replace military concerns on the world's agenda." Somewhat greater disagreement, with a 10 percent partisan gap, emerged on the prospects for neglect and increasing impoverishment of the Third World as a consequence of vanishing

Cold War rivalries in that part of the world. Whereas a slight majority of Democrats agreed that this dismal scenario was likely to occur, slightly more than two-fifths of the Republicans did so.

Finally, responses to two items with strong military overtones reveal very strong partisan differences. The proposition that military threats are no longer effective elicited agreement from a 52 percent majority of Democrats but from only one Republican in five. A slim majority of Democrats also agreed that the United States, as the dominant power, can channel the direction of change toward a "new world order"; the comparable figure among Republicans was almost four out of five. These results are wholly consistent with the finding (see table 5.4) that Republicans and Democrats have strikingly different orientations toward the military dimensions of international affairs.

The data to this point indicate that Democrats and Republicans tend to have rather similar views on the nature of the post–Cold War international system, even though the former are somewhat more likely than the latter to predict fundamental changes. In contrast, the most significant partisan differences arise from questions about military issues and the U.S. role in the system.

Approaches to Peace

As for the perceived effectiveness of various approaches to peace, opinion leaders in the 1992 survey were offered a broad array of options. The actual items in this cluster of questions are listed in table 4.5. These span the full range of views from a basic realpolitik perspective (military superiority, alliances, balance of power) to key aspects of traditional liberal positions (trade, international organizations, better international communication and understanding, arms control).

Some elements of bipartisan agreement emerge from the responses to this cluster of items. Two approaches that have usually found favor among liberals—trade and technical cooperation and enhanced international communication—were rated as "very effective" by exactly half of the leaders in the former case and by 45 percent in the latter. For example, trade was ranked as the most effective path to peace by Democrats, and it was rated third highest by Republicans. Although Democrats were more sanguine about both approaches, in neither case was there a significant partisan gap. It might be worth noting that the 1994 congressional votes on the GATT/World Trade Organization agreement provide further evidence that, among leaders, trade issues cut across rather than along party lines. In the Senate,

Democrats and Republicans recorded favorable votes in identical proportions—76 percent. In the House of Representatives, 68 percent of GOP members supported the agreement, as did 65 percent of the Democrats.

In contrast, the most striking example of partisan discord is the different assessments accorded to "American military superiority" by members of the two major parties. Well over half of the Republicans rated military superiority as a "very effective" approach to peace, and it was by a considerable margin their preferred approach. In dramatic contrast, Democrats as a group rated military superiority as the *least* promising strategy for peace, with only 15 percent of them giving it a "very effective" rating. Another partisan divergence of views arose from assessments of the effectiveness of narrowing the gap between rich and poor nations. In contrast to the 44 percent of Democrats who gave this approach the highest rating, only 16 percent of Republicans did so. Two of the traditional instruments of foreign policy, collective security through alliances and balance-of-power politics, received rather different assessments. Forty percent of the leaders in the 1992 survey rated the former as "very effective," whereas only half that many expressed the same judgment about policies directed at achieving a balance of power. Partisan differences were insignificant in both cases.

In summary, these responses generally fall along lines that are familiar to theorists of international relations. Republicans accorded their highest rating to an approach with a strong realpolitik flavor, whereas Democrats favored liberal strategies for peace. The primary point of convergence across party lines was on trade and technical cooperation. These results are also consistent with the finding that most Republicans can be classified as *internationalists* and *hard-liners*, whereas Democrats are predominantly *accommodationists*.

Implications for U.S. Foreign Policy

When asked to explore the implications for U.S. policies of the end of the Cold War and the collapse of the Soviet empire, it is clear that few opinion leaders believe that the appropriate answer is a significant retrenchment from international activism toward isolationism. The proposition that the United States should limit its involvement in world affairs to military undertakings for peace and stability was rejected by an overwhelming bipartisan majority; it garnered the assent of fewer than one respondent in six. Nor was there much support for the self-centered approach represented by columnist Patrick Buchanan's (1990) call for a new foreign policy that "puts America first, and second and third as well." Given Buchanan's status as a highly visible candidate for the 1992 Republican presidential nomination, it is perhaps not surprising that members of the GOP recorded a higher level of agreement with his prescription, although among that group, only about one-third agreed, whereas even fewer (14 percent) of the Democrats did so. There was, however, considerable support for a proposition with at least some isolationist overtones: because America's allies are now capable of defending themselves, the U.S. can focus its attention on domestic issues rather than external threats to its well-being. One-half of the Republicans and two-thirds of the Democrats agreed.

A second major point of convergence across party lines emerged on two propositions to expand the nation's foreign policy agenda to give greater emphasis to economic and social issues, including hunger and poverty. Although support among Democrats outstripped that among Republicans at a statistically significant level, these differences are less salient than the much more important agreement with these propositions by well over 80 percent of opinion leaders in both political parties. The 1992 FPLP survey was completed months before the Bush administration launched Operation Restore Hope in Somalia, but these figures indicate that such undertakings are likely to gain strong bipartisan support, at least as long as the mission is a purely humanitarian one that does not involve the risk of being drawn into a civil war and suffering the casualties that are almost certain to follow.

Points of strong partisan differences emerge, not surprisingly, on questions about the role of the military in the post–Cold War era. Given their sanguine appraisal of U.S. military superiority as an approach to peace, it is not surprising that Republicans strongly (74 percent) supported the maintenance of substantial military forces and rejected by a narrower margin of 53 to 45 percent the view that the United States should replace its reliance on military force with a commitment to diplomacy and negotiation. The Democrats took precisely the opposite position, and the partisan gap exceeded 30 percent on both issues. An almost equally large chasm emerged on the question of ceding additional power to the United Nations and other international organizations. The overall leadership sample divided evenly on the issue, but almost twice as many Democrats (64 percent) as Republicans (33 percent) supported it.

The U.S. Roles and Interests
Responses to questions about U.S. roles and interests indicate once again that most Democrats and Republicans reject an indiscriminate

retreat to isolationism as an appropriate reaction to the end of the Cold War. Both Republicans (57 percent) and Democrats (56 percent) agreed that "The best way to encourage democratic development in the Third World is for the U.S. to solve its own problems," but four additional questions yielded strong majorities in opposition to various isolationist positions. Specifically, relatively few leaders in either party expressed agreement with the following propositions:

> We shouldn't think so much in international terms but concentrate more on our own national problems (34 percent agreed).
> Vital interests of the United States are largely confined to Western Europe, Japan, and the Americas (29 percent agreed).
> The United States should only be involved in world affairs to the extent that its military power is needed to maintain international peace and stability (15 percent agreed).
> Third World conflict cannot jeopardize vital American interests (14 percent agreed).

In none of these cases did Republicans and Democrats differ by more than an insignificant 3 percent.

Although both Republicans and Democrats spurn an American retreat to isolationism and a narrow, self-regarding definition of the national interest, this agreement does not extend to the *type of role* that the United States should play in the international system. When asked whether the United States should scale down its leadership position, Republicans overwhelmingly responded in the negative whereas more than two-thirds of the Democrats agreed. The closely related proposition that the country should quit acting like a superpower elicited little agreement (22 percent) among Republicans, while splitting Democrats almost evenly.

Foreign Policy Goals

A more specific perspective on policy preferences emerges from responses to a cluster of questions asking for an assessment of American foreign policy goals. These questions, cited earlier in chapters 3 (see table 3.2) and 4 provide an opportunity to assess the level of elite partisan differences across a broad array of Cold War and post–Cold War concerns, including world order security issues, global economic and environmental issues, and U.S. economic and value issues.

Opinion leaders of all partisan loyalties agreed overwhelmingly that preventing nuclear proliferation is a "very important" foreign policy goal, and only slightly smaller majorities accorded worldwide

TABLE 5.5. The Importance of Foreign Policy Goals as Assessed by American Opinion Leaders in 1992: The Effects of Party

Here is a list of possible foreign policy goals that the U.S. might have. Please indicate how much importance you think should be attached to each goal.

	All Respondents (N = 2,312)	Republicans (N = 721)	Independents (N = 592)	Democrats (N = 895)	Partisan gap (Rep-Dem)
			Very Important (%)		
World order security issues					
A. Preventing the spread of nuclear weapons	87	86	87	87	−1
B. Worldwide arms control	73	63	74	80	−17*
C. Strengthening the United Nations	44	31	42	55	−24*
D. Protecting weaker nations against foreign aggression	28	28	26	30	−2
World order economic and environmental issues					
E. Fostering international cooperation to solve common problems, such as food, inflation, and energy	71	58	73	81	−23*
F. Protecting the global environment	66	49	68	78	−29*

G. Combatting world hunger	55	40	53	68	−28*
H. Helping to improve the standard of living in less developed countries	43	27	44	56	−29*
U.S. economic interests					
I. Securing adequate supplies of energy	68	76	69	62	14*
J. Reducing the U.S. trade deficit with foreign countries	49	58	46	43	15*
K. Protecting the jobs of American workers	32	34	29	32	2
L. Protecting the interests of American business abroad	24	36	23	14	22*
U.S. values and institutions issues					
M. Promoting and defending human rights in other countries	39	25	35	52	−27*
N. Helping to bring a democratic form of government to other nations	23	21	21	26	−5
Cold War/security issues					
O. Defending our allies' security	34	45	31	28	17*
P. Matching Russian military power	18	30	17	10	20*
Q. Containing communism	12	22	10	6	16*

*Difference significant at the .001 level.

arms control the same rating, but on the latter issue the partisan gap reached 17 percent with more Democrats (80 percent) according the issue the top rating. Assessment of the United Nations gave rise to very substantial partisan differences; a majority of the Democrats gave a top rating to strengthening that organization, whereas fewer than one-third of the Republicans did so. Although the Gulf War had restored Kuwait's independence only a year before the 1992 FPLP survey, not even one-third of the Republicans, Democrats, or independents gave a very high priority to "protecting weaker nations against aggression."

Assessments of all four "world order economic issues" gave rise to huge partisan differences; in each case, ratings from Republicans were significantly less enthusiastic than those of the other respondents. A majority of Democrats and independents but a far smaller proportion of Republicans accorded the top rating to international economic cooperation, protecting the global environment, combating world hunger, and improving the standard of living in LDCs. Only the first of these goals received a "very important" rating from a majority of Republicans. The gap between Democrats and Republicans ranged between 23 and 29 percent on these four goals.

The four issues that focus on American economic interests— energy, the trade deficit, jobs, and business interests abroad—yielded precisely the opposite pattern of responses, as Republicans' ratings outstripped those of Democrats in each case. Energy security was judged to be "very important" by most Democrats (62 percent) and by even more Republicans (76 percent). The goal of reducing America's chronic trade deficit was judged to be "very important" by one-half of the leadership sample, and it resulted in similar partisan differences. The last two economic goals share strong protectionist overtones. Neither protecting American jobs nor U.S. business interests abroad was rated as "very important" by even one-third of the opinion leaders; only the latter goal resulted in a substantial partisan gap.

Two additional questions focus on promoting "human rights in other countries" and "a democratic form of government" in other nations. Neither goal ranked very high on the foreign policy agenda of opinion leaders. Whereas a slim majority of Democrats accorded the top rating to promotion and defense of human rights abroad, only a quarter of the Republicans did so. Members of the two major political parties shared a very limited enthusiasm for exporting democracy, and partisan differences were not significant.

Most opinion leaders believe that the Cold War has ended. This view is clearly reflected in responses to three security goals that ranked high on America's foreign and defense policy agenda during more than four decades of confrontation between Washington and Moscow: defending allies, matching Russian military power, and containing communism. Not one of the three goals was rated as "very important" by even 40 percent of the opinion leaders taking part in the 1992 survey, nor were any of the goals accorded that rating by a majority in any of the partisan groups. Nevertheless, responses to all three of them gave rise to very substantial and significant partisan differences; Republicans outstripped Democrats by margins ranging from 16 to 20 percent in their assessments of these goals. These differences aside, however, the most striking result is the fact that not even one leader in five accorded a "very important" rating to the two goals most closely related to the Cold War—matching Russian military power and containment.

International Interventions and Commitments
Nine items in the 1992 leadership survey focus on specific U.S. international commitments and undertakings. The data indicate bipartisan agreement on several of them. Two-thirds of the opinion leaders endorsed the proposition that the "U.S. has a moral obligation to prevent the destruction of the state of Israel"; this is the only international commitment that elicited stronger Democratic (71 percent) than Republican (63 percent) support. Even before Harry Truman's recognition of Israel within hours of its declaration of statehood in 1948, members of the American Jewish community tended to support the Democratic party. Although some visible Jewish leaders subsequently have become outspoken conservative Republicans—Norman Podhoretz and his *Commentary* magazine provide a prominent example—strong support for Israel among Democratic opinion leaders is not very surprising. Even Democrats who are critical of other American security undertakings abroad (recall from table 5.4 that most Democrats are *accommodationists*) may point to the fact that, unlike some other allies, Israel is a democratic country that has shown a willingness to defend itself without requesting that U.S. troops be deployed there. In contrast, although President Truman also threw American support behind South Korea immediately following the North Korean invasion in 1950, a much larger proportion of Republicans (74 percent) than Democrats (53 percent) agreed that the United States has a comparable obligation to maintain its security commitment to that country. Finally, the general proposition that the United States should not hesitate to intrude into the domestic affairs of other countries in support of a "democratic world order" gained

approval from fewer than one-quarter of adherents to either political party.

Responses to questions about three additional security commitments reveal strong partisan differences. Although preservation of NATO received strong bipartisan support, Democrats were evenly divided on a complete withdrawal of U.S. troops from Europe, whereas fewer than one-third of the Republicans supported such a policy. Proposals to protect Taiwan from invasion and to maintain an American military presence in the Middle East to protect oil fields were highly controversial—in both cases, the entire leadership sample was divided almost equally between supporters and opponents— but by margins of 21 and 28 percent, respectively, Republicans expressed far greater enthusiasm for both undertakings than did Democrats.

Finally, two additional items with a strong realpolitik tenor also brought forth very large partisan gaps. Two-thirds of the Republicans agreed that "There is nothing wrong with using the C.I.A. to try to undermine hostile governments," but only 28 percent of the Democrats supported that policy. The proposition that "The U.S. may have to support some dictators because they are friendly toward us" yielded almost similar responses. Whereas fewer than three Democrats in ten expressed agreement, more than twice that proportion of Republicans did so.

These results indicate that, although evidence of a bipartisan consensus may be found on such general questions as the structure of the post–Cold War international system, agreement does not necessarily extend to more specific policy-oriented areas, including the appropriate post–Cold War roles for the United States and the priorities that should be attached to various international goals. Substantial majorities among both Republicans and Democrats may oppose an undiscriminating retreat into a post–Cold War isolationism role for the country, but there is considerable disagreement on *what kind of international role* is most appropriate, as well as on strategies and means for pursuing U.S. interests abroad. These differences also extend to the types of international undertakings and interventions that Republicans and Democrats are prepared to endorse. More generally, Republicans tend to favor a leadership role consistent with American superpower status, whereas Democrats are more supportive of a U.S. role as a "normal nation" that pursues its interests in conjunction with others, including through the United Nations. Stated somewhat differently, members of the GOP appear more inclined to favor unilateral action in the pursuit of national interests, whereas multilateralism finds stronger support among Democrats.

Ideology

The data reviewed to this point support the lament of Destler, Gelb, and Lake (1984) about the increasingly partisan nature of foreign policymaking, but the other part of their diagnosis—the role of ideology—has yet to be explored. Some anecdotal evidence would seem to suggest that for several decades each of the two major parties has become ideologically less diverse as the GOP has moved sharply toward the right and the Democrats to the left; it includes the presidential nominees in recent campaigns, the defections of some prominent conservative Democrats to the Republican party—Strom Thurmond, John Connally, Phil Gramm, Richard Shelby, and Ben Nighthorse Campbell are some of the more visible switchers—and the growing use of such "litmus tests" on candidates as positions on taxes or abortion.

The 1994 congressional elections appear to provide further evidence of this trend. Indeed, there is some evidence that ideology may even dominate partisanship. In the early 1980s, the Republican chairman of the Senate Foreign Relations Committee, Charles Percy of Illinois, called for a revival of bipartisanship in foreign policymaking (Percy, 1981–82). Not long thereafter, Percy was defeated in his bid for reelection, in part because conservative Republicans such as his Foreign Relations Committee colleague Jesse Helms (Republican, North Carolina), hoping to purge the GOP of moderates, supported Percy's liberal Democrat opponent; that support included substantial financial aid from Helms's fund-raising Congressional Club to Percy's opponent. Can these tendencies toward increasing ideological cleavages also be found in public attitudes toward foreign policy issues and in the views of opinion leaders?

The General Public

Wittkopf's extensive secondary analyses of the CCFR surveys examined the relative potency of party and ideology on foreign policy attitudes. His conclusion was that the latter tends to dominate the former: "Compared with ideology as a source of the divisions that so often seem to have plagued recent American foreign policy, partisanship is again shown to be the less important factor" (Wittkopf 1990, 48). More specifically, he found that liberals tend to have an *accommodationist* orientation toward foreign affairs, supporting cooperative internationalism while opposing militant internationalism. In contrast, conservatives typically take precisely the opposite positions and thus are *hard-liners*. He further found that political moderates are likely to be *internationalists* owing to their support for both varieties of internationalism (Wittkopf 1990, 46). The potency of ideology remained fairly stable through the 1974–86 period covered by the first four CCFR surveys. Similar findings about the powerful impact of ideology on public attitudes emerge from the Americans Talk Security and Americans Talk Issues surveys initiated prior to the 1988 presidential campaign and continuing into the mid-1990s (Americans Talk Security 1987–91; Americans Talk Issues 1991–94). Finally, an analysis of the 1994 CCFR survey confirms again that party and ideology remain powerful correlates of foreign policy beliefs, with the sharpest polarization between liberal Democrats and conservative Republicans. However, a somewhat more complex pattern also may be emerging; when partisanship was held constant, the most liberal and conservative respondents were the only political groups with strong *isolationist* tendencies (Wittkopf 1995, 14).

The Gallup surveys on the Persian Gulf War provide an opportunity to assess the impact of ideology following the end of the Cold War. As I demonstrated earlier, responses to these questions revealed that strong partisan differences emerged on virtually all questions posed before, during, and after the 1991 war (table 5.3). When responses to the same questions are reported on the basis of the respondents' ideology, the results bear a very strong resemblance to those on the impact of political party. In brief, conservatives were uniformly more supportive of U.S. policy, including the decision to initiate hostilities after the January 15, 1991, deadline passed without an Iraqi withdrawal from Kuwait. Whereas on January 13 almost 60 percent of conservatives favored going to war instead of relying on sanctions or withdrawing from the conflict, fewer than half of the liberals supported that policy option. Once the air war had begun, approval from the conservatives outstripped that of liberals by 16 percent, and approximately similar gaps emerged from three questions asking for an appraisal of U.S. policy toward Iraq several months after the fighting had ended. The two questions relating to the use of tactical nuclear weapons against Iraq gave rise to minuscule partisan differences; the ideological chasm on these questions was similarly insignificant. In short, the data suggest a convergence of partisan and ideological positions on the Persian Gulf War, with Republicans and conservatives providing the strongest support for U.S. policies.

Opinion Leaders

Evidence reviewed in chapter 4 indicates that, compared to the general public, opinion leaders are more likely to think about public affairs in coherent ideological terms. For example, the consistently strong correlations between attitudes on domestic and on foreign policy issues would appear to indicate the existence of coherent underlying ideological beliefs. The question to be addressed here is the relationship between partisanship and ideology. How do they interact? Does one of them dominate the other? Has the end of the Cold War significantly altered the relationship? Data from the five FPLP surveys conducted between 1976 and 1992 will be examined in order to address these questions.

Respondents to the FPLP surveys were asked not only to identify preferences among political parties but also to locate themselves on a standard seven-point ideological scale, the end points of which were "far left" and "far right." Because so few respondents placed themselves in the two extreme positions on the scale, "far left" and "far right" were combined with the adjoining categories of "very liberal" and "very conservative," thereby collapsing a seven-point ideology scale into one with five categories.

When party preferences of opinion leaders are cross-tabulated against ideological self-placement, the strong relationship between the two attributes clearly emerges (table 5.5). Members of the GOP are overwhelmingly conservatives, and a vast majority of Democrats identify themselves as liberals. Indeed, conservative Democrats and liberal Republicans appear to represent endangered species. Moreover, the relationship between party and ideology, as measured by the correlation between them, has steadily strengthened during the sixteen-year span of the five FPLP surveys. The end of the Cold War has witnessed no erosion of the trend toward increasing confluence of party and ideology among opinion leaders.

The distribution of opinion leaders in table 5.6 does not, however, provide any clues about the relative potency of partisanship and ideological positions. An initial answer may be obtained by examining how leaders of all combinations of party identification and ideological preference are distributed across four foreign policy orientations—*hard-liners, isolationists, internationalists,* and *accommodationists* (table 5.7). As was true of the general public, ideological preferences dominate party identification among leaders taking part in the 1992 FPLP survey. The same was also true of the previous four FPLP surveys. Irrespective of party loyalties, liberals are overwhelmingly in the two groups that support cooperative internationalism—*accommodationists* and *internationalists.* Conservatives, on the other hand, are almost equally likely to be found among the two groups—*hard-liners* and *internationalists*—that support militant internationalism. Although there are relatively few cross-pressured

TABLE 5.6. The Relationship between Party and Ideology among American Opinion Leaders, 1976–92

Of the leaders who identify themselves as . . .		the percentage who also identify themselves as . . .				
	Year	VL	SL	Mod	SC	VC
Republicans	1976	1	5	23	58	13
	1980	0	4	20	60	17
	1984	*	2	18	63	18
	1988	*	3	18	57	22
	1992	1	2	18	64	15
Democrats	1976	20	46	23	10	1
	1980	12	49	27	12	1
	1984	15	50	27	8	1
	1988	18	51	24	6	*
	1992	19	50	23	7	*
Independents	1976	7	24	33	30	6
	1980	6	20	34	34	6
	1984	5	23	39	29	3
	1988	5	20	38	32	4
	1992	3	21	45	28	2

*Fewer than 0.5 percent.
Key: VL = Very liberal; SL = Somewhat liberal; Mod = Moderate; SC = Somewhat conservative; VC = Very conservative.
Note: Phi for 1976 = .64; 1980 = .67; 1984 = .70; 1988 = .72; 1992 = .75.

leaders (liberal Republicans and conservative Democrats) their foreign policy orientations are revealing; they tend to resemble the orientations of their ideological brethren far more than they resemble the orientations of those with whom they share a party identification. Among the "very liberal" opinion leaders, only two respondents (both Democrats) are classified as *hard-liners;* conversely, an almost equally small number of the "very conservative" leaders taking part in the 1992 survey had an *accommodationist* foreign policy orientation.

Finally, a more extensive multivariate analysis that includes all 182 questions in the 1992 FPLP survey confirms that ideological self-identifications outweigh partisan loyalties. More specifically, two-way analyses of variance revealed that ideological differences alone were significant at the .001 level on 46 percent of the questions, including both domestic and foreign policy issues. The comparable figures for party alone, both ideology and party, and neither ideology nor party were 2 percent, 32 percent, and 20 percent, respectively. The latter category—questions for which neither ideology nor party are sources of significant differences—includes virtually all of the trade issues.

TABLE 5.7. Ideology, Party, and Foreign Policy Orientations in the 1992 Foreign Policy Leadership Project (FPLP) Survey

Ideology	Party	N	Hard-liners	Isolationists	Internationalists	Accommodationists	Total*
Very liberal	Republican	4	0%	0%	0%	100%	100%
	Independent	18	0	0	0	100	100
	Democrat	171	1	0	4	95	100
Somewhat liberal	Republican	17	6	12	41	41	100
	Independent	120	4	3	19	73	99
	Democrat	444	1	3	14	82	100
Moderate	Republican	129	5	2	53	40	100
	Independent	263	5	9	28	58	100
	Democrat	202	6	4	33	57	100
Somewhat conservative	Republican	457	17	7	54	23	101
	Independent	164	18	6	41	35	100
	Democrat	61	15	5	41	39	100
Very conservative	Republican	105	31	10	50	10	101
	Independent	14	43	0	50	7	100
	Democrat	2	50	0	50	0	100

*May not equal 100 percent because of rounding error.
Note: Phi = .57

In summary, then, the Destler, Gelb, and Lake (1984) diagnosis, although published more than a decade ago and well before the end of the Cold War, has lost none of its validity. Partisan and ideological differences continue to characterize the foreign policy attitudes of the general public and, to an even greater extent, those of opinion leaders.

Generation

A generational interpretation of American foreign policy views appears to offer an attractive way to account for periodic shifts in public attitudes on foreign affairs. It seems to provide an explanation for the long-term cycles in which public moods have been described as swinging between internationalism and isolationism at intervals of approximately a generation in length throughout the history of the Republic (Klingberg 1952, 1979, 1983; Holmes 1985). It is also consonant with the observation that members of each generation view the world in the light of the critical events that marked their coming to maturity.

Although generational analyses of American foreign policy were given an impetus by domestic divisions arising from the Vietnam War, they antedated that conflict. Some years ago, Karl Mannheim (1952, 291) suggested that generation is one of the most important factors shaping social beliefs and action.

> The fact of belonging to the same class, and that of belonging to the same generation or age group, have this in common, that both endow the individual with a common location in the social and historical process, and thereby limit them to a specific range of experience, predisposing them for a certain characteristic mode of thought and experience, and a characteristic type of historically relevant action.

His thesis is especially germane for analyses of public opinion and foreign policy because it posits explicit linkages between age and "lessons of history."

Mannheim's injunction has not gone unheeded. In recent decades the concept of generation has played a central role in analyses ranging from the political right in interwar Finland to a proposed new paradigm for the entire course of American history, and from the Sino-Soviet conflict to the political views of American students. Even turmoil in Poland before the collapse of its communist regime has been explained by reference to generational differences (Rintala 1962; Huntington 1974; Taylor and Wood 1966; Lipset and Ladd 1971; Spivak 1981a, 1981b). And, as befits its growing prominence in social research, the concept also has spawned a critical literature and several controversies (Spitzer 1973). Finally, interest in the characteristics of the so-called Generation X has also stimulated speculation and analysis from a generational perspective (Strauss and Howe 1991; Howe and Strauss 1992).

American involvement in Vietnam and the resulting domestic conflict generated a good deal of speculation about generational differences and, more specifically, about the divergent lessons that Americans of different ages have drawn from the most salient foreign policy episodes they have experienced. "Generation gap" has thus joined those other famous gaps—bomber, missile, and credibility—in the vocabulary of many foreign policy analysts. The most visible lines of cleavage quite often have been described as falling between persons whose views were shaped by events leading up to World War II, on the one hand, and, on the other, those whose outlook was molded by the war in Southeast Asia (Allison 1970–71; Roskin 1974; Handberg 1972–73; Knight 1977; Kelman 1970; Russett 1975; Gergen and Back 1965; Bobrow and Cutler 1967; Cutler 1970). The interpretation that links post-Vietnam dissensus on matters of foreign policy to the lessons that each generation has adduced from dramatic and traumatic episodes was summarized by former White House National Security Adviser Zbigniew Brzezinski:

> There is a tendency in America to be traumatized by international difficulties. The generation of the Nineteen-forties was always thinking about the failure of the League of Nations. I'm talking about leadership groups now. The leadership of the sixties was always thinking about Munich. Now there is a generation worried by Vietnam, with consequences of self-imposed paralysis, which is likely to be costlier in the long run.[10]

To be more specific, the "Munich generation versus Vietnam generation" thesis usually takes some variant of the following line of reasoning. Those who experienced the bitter fruits of appeasement and American isolationism during the 1930s tended to identify British and French concessions to Hitler at the 1938 Munich Conference as the paradigmatic example of how not to deal with expansionist totalitarian regimes. When faced after World War II with the Soviet occupation of Eastern Europe, the absence of any liberalization within the USSR, as well as periodic crises in Berlin and elsewhere, persons of this generation were prepared to support an active American foreign policy to meet challenges from the Soviet Union and its satellites.

In contrast, according to this thesis, persons of a more recent generation—for whom World War II and its genesis, as well as the origins of the Cold War, are merely distant historical events rather than episodes experienced firsthand—are more likely to look to the war in Southeast Asia as a source of guidance on the proper and improper conduct of foreign relations. According to this description of contemporary American society, then, what the parents regarded as indispensable commitments to maintain a viable world order their offspring view as indiscriminate (if not incriminating) undertakings against ill-defined, often phantom threats that have no intimate connection to legitimate American interests, let alone the propagation or preservation of democratic values and institutions abroad.[11] Unencumbered by the memories and ideological baggage accumulated during World War II and the Cold War, the Vietnam generation is sometimes described as concerned with not only the physical safety of the nation but of this fragile "spaceship earth" as well; as ready to give up the hidebound political shibboleths of their elders in favor of a more enlightened worldview; as eager to renounce a materialistic lifestyle that eats up a disproportionate share of the world's resources in favor of simpler pleasures; and as inclined to respond to the sound of falling dominoes with a bored, "so what?" To some, this is a harbinger of better days to come, and to others it is no doubt a profoundly threatening one.

This is, of course, a vastly oversimplified summary of a rather complex line of reasoning. Nevertheless, even if it is something of a caricature, it does capture some central elements of the thesis that in important respects the cleavages on foreign policy issues in this country represent a confrontation of two distinct worldviews, each rooted in and sustained by the experiences of different generations.

The generational thesis, if valid, has some important implications for the conduct of American foreign policy because it suggests that members of the "Vietnam generation," as they achieve positions of leadership and influence, bring to their roles an intellectual baggage radically different from that of the leaders they are replacing. Under these circumstances, moreover, the prognosis is that as the next generation of leaders replaces those currently in positions of influence, a new consensus reflecting the sensibilities of the younger group will emerge.[12] Specifically, barring the election of Bob Dole in 1996, George Bush was almost certainly the last president with military service during World War II, and Bill Clinton was the first born after the end of that conflict. Recall also that persons who had reached voting age at the time of the Munich Conference reached retirement age during the 1980s. It remains to be seen to what extent the evidence supports the generational thesis.

The General Public

However theoretically plausible the generational interpretation of foreign policy differences may be, it is not unambiguously supported by empirical evidence. Both survey and voting data suggest that, at least within the general public, cleavages do not fall quite so neatly along age lines. Thus, the popular image of a dovish or isolationist generation of students demonstrating on college campuses in the midst of the Vietnam War to protest against the excessive foreign policy commitments of their elders provides a skewed, if not inaccurate, picture of American society. The generational interpretation of positions on U.S. policy in Vietnam received little support from surveys conducted during the decade before the 1973 Paris agreement that was to have ended the war. Indeed, these surveys revealed that, compared to their elders, the younger respondents were usually *more* inclined to support American policy in Southeast Asia, as well as to oppose withdrawal from Vietnam (Erskine 1970; Converse and Schuman 1970; Mueller 1973; Lunch and Sperlich 1979). Moreover, the allegedly dovish younger generation provided stronger support than other age groups for the decidedly hawkish George Wallace-Curtis LeMay ticket in the 1968 presidential election. More generally, a broad-scale study of American public opinion during the final three decades of the Cold War found little evidence of a generational basis for changes in public opinion about world affairs. Specifically addressing the "Munich versus Vietnam generation" thesis, Mayer (1992, 166–67) concluded that "If the experience of the last three decades is any guide to the future, the destiny of détente and the 'new world order' depends considerably more on the kinds of external events and conditions that cause intracohort change than on the workings of generational replacement."

Public opinion surveys of the post-Vietnam period also reveal few, if any, striking age-based differences on foreign and defense issues. Even when small differences appear, they do not consistently fit the pattern implied by the "Munich generation versus Vietnam generation" thesis. For example, a Gallup survey in 1975 asked whether the United States should continue a policy of protecting other nations against communist takeovers. There were virtually no differences in levels of support among the three youngest age groups: 18–24, 25–29, and 30–49. In each case, about four respondents out of seven agreed that containment should be maintained. In contrast, respondents over the age of fifty expressed somewhat *more*, rather than less, skepticism; only 47 percent of them supported that policy. Later surveys dealing with such controversial Cold War issues as the proper level of defense spending and the appropriate American role in Central American civil wars also failed to reveal any sharp age-based discontinuities.

Finally, the end of the Cold War has not significantly widened systematic age-based differences on foreign policy issues. Questions concerning U.S. involvement in Bosnia yielded quite similar responses from the various age groups, with some exceptions; proposed American air strikes against Bosnian Serbs failed to win approval of respondents in any age group, but the gap between supporters and opponents of such military action was widest among the oldest ones (Gallup 1993). By 1995, the oldest respondents were most inclined to assess the level of American involvement in Bosnia as too great (Saad 1995). A plurality of Americans supported lifting economic sanctions against South Africa after Nelson Mandela was released from jail (Gallup 1991), and a strong majority favored reducing immigration (Gallup 1993). Age-based differences on both questions were negligible.

Evidence from other studies also reveals mixed results. An analysis based on the first CCFR survey found that the under-thirty age group was almost evenly divided between "liberal internationalists" (30 percent), "conservative internationalists" (32 percent), and "non-internationalists" (38 percent). Indeed, compared to the thirty-to-sixty-four and over-sixty-four age groups, those of the youngest generation were the most evenly divided among these three categories (Mandelbaum and Schneider 1979).[13] On the other hand, a fuller analysis of the first four CCFR surveys did uncover some generational differences. Wittkopf (1990, 42–44) found that the oldest age group tended to be *hard-liners* in its foreign policy orientations, whereas the youngest was more inclined toward an *accommodationist* stance. Responses to the 1994 CCFR survey revealed, however, that significant generational differences did not survive multivariate analyses that included other sociodemographic variables (Wittkopf 1995, 14).

An especially interesting study from a generational perspective analyzed the analogies used to depict the situation in the Persian Gulf: World War II, in which Saddam Hussein's Iraq is viewed as playing an unremittingly expansionist role similar to Hitler's Germany; and the Vietnam War, in which an initial small commitment runs the risk of years of conflict without a clear outcome (Schuman and Rieger, 1992). After being asked to assess the relevance of the two analogies, respondents were asked: "Which of the two comparisons do you think best fits the Middle East situation with Iraq—the comparison to Hitler and Germany in the 1930s or the comparison to Vietnam in the 1960s?" The results revealed significant generational effect on the choice of analogy before the start of the war against Iraq, with older respondents more likely to choose the Hitler comparison, even when education, race, gender, and region were controlled, whereas the younger ones were more inclined to select the Vietnam analogy. That relationship faded considerably, however, once the war began. The analysis further found that the choice between the Hitler and Vietnam analogies was strongly correlated, both before and during the war, with support for or opposition to U.S. military action against Iraq. Despite the significant relationship between age and the choice of analogies, however, the results also indicated a very modest relationship between generation and support for policy choices before and during the conflict. The authors conclude:

> we have demonstrated the influence of generational experience in directing attention to one historical analogy or another—and also its limitation in influencing support for policy choices. Rather than past experience controlling the present, the present controlled the past, as most Americans of all generations came to accept the analogy to World War II—an analogy that justified massive military action against an enemy that was almost unknown a few months earlier (Schuman and Rieger 1992, 325).

The widespread propensity to use familiar analogies also emerges from a 1993 Gallup survey. Respondents were asked whether the conflict in Bosnia is more like the Vietnam War or the Persian Gulf conflict. Presumably, the outstanding difference between the two events was that the former was a protracted and failed American undertaking, whereas the latter resulted in a quick victory. By a margin of 57 to 34 percent respondents in the eighteen-to-twenty-nine age group chose the Persian Gulf analogy, whereas those aged fifty and higher (all of whom had reached adulthood before the American pullout from Saigon in 1975) were split evenly on the choice between the two historical analogies. However, these generational differences in choice of analogy did not translate into consistently different policy preferences on Bosnia. Another Gallup survey less than three weeks later did indeed find that the youngest age groups were most inclined to judge a Clinton plan for Bosnia involvement as "about right" (49 percent), whereas only about a third of the older respondents came to a similar judgment. But when the question was posed two weeks later, in this instance without reference to President Clinton, generational differences in judgments about the appropriate level of U.S. involvement in Bosnia virtually disappeared.[14]

The extensive surveys on the Persian Gulf War provide a further opportunity to assess the impact of age on a major post–Cold War undertaking as well as to confirm the results of the Schuman-Rieger study. Gallup surveys placed respondents into three groups based on age: eighteen to twenty-nine, thirty to forty-nine, and fifty and over. (The questions are described in table 5.3.) The cutting points for these groups do not coincide very precisely with crucial events experienced during formative years, as posited by some generational hypotheses. The youngest, born in the years 1962–73, clearly constitute a post-Vietnam generation. Those in the middle group were born between 1942 and 1961; thus, only the older members of this cohort might be considered members of the Vietnam generation. The oldest group, born before 1942, would include some respondents of the World War II generation but would not be limited to them.

The results of these Persian Gulf War surveys fail to provide a great deal of support for a generational interpretation of foreign policy preferences. Perhaps the results reflect, at least in part, the imperfect correspondence between age groups and the "critical" events that are central to some generational explanations. With a single exception, the variance of responses across the three age groups is less than 10 percent. Moreover, respondents in the thirty-to-forty-nine group, which includes the Vietnam generation, in fact tended to be slightly more rather than less supportive of U.S. policy, including the decision to launch a war against Iraq. Eighty-five percent of that age group approved of "The U.S. decision to go to war in order to drive the Iraqis out of Kuwait," whereas 74 percent of those aged fifty or older did so.

Opinion Leaders

Although evidence for a generational interpretation of the general public is at best mixed, perhaps the search for age-based cleavages is more fruitfully pursued among opinion leaders. At least some advocates of the generational perspective suggest that, irrespective of its relevance for the general public, it accurately describes the cleavages among elites, actual and emerging (Allison 1970–71). The Vietnam protests among the young were more often found at the "elite" universities—Stanford, Harvard, Berkeley, and the like—than at state and community colleges or in noneducational settings. There is evidence, moreover, that the generational hypothesis appears to fare best when applied to such specific groups as political activists or protesters (Jennings 1987). Some anecdotal evidence would also seem to raise questions even about a generational interpretation of elites, however.

As is well known, Bill Clinton was among the vocal opponents on university campuses of American policy in Vietnam, and by a combination of educational deferments and a high number in the draft lottery he avoided being called to military service in that conflict. But many of Clinton's most visible and outspoken current critics—among them, Senator Phil Gramm, House Speaker Newt Gingrich, and columnist George Will—also sat out the war by pursuing postgraduate education during the years they were eligible for military service. In short, membership in the same generation and at least one important shared experience during their formative years did not stamp these leaders with similar worldviews.

The five FPLP surveys will again provide evidence about opinion leaders. To assess the effects of age on foreign policy attitudes, the division of respondents into age groups was based on two premises. Three wars in which the United States had been involved since 1941 were assumed to provide significant benchmarks. The "Munich generation versus Vietnam generation" thesis also identifies two of these wars as watershed points in American thinking about external affairs. The second premise is that late adolescence and young adulthood may have special significance. Because that period encompasses for many the beginning of eligibility for military service, consciousness of and interest in foreign affairs may be enhanced when prospects for personal involvement hinge upon the outcome of foreign policy undertakings. More generally, those years in the life cycle have often been identified as especially crucial in the formation and development of political beliefs.[15]

Following this reasoning, three cutting points, 1923–24, 1932–33, and 1940–41, divided the respondents into four groups. Even the youngest of the World War II generation—those born in 1923—had reached the age of eighteen when the attack on Pearl Harbor brought the United States into World War II. By the end of that war they would have been likely, if otherwise eligible, to have experienced military service. But even those who were not on active military duty could scarcely have lived through the war without having taken cognizance of it. Leaders born between 1924 and 1932 would at least have reached the age of twenty-one during the Korean War. The older among them would also have been young adults during World War II, but for this group the Korean War would presumably have been an especially salient experience. Persons born between 1933 and 1940 would, if inducted into the armed forces, most likely have served during the period following the Korean armistice of 1953 and before the rapid escalation in 1965 of the Vietnam conflict. Hence, this group is labeled the "interim generation." Those born between 1940 and 1954 have been designated the "Vietnam generation." Even the oldest persons in this group would have been only thirteen years old when the fighting in Korea ended. For them, "the war" almost certainly refers to the conflict in Southeast Asia. For the 1992 survey, an additional cutting point (1954–55) was added, and those born after 1954 were designated as members of the "post-Vietnam" generation.

Evidence from the five FPLP surveys provides rather limited support for the generational thesis. The relationship between the age groups described above and the four foreign policy orientations— *hard-liners, internationalists, isolationists,* and *accommodationists*— has been consistently quite weak.[16] More detailed analyses, summarizing appraisals of four possible U.S. foreign policy goals, can provide further insight into the strengths and limitations of the generational perspective. Two of them—"containing communism" and "defending our allies' security"—are quintessential Cold War goals, whereas the other two address nonstrategic-military concerns: "helping to improve the standard of living in less developed countries" and "strengthening the United Nations."

Assessments of containment as a foreign policy goal resulted in only minor differences among the generational groups. Variations in ratings of that goal during the five surveys over the 1976–92 period clearly reflected the nature of relations between Washington and Moscow; by 1992, only one leader in eight rated that goal as "very important." Generational differences within any single survey were quite muted, however, and the correlations (*phi*) between appraisals of containment and generation never even reached .10 in any of the surveys. Moreover, even these minor variations did not fall into a consistent pattern; members of the World War II generation were by a very thin margin strongest supporters of containment in several surveys, but in 1984 their "very important" ratings lagged behind those of the other groups, again by the scantest of margins. Nor did appraisals of "defending our allies' security" yield much support for the generational thesis. The end of the Cold War was reflected in the declining urgency attributed to either containment or the defense of allies by respondents in all age groups.

The other two goals did yield somewhat wider generational differences, as well as a tendency for members of the oldest generation to accord the highest ratings to both development assistance for helping to improve the standard of living in the Third World and strengthening the United Nations. These differences also may reflect generational experiences; both the creation of the United Nations and the initiation of aid to LDCs (for example, President Truman's Point Four program) took place during the formative years of the World War II generation. In 1992, 60 percent of that age group rated assistance to LDCs as a "very important" foreign policy goal, and 64 percent of them judged strengthening the United Nations in similar terms. On the other hand, the Vietnam generation is apparently least enthusiastic about these goals for U.S. foreign policy; their "very important" ratings failed to reach 40 percent for either goal.

The word *apparently* is used advisedly here. Before accepting any evidence of generation gaps as definitive, it behooves us to consider whether or not the age groups in elite surveys also differ significantly with respect to other possible explanations for variations in their responses. In order to assess conclusively the impact of age on foreign policy attitudes, each of the generational groups should be as similar as possible with respect to other background attributes that might serve as competing explanations. For several reasons this is not true of the FPLP samples. Occupational differences offer a case in point. The sociology of occupations is such that prominence or leadership positions tend to come earlier in some professions or institutions than in others. For example, business executives typically do not reach the top levels of management before an age (mid to late fifties) at which many senior military officials, even those who achieved flag rank, have already retired. The suspicion that responses to the four issues discussed here may not accurately reflect the impact of age is supported by multivariate analyses. Occupational differences are highly significant for all four questions, whereas they are not for generations.[17]

This point can be further illustrated by expressions of policy preferences for dealing with Iraq's invasion of Kuwait in 1990. The 1992 FPLP survey asked respondents whether they favored using force, relying on economic sanctions, or staying out of the conflict in the Persian Gulf region. As table 4.7 shows, opinion leaders expressed an overall preference, both before and after the war, for using force against Iraq rather than giving economic sanctions more time to work. Their responses also indicate rather sharp differences between the Vietnam and post-Vietnam generations. Before January 15, 1991, 62 percent of the Vietnam generation's opinion leaders favored using force right away, but only 38 percent of those in the post-Vietnam generation expressed support for that option. This gap narrowed only slightly when leaders were asked about their policy preferences after the war had ended. Support for the use of force increased to 69 percent for those in the Vietnam generation and to 50 percent for the

members of the post-Vietnam age group. But these age-based differences once again melt away when occupation is introduced into the
analysis. The reasons are not hard to find. Military officers account for
over 20 percent of the Vietnam generation elites—indeed, over 88
percent of the military officers taking part in the 1992 FPLP survey are
within that age group—but they constitute fewer than 4 percent of the
youngest, post-Vietnam generation. Conversely, the latter age group
includes a significantly higher proportion of labor leaders, State Department officials, and media leaders. These results are not atypical.
Multivariate analyses of the FPLP surveys have generally reduced
rather than enhanced the impact of age on responses to most issues.[18]

In summary, there is little evidence presented here to sustain the
hopes—or fears—that the inevitable replacement of one generation
by its successor will give rise to significant changes in public or elite
attitudes toward foreign affairs. These attitudes may well change over
any extended period of time, as they have in recent years on a number
of central Cold War issues, but generational differences may not be
the most fruitful place to look for the dynamics of change.

Gender

One of the pioneers of public opinion research wrote almost a half
century ago that "more women than men seem to be ignorant of or
apathetic to foreign policy issues" (Almond 1950, 121). More than
thirty years later, Donald Regan, President Reagan's hapless chief of
staff, offered similar observations about women being more interested
in shopping than in foreign affairs. But the ignorance-apathy thesis is
not the only such stereotype. A strong and systematic correlation
between gender and warlike or pacifist attitudes is often alleged but
much less frequently supported with systematic evidence.

Although such stereotypes may still be found in the literature,
there are also signs that serious interest in the impact of gender on
politics has grown substantially in recent years (for example, Beckman and D'Amico 1994; Brandes 1994; D'Amico and Beckman
1995.) One obvious reason is that women are playing a more important, if not yet equal, leadership role in politics. Margaret Thatcher
was England's longest-serving twentieth-century prime minister, and
women have led governments in countries as diverse as Sri Lanka,
Norway, Israel, Canada, France, Poland, Iceland, the Philippines,
Nicaragua, Yugoslavia, Turkey, and India. At the same time, there is a
growing sense among students and observers of political behavior that
much of the received wisdom, such as the stereotypes just cited, merit

serious empirical examination. However, the interest in and literature about gender politics has not necessarily yielded a consensus. With respect to public opinion, for example, differences exist on such basic questions as the following:

1. Is there a "gender gap" or, more precisely, which issues give rise to consistent and substantial differences between men and women? There is some evidence of a systematic gender gap. For example, Converse (1987a) found substantial gender differences and that "'Rambo' themes come very disproportionately from males." According to Baxter and Lansing (1980), war/peace concerns are an exception to the general rule that men and women agree on most issues, and a study by Fite, Genest, and Wilcox (1990) identified gender as among the most important demographic predictors of foreign policy attitudes. Brandes (1994) also found large, stable, and significant gender gaps on security policy attitudes in the United States and Great Britain throughout the period since the end of World War II. A broad examination of survey data led Shapiro and Mahajan (1986) to conclude that systematic gender differences also emerge from "compassion" issues and those involving regulation and protection. Wittkopf's analyses of the CCFR data during the 1970s and 1980s found some gender-based differences along both the militant internationalist and cooperative internationalist dimensions, but that was no longer the case in 1994 when gender was combined with other background variables (Wittkopf 1990, 1995). Finally, Conover (1988) argues that "feminism," an ideological predisposition toward a certain stance on women's issues, overshadows gender in explaining beliefs and values.

A number of Americans Talk Security (1988) surveys also cast some doubt on stereotypical views of gender differences. Women consistently expressed more skeptical opinions about the USSR than did men. Although women were more inclined to describe themselves as "doves," men offered more support on all five arms control items by an average margin of 6 percent; expressed more trust in the USSR on six of seven items (6 percent); assessed Gorbachev more favorably on eight items (9 percent); had more benign views of Soviet motives on six of nine items (3 percent); assessed relations between the superpowers more favorably on ten of thirteen items (5 percent); and expressed a more optimistic view on the likelihood of nuclear war (10 percent). In the only exception to this pattern, women were more critical on three items relating to the impact of defense spending (6 percent).[19]

2. Have gender differences widened or narrowed during recent years? There appeared to be somewhat greater agreement on this issue, at least through the middle 1980s, as the evidence seemed to indicate that the gender gap was in fact widening (Baxter and Lansing 1980; Shapiro and Mahajan 1986; Klein 1984).

3. To the extent that there is a gender gap, is it the result of changing attitudes and behavior among women? Conversely, does the gender gap arise as a result, for example, of growing conservatism among men? According to Ehrenreich (1984), the gender gap will increase because a growing number of women will defect from conservative positions on three broad classes of issues—"peace, environmental protection, and social justice"—which correspond almost exactly with those on which Shapiro and Mahajan (1986) found evidence of significant gender differences. Conversely, Wirls (1986) proposed a male-oriented explanation of emerging gender differences on the same classes of issues, arguing that they have developed because of growing conservatism and Republicanism among men, rather than a movement to the political left by women. A similar interpretation may be found in Boyce (1985).

4. Are gender differences more pronounced among the general public or among leaders? Randall (1982) and Ehrenreich (1984) indicate that gender differences are widest among the most highly educated. On the other hand, an elite survey undertaken in 1976 found relatively limited evidence of such differences on foreign policy issues (Holsti and Rosenau 1981).

There is, in short, a rather striking lack of consensus among those who have pondered these issues. The differences are all the more striking because, with the exception of Nevitte and Gibbins (1987), who undertook surveys of both Canadian and American students, and Brandes's (1994) study in the United States and Great Britain, the others are all focused on a single country (the United States), and they cover a relatively short span of time (since the 1960s).

The General Public

As most of these findings reflect results from the mid-1980s or earlier, it may be worth examining more recent data with a view to assessing the nature and strength of gender differences on foreign and defense policy issues. Several points emerge from a number of surveys of the general public.

First, the differences between women and men are quite limited

on questions spanning a wide range of issues, including Soviet motives in world affairs (39 percent of men and an equal percent of
women judged it to be "world domination"), the impact of eliminating
all nuclear weapons (46 percent of both women and men believed it
would make no difference, and 22 percent of both groups stated that it
would reduce the chances of a war with the USSR), the appropriate
criteria and levels of defense spending (62 percent of men and 58
percent of women agreed that the United States should spend whatever is necessary rather than only what we can afford), assessments of
U.S. participation in the Bosnian war (46 percent of men and 51
percent of women judged it to be "about right," and 30 percent of each
group thought it was "too much"), proposals to send twenty thousand
U.S. troops to Bosnia (opposed by more than two-thirds of both
women and men), immigration (more than 60 percent of both men and
women felt it should be reduced), and economic competition as "more
of a threat to our nation's future than communism" ever was (45
percent of men and 44 percent of women agreed). Finally, after the
government in Kuwait arrested several Iraqi agents and charged them
with plotting the assassination of President Bush, a June 1993 Gallup
poll asked whether the United States should have Saddam Hussein
assassinated to remove him from power. Women were very slightly
more inclined to support that option (54 percent to 53 percent).[20]

A second conclusion is that moderate gender differences characterized assessments of the Soviet threat; compared to men, women
regarded it as more serious. Thirdly, substantial gender gaps appeared
on five issues.

President Reagan's military policies in Central America received
the approval of a slight majority among men, but only 38
percent of the women (Americans Talk Security 1988, No. 5).

The Strategic Defense Initiative ("Star Wars") program was approved by 61 percent of men and only 42 percent of women
(Americans Talk Security, 1988, No. 6).

The proposition that "the U.S. has a special moral responsibility
to help the disadvantaged of the world even if this means
putting off some spending on our own domestic problems" was
supported by only 35 percent of the men and an even smaller
number (26 percent) of women (Americans Talk Security
1988, No. 8).

The Bush administration's decision to lift economic sanctions on
South Africa in 1991 gained the support of more than half of
the men but only 37 percent of the women (Gallup, July 1991).

A proposal for U.S. air strikes against Bosnian forces attacking

Muslim towns was favored by only 44 percent of the men and 28 percent of the women (Gallup, May 1993).

An Americans Talk Security survey during the waning days of the Cold War provides additional evidence about the impact of gender. Respondents were asked to assess the severity of several potential national security threats. The results reveal rather modest gender differences on most issues. Women tended to see somewhat greater dangers in drug trafficking, domestic threats, and U.S. meddling in conflicts abroad. Most notably, women expressed strikingly greater concern about Soviet aggression and that country's military strength relative to the United States. The results in table 5.8, which further distinguish respondents by age, also reveal that older women—those aged forty or more—were consistently the most apprehensive among the four gender-age groups. On balance, however, men and women agree far more than they disagree on which are the more severe and less severe threats to national security.

The Persian Gulf War of 1991 provides still another opportunity to assess gender differences. Responses to Gallup surveys conducted before, during, and after the war reveal the existence of a quite considerable gender gap prior to the initiation of the war when the January 15 deadline for Iraqi evacuation of Kuwait expired (the questions are listed in table 5.3). In contrast to the strong support among men for the policies of the Bush administration, women were almost evenly divided on most issues. Once the war began, there was a tendency for opinions to converge, with a notable gain in support for U.S. policies among women. When asked a hypothetical question about the use of tactical nuclear weapons "if it might save the lives of American troops," by a very narrow margin of 46 to 44 percent women expressed greater approval for that option, but when the same question was posed three weeks later without the clause about saving lives, support fell among women (to 25 percent) even more than among men, one-third of whom favored using such weapons.

Although men have continued to be somewhat more supportive of the Gulf War undertaking, postwar assessments also revealed a relatively small gender gap. When asked, "Do you approve or disapprove of the way George Bush has handled the situation in Iraq since the war in the Persian Gulf ended," responses among women and men were identical—63 percent approved. Strong majorities also gave an affirmative answer to the question, "All in all, was the current situation in the Mideast involving Iraq and Kuwait worth going to war over?" In this case, however, men were somewhat more inclined to say "yes"—by a margin of 71 to 62 percent.

TABLE 5.8. Assessments of Threats to U.S. National Security in 1988: The Impact of Gender

I would like to get your assessment of some of the national security threats (and other challenges) the United States will face in the next five years or so. Please tell me whether [*threat*] poses an extremely serious, very serious, somewhat serious, or not very serious threat to our country's national security interests.

		Men		Women	
		Extremely serious + Very serious (%)			
Threat	All Respondents	Under 40	40 and over	Under 40	40 and over
International drug trafficking	87	78	89	87	93
The spread of nuclear weapons to Third World countries	81	83	89	83	78
Terrorist activities around the world	79	80	76	77	83
Damaging our environment from things like air and water pollution or the heating of the earth's atmosphere known as the greenhouse effect	77	72	77	76	81
Domestic problems like unemployment, homelessness, and crime	73	68	68	71	83
The undermining of our constitutional government	59	59	59	56	61
The economic competition from countries like Japan and West Germany	55	53	57	44	65
Unnecessary U.S. involvement in conflicts around the world	52	48	49	53	56
Soviet aggression around the world	50	47	43	52	57
An increase in Soviet military strength relative to the United States	50	41	49	56	55
The spread of religious fanaticism in Third World countries	36	29	40	33	41

Source: Constructed from data in Americans Talk Security, National Survey No. 8, September 1988, 93–103.

The evidence reviewed here neither wholly refutes nor strongly confirms the gender gap thesis. Women consistently expressed less support for such American interventions as assistance to the contras in Nicaragua or the invasion of Iraq to force Saddam Hussein's forces out of Iraq, but they were no less willing to have the United States involved in efforts to end the civil war in Bosnia. Perhaps the latter undertaking appeared more attractive because its primary goal could be portrayed as a largely humanitarian project to prevent "ethnic cleansing" and the related horrors of that conflict. It is less clear, moreover, that the roots of women's attitudes on interventions are to be found in an aversion to the use of force. There was, to be sure, a huge gender gap on proposals to initiate air strikes against Bosnian Serbs who were shelling Muslim cities, but women were no less prepared than men to use tactical nuclear weapons in order to reduce U.S. casualties in Operation Desert Storm or to remove Saddam Hussein from power by assassination. Nor did women express more empathetic attitudes toward U.S. Cold War adversaries or greater support for foreign assistance to poorer countries. And despite some evidence that gender and age combined to affect assessments of threats to national security, the more impressive pattern that emerges from the data in table 5.8 is the striking similarity in rankings of threats by men and women, whatever their ages.

Opinion Leaders

The four FPLP surveys of opinion leaders undertaken between 1976 and 1988 provided only very modest evidence of strong and persistent gender gaps on foreign policy issues. The militant/cooperative internationalism classification scheme was shown earlier to be strongly related to party and ideology. In contrast, the distribution of men and women in the MI/CI scheme consistently yielded very low correlations.[21] More generally, evidence of a gender gap in the first four FPLP studies can be summarized briefly.

Women consistently expressed a greater degree of concern for protecting the environment. There has been some narrowing of gender differences on these issues, a trend that arises largely from men catching up with women rather than from a declining environmental sensitivity among women. At least on this cluster of issues, the results run counter to the hypothesis that the gender gap arises from a change in men's attitudes. Specifically, that it is the result of men having moved toward more conservative positions during the 1980s (Wirls 1986).

As shown earlier, compared to the general public, opinion leaders are significantly less protectionist on trade issues. Within the leadership samples, women have been consistently more inclined toward efforts to protect jobs and industries by imposing some kind of trade barriers. Trade policy is one of the few issues on which there are neither strong partisan nor ideological differences, and thus the strong gender gap on this issue stands out rather sharply.

Women tended to be more wary of America's Cold War adversaries—both China and the Soviet Union—a finding that survived even when the data were subjected to multivariate analyses. This wariness and skepticism about the USSR was no less evident during the Gorbachev years just prior to disintegration of the Soviet Union.

Hypotheses about a greater sensitivity among women to international "compassion issues" such as combating world hunger or providing Third World development assistance received very little support from the FPLP data.

Perhaps the most consistent finding was a greater aversion among women for foreign entanglements, including, but not limited to, military interventions abroad. The evidence suggests that the gender gap arises less from a general aversion to the use of force and more from a greater skepticism toward commitments and interventions that might entangle the United States in undertakings abroad. This orientation manifested itself in a number of specific ways in which women differed from men, including less support for American responsibility for the defense of allies or commitments to specific nations and a more skeptical attitude toward both military and economic assistance programs abroad. Women were also more inclined than men to favor imposition of economic sanctions; because economic sanctions reduce or eliminate trade, aid, and related interactions with the target country, choice of that policy instrument can be viewed not only as a less violent alternative to war, but also as a form of withdrawal from foreign entanglement. Thus, although women differed little from men in placement in the MI/CI scheme—specifically, there was no evidence of women being disproportionately in the *isolationist* quadrant of that scheme—they did express less support for various forms of American involvement abroad.[22]

One significant reason for a skeptical view of internationalist undertakings is that they might lead to confrontations, crises, and conflict among major powers. Because the end of the Cold War and disintegration of the Soviet Union substantially reduced those risks, they might also have had an impact on the nature and magnitude of gender differences. A brief examination of some data from the 1992 FPLP survey will offer some clues about whether they are in fact widening or narrowing.

Unlike most Middle East confrontations of the previous four decades, the conflict arising from Iraq's invasion of Kuwait did not carry the risk of an escalating crisis between Washington and Moscow. Moreover, when President Bush ended the short military campaign after Iraqi forces had been expelled from Kuwait, American casualties had been lower than even the most optimistic projections. The reduced risks of a confrontation with the USSR and low casualties might have been expected to narrow gender differences on the war, but in fact they did not. When asked about their policy preferences before the start of the war, men among the opinion leaders favored the immediate use of force over giving economic sanctions more time to work by a margin of 58 to 41 percent; only 5 percent opposed getting involved at all. Policy preferences among women were significantly different; a plurality of 46 percent favored the economic sanctions option, whereas only 41 percent supported the immediate use of force, and 11 percent opposed any American involvement.

The successful end of the war against Iraq increased retrospective support for the use-of-force option, but it also slightly widened the gender gap. Whereas 64 percent of the men preferred the force option after the war, only 45 percent of the women did so. Moreover, by a margin of 16 to 7 percent, women outstripped men in their opposition to having been involved in the conflict at all. These significant gender differences persisted even when responses were controlled for ideology. That is, within each ideological group (very liberal, somewhat liberal, moderate, somewhat conservative, very conservative), women were less enthusiastic about the immediate use of force against Iraq.

A cluster of questions asking opinion leaders to assess the consequences of the Persian Gulf War provides additional evidence of a gender gap and the reasons for it. The first five items in table 5.9 emphasize various positive outcomes of the war, and the next five focus on less favorable ones. Majorities among male opinion leaders agreed with each of the favorable assessments, and they also rejected the negative ones. In striking contrast, women were significantly less inclined to agree that the conflict increased U.S. influence in general or more specifically in the Middle East, and a majority rejected the

TABLE 5.9. Assessments of the Persian Gulf War: The Impact of Gender

Here are some assessments of the Persian Gulf War. Please indicate how strongly you agree or disagree with each statement.

	Agree Strongly + Agree Somewhat (%)	
	Men	Women
It increased the influence of the United States with other nations	82	66*
Soviet-American cooperation before and during the war helped to establish firmer foundations for a new world order	80	76
It was a great victory for the United States	62	43*
It has given the U.S. the leverage needed to gain settlement of other Middle Eastern issues such as the Arab-Israeli conflict	60	46*
It put the Vietnam War behind us	56	48
The U.S. spent money abroad that needed to be spent at home	37	58*
Too many Iraqis were killed	37	47*
The U.S. will be too ready to use military force and go to war again	35	43
It increased frustration and hatred in the Middle East and will bring more violence and terrorism	31	44*
The U.S. will be too confident and drop its guard against foreign threats	21	19

*Gender differences significant at the .001 level. Differences are significant after controlling for ideology.

judgment that the war "was a great victory for the United States." The largest gender difference emerged on the proposition that "The U.S. spent money abroad that needed to be spent at home." Women were also far more prone to agree that too many Iraqis had been killed in the war and to express the fear that the conflict had increased the prospects for violence and terrorism in the Middle East. It is again noteworthy that, while each of the items in table 5.9 gave rise to significant ideological differences, in six cases the gender differences persisted even after multivariate analyses had controlled for ideology.

Some further evidence of a gender gap emerges on several questions in the 1992 FPLP survey about American commitments and undertakings abroad. Opinion leaders split sharply along gender lines on eight of them. Almost half of the women agreed that, "we shouldn't think so much in international terms but concentrate more on our own national problems," whereas only a third of the men expressed support for this proposition. These gender differences also manifested themselves in levels of approval for several items related to international commitments and undertakings.

The United States has a moral obligation to prevent the destruction of the state of Israel (men: 67 percent; women: 46 percent).

The United States should maintain its military commitment to South Korea (men: 63 percent; women: 46 percent).

Selling arms to Saudi Arabia (men: 61 percent; women: 35 percent).

The United States should give economic aid to poorer countries even if it means higher prices at home (men: 58 percent; women: 43 percent).

The United States has a moral obligation to prevent the military conquest of Taiwan (men: 50 percent; women: 33 percent).

Military aid programs will eventually draw the United States into unnecessary wars (men: 35 percent; women: 50 percent).

This pattern of responses is especially significant because, unlike most of the gender differences that have emerged from to the FPLP surveys, they did *not* disappear when the responses were controlled for ideology. The single exception to the consistently more skeptical attitude toward international undertakings among women—the significantly stronger support among men for bringing home all U.S. troops from Europe (43 percent versus only 34 percent among women)—defies easy explanation.

In contrast to this evidence of a gender gap, four additional items that advocate at least some retrenchment of U.S. international commitments gained the support of majorities among both men and women, without significant differences between them. These questions focus on deploying troops abroad, letting allies defend themselves, scaling down America's leadership role, and serving as a model for democratic development in the Third World by solving domestic problems. Additionally, huge majorities among both groups rejected the proposition that "The U.S. should not hesitate to intrude upon the domestic affairs of other countries in order to establish and preserve a more democratic world order."

Finally, a cluster of questions asking opinion leaders to evaluate a series of potential threats to U.S. national security may be especially telling because it offers a varied menu, including three threats that are at least in part residues from the Cold War (nuclear weapons in the former Soviet Union and the Third World, and Middle East conflicts), two environmental issues, five potential dangers with a strong "post–Cold War" flavor (drugs, population, the rich nation/poor nation gap, economic competition, and mass migrations), two domestic issues, and one that addresses the possibility that this country will meddle in conflicts that are "none of our business." Judgments about such a broad range of potential national security threats should reveal a good deal about the scope and magnitude of gender gaps.

TABLE 5.10. Assessments of Threats to U.S. National Security in 1992: The Impact of Gender

This question asks you to evaluate the seriousness of the following issues as threats to American national security during the remaining years of this century. Please indicate how serious you regard each possible threat.

	Extremely serious + Very serious (%)	
	Men	Women
An inability to solve such domestic problems as the decay of cities, homelessness, unemployment, racial conflict, and crime	89	91
The possession of nuclear weapons by Third World countries and terrorists	87	88
The federal budget deficit	84	82
Environmental problems like air pollution and water contamination	76	82*
International drug trafficking	72	78**
Uncontrolled growth of the world's population	66	66
A growing gap between rich nations and poor nations	58	63
Armed conflicts in the Middle East	57	62*
The greenhouse effect and other changes in the global climate induced by human activities	56	66*
Nuclear weapons in republics that seceded from the former Soviet Union	56	61
Economic competition from Japan and Europe	46	44
Mass migrations	33	38
American interventions in conflicts that are none of our business	31	42*

*Gender differences significant at the .001 level, but not after controlling for ideology.
**Gender differences significant at the .001 level only after controlling for ideology.

The responses of opinion leaders summarized in table 5.10 provide evidence of a gender gap on both environmental dangers and threats arising from Middle East conflict and unwarranted American meddling abroad, but further examination of the data reveals that these differences disappear once ideology is introduced into the analysis. Compared to men, women among opinion leaders tend to regard most of these thirteen threats as more serious, but the differences between their judgments are very small. In fact, the most striking feature that emerges from assessments of these future threats to U.S. national security is *gender similarities,* not gender differences. Men and women have almost identical assessments of these national security dangers; the rank-order correlation between the two columns is a very high .96.

In summary, opinion leaders tend to resemble the general public with respect to many aspects of gender differences. On some issues—the Persian Gulf War is a good example—the gaps between men and women are substantial, and they do not vanish when other background attributes such as ideological preferences are introduced into the analysis. On most issues, however, gender-based cleavages pale in size and persistence when compared to those defined by other background attitudes. Although gender does not rival ideology and party as a potent source of foreign policy attitudes, neither is it irrelevant. Indeed, it may be most relevant on precisely the issues that are central to post–Cold War foreign policy debates on the scope and nature of American commitments to international undertakings.

Other Background Attributes

Education

One of the best-supported generalizations about foreign policy attitudes is that increasing levels of education are associated with stronger support for internationalism. Foreign policy questions during the first decade of systematic polling were largely directed at attitudes toward various aspects of American involvement in world affairs such as participation in World War II and active participation in international affairs after that conflict, including but not limited to membership in the United Nations. These early surveys found a consistent pattern wherein the least educated segments of the public were also the least likely to support an active international role for the United States (Bruner 1944; National Opinion Research Center 1947). Although immense international changes have occurred in the half century since those pioneering studies, the link between the level of education and internationalism has persisted (Hero 1959, 1969; Hughes 1978; Watts and Free 1973).

Even with the development of a more differentiated concept of internationalism—for example, when a distinction is drawn between militant and cooperative internationalism—the link to education has persisted, although in a somewhat modified form. Higher education is strongly correlated with support for cooperative internationalism, but the association with militant internationalism is somewhat weaker and more tenuous (Wittkopf 1990, 37–39; 1995, 14).

The many surveys on the Persian Gulf War provide an opportunity to examine the impact of education on a recent issue. The Gallup polls undertaken before, during, and after military operations against Iraq indicate that, even on an issue with strong military internationalist overtones, the links between education and approval of international undertakings persist, although the relationship is not linear. Before the war, levels of support for military action to drive Iraq out of Kuwait were consistently highest among those with some college experience, followed by college graduates, high school graduates, and those with less than a high school diploma. These differences narrowed during the war and in retrospective assessments of the conflict. A July 1991 Gallup survey found that 78 percent of the general public approved of the U.S. decision to go to war; appraisals from the four education-level groups fell within a very narrow range of approval—75 to 79 percent. The most striking differences in these surveys concerned questions about the possible use of tactical nuclear weapons if it would reduce American casualties (50 percent of high school graduates approved versus 35 percent of college graduates) and a hypothetical law to ban peace demonstrations during a war (51 percent of those without a high school diploma agreed, whereas only 16 percent of college graduates did so).

Because opinion leaders tend to have very high levels of educational attainment, analyses to unearth links between education and foreign policy attitudes are not very meaningful. In the 1992 FPLP survey, for example, virtually all respondents had graduated from college and more than three-fourths of them had earned at least one graduate degree. Analyses based on a differentiation of graduate degrees—for example, distinguishing between the M.A., M.B.A., Ph.D., J.D., M.D. and other degrees—would probably provide a better understanding of the impact of occupation than of the effects of education on foreign policy attitudes.

Region

Region has traditionally been linked to foreign policy attitudes (Lowell 1923, 292). The conventional wisdom has been that midwesterners have an isolationist foreign policy orientation, southerners share internationalist and martial attitudes, and those living on the East and West Coasts are most receptive to such cooperative forms of internationalism as membership in international organizations. On trade issues, the manufacturing North was regarded as the natural home for protectionist sentiments, whereas the agricultural south, dependent on cotton and other exports, was seen as the champion of free trade. Hard evidence supporting these characterizations is often less than definitive, and in some cases it is subject to alternative interpretations. Although we are lacking systematic survey evidence from the 1919–21 period, it is probably true that opposition to the Treaty of Versailles and the League of Nations was strongest in the Midwest. But ethnicity may provide a plausible alternative to explanations based on geography. German-Americans and Irish-Americans, two ethnic groups that were heavily concentrated in the Midwest, tended to oppose the treaty and the league, the former because it placed responsibility for World War I on Germany, the latter because the league was perceived to be an instrument of British policy that would do little to enhance the cause of Irish independence.

Evidence to substantiate the regional thesis is at best mixed. Support in the Midwest for American membership in the United Nations equaled that in other regions (Gallup 1972, 451–52), and bipartisan cooperation between two midwesterners, Harry S. Truman and Arthur Vandenberg, contributed significantly to the major undertakings that formed the pillars of an internationalist post–World War II foreign policy, including the Truman Doctrine, the Marshall Plan, and NATO. The experience of World War II; the emergence of national media, first with radio networks and followed by television networks; and the increasing mobility of Americans, a process that was accelerated by World War II, were among the factors that probably contributed to the erosion of whatever distinct regional orientations toward foreign affairs may have existed. Almond's analysis of surveys during the early years of systematic polling led him to conclude that "Regional differences in foreign policy attitudes were quite pronounced in the period before World War II, but the evidence for the period since Pearl Harbor shows regional differences to be of declining importance." In place of a regional explanation, he suggested an alternative geographical thesis that emphasized rural/urban differences (Almond 1950, 131, 133; see also Hughes 1978; Watts and Free 1973).

Although regionalism appears to be a declining factor in shaping foreign policy attitudes, there is some evidence that it has not wholly disappeared. Congressional votes have pitted the "manufacturing belt" against the "sun belt" on foreign policy issues since the 1960s (Trubowitz 1992), and Wittkopf's secondary analyses of the first four CCFR surveys found some regional differences in orientations toward militant and cooperative internationalism, but these variations appear to be situational rather than consistent. While easterners tended to be somewhat more *accommodationist* than respondents from other regions in all four surveys, for example, both midwesterners and westerners leaned toward three different foreign policy orientations over the course of the twelve-year period (Wittkopf 1990, 39–41, 49).

The Gallup Persian Gulf surveys also provide some support for the regional thesis, but it is very weak. The prewar surveys typically found that southerners were slightly more supportive of military action to drive Iraq out of Kuwait, whereas easterners were slightly less supportive of the military option. Wartime and postwar surveys revealed a further narrowing of the already small regional differences. A few months after the end of military operations, approval for the U.S. decision to go to war with Iraq ranged from 74 percent in the East to 82 percent in the South (Gallup 1991).

Race

For obvious reasons, much of the attention on race and political attitudes has focused on a broad range of domestic issues that touch in some way upon civil rights and efforts to overcome the long legacy of segregation and second-class citizenship for black Americans. It sometimes was assumed that these issues rather than foreign policy topped the political agenda of black Americans and their leaders. Martin Luther King's public criticism of the Johnson administration's policy in Vietnam may have been something of a watershed event in this respect. Moreover, several developments since the Vietnam War have increased the probability that black Americans would take an active interest in foreign affairs: the end of conscription, leading to a professional military that is both disproportionately black and one of the most effective institutions for professional advancement of minorities; increasing controversy about American policy in Africa, especially toward, but not limited to, South Africa; and increasing activism by black Americans within Congress and congressional lobbying groups on such foreign policy issues as sanctions on South Africa and the treatment of refugees from Haiti.

Much of the evidence indicates that black Americans tend to be more isolationist than the public as a whole, but, as one analyst has pointed out, it is sometimes unclear whether there are equally plausible explanations, including class and education, that may account for differences in foreign policy attitudes (Hero 1959; Watts and Free 1973; Hughes 1978; Wittkopf 1990, 41, 44; Wittkopf 1995, 14). However, responses to the Persian Gulf surveys appear to indicate that race may well be emerging as one of the more powerful sources of foreign policy cleavages. The evidence summarized in table 5.11 reveals that, although the gaps between whites and nonwhite minorities—for example, Asian-Americans or Latinos—are consistent but of moderate magnitude, those between white and black Americans can only be described as enormous. The racial gap was only partially bridged by the onset of the war. Although the United States achieved

TABLE 5.11.   Attitudes on Selected Issues Relating to the Persian Gulf Conflict, before, during, and after the War: The Impact of Race

Date	Question	All	White	Nonwhite	Black
Prewar surveys					
Jan. 13	Do you think the United States made a mistake in sending troops to Saudi Arabia, or not? [% yes]	29	25	34	62
Jan. 13	Which of the following comes closest to your opinion? Favor: Withdraw; sanctions; war. [% initiate a war]	50	54	42	25
Wartime surveys					
Jan. 20	Do you approve or disapprove of the U.S. decision to go to war in order to drive the Iraqis out of Kuwait? [% approve]	80	83	81	59
Jan. 26	Do you favor or oppose using tactical nuclear weapons against Iraq if it might save the lives of U.S. troops [% favor]	45	45	45	45
Jan. 26	Would you favor or oppose a law to ban peace demonstrations while U.S. troops are fighting overseas? [% favor]	31	31	27	41
Feb. 17	Do you favor or oppose the U.S. use of tactical nuclear weapons in the Persian Gulf War [% favor]	28	29	31	26
Postwar surveys					
July 14	All in all, was the current situation in the Mideast involving Iraq and Kuwait worth going to war over, or not? [% yes]	66	71	40	37
July 21	Looking back, do you approve or disapprove of the U.S. decision last January to go to war with Iraq in order to drive the Iraqis out of Kuwait? [% approve]	78	82	46	37

Source: Gallup surveys. The typical survey was spread out over a 3–4-day period. The left-hand column reports the final date of the survey.

its goal of forcing Iraq out of Kuwait, and it did so with minimal casualties, postwar appraisals of the American undertaking yielded striking cleavages that tended to coincide with race. Whereas more than four-fifths of whites approved in retrospect of the decision to initiate the war against Iraq, the comparable figure among black Americans was 37 percent. Race has also been a source of divisions on at least four other recent foreign policy issues: South Africa, Haiti, Somalia, and Bosnia. Compared to whites, black Americans were more supportive of U.S. intervention in the first three cases, whereas the opposite pattern emerged with respect to the civil war in Bosnia.[23] It remains to be seen whether the racial divide on the Persian Gulf War and these other issues is an anomaly or a harbinger of deep and persisting racial cleavages on future foreign policy undertakings.

Conclusion

This exploration of the sources of foreign policy opinions began with the Destler-Gelb-Lake lament of more than a decade ago about the increasingly partisan and ideological character of debates about international issues. The evidence presented here largely sustains their diagnosis, whether the focus is on the general public or opinion leaders. Among both groups the closely linked attributes of ideology and party identification consistently have been the most powerful correlates of attitudes on a wide range of foreign policy issues. That generalization has withstood repeated multivariate analyses that included other background attributes. Notwithstanding that overall theme, some beliefs transcend party and ideology, and these are far from trivial aspects of international relations; for example, the end of the Cold War and the multipolar nature of the international system that has emerged as that decades-long conflict ended. Presumably such events as the demolition of the Berlin Wall and disintegration of the Soviet Union were of such an unambiguous nature and compelling importance that their impact on beliefs transcends partisanship and ideology. Although efforts to claim partisan or ideological advantage from the successful denouement of the Cold War were never in short supply—many a Canadian forest has been felled just to print polemics affirming or denying that the Reagan military buildup contributed to the end of the Cold War—the fact of Soviet collapse has not been controversial. Surveys of opinion leaders also have revealed that cleavages on international trade and Middle East issues revolving around Israel and its security divide leaders and the public in other ways. But these are exceptions to the general rule of powerful partisan and ideological cleavages.

In contrast, although the other background factors discussed earlier—gender, generation, region, education, and race—are not irrelevant for explaining foreign policy views, they appear to do so less consistently and, when they do, they only rarely serve to bridge the dominant partisan and ideological cleavages. The so-called gender gap provides a good example. Men and women often differ on specific U.S. security commitments, trade, and the environment, but it is much harder to find comparable evidence of consistent differences on basic orientations toward international affairs, assessment of threats, images of adversaries, the use of force, and foreign aid. More generally, liberal Democrats, whether men or women, usually have similar foreign policy beliefs, which, in turn, differ sharply from those of conservative Republicans of either sex.

One should nevertheless be cautious about assuming that attributes that contribute only modestly to understanding foreign policy opinions will be equally irrelevant for all issues. Consider the generational hypothesis, wherein it is suggested that because major differences in worldviews are linked to age, the replacement of one cohort with another will account for major changes in attitudes. The evidence has rarely confirmed that this is an especially rewarding way of analyzing U.S. foreign policy attitudes. But it may well be that other important issues do in fact divide the public, opinion leaders, or both along generational lines. For example, Mayer (1992) has demonstrated that although generational replacement had little impact on foreign policy attitudes, it was a major source of change on some social and cultural issues.

If, as seems likely, the foreign policy agenda during the post–Cold War era will be characterized by a widening array of crucial issues and a continued blurring of the lines between the domestic and international arenas, we might also expect some shifting linkages between foreign policy beliefs and socio-demographic variables. Trade issues may be used to illustrate this hypothesis. Evidence through the middle 1990s indicated that there were substantial differences between the general public and leaders, with the latter far more supportive of efforts to liberalize trade (see table 4.2). The gap no doubt reflected at least in part different personal vulnerabilities to dislocations arising from reduction or removal of trade barriers; blue-collar workers in the textile, steel, and automobile industries, for example, have been more likely to lose jobs to foreign competition than bankers, insurance executives, highly educated workers in advanced technology firms, and employees in the "knowledge industries." However, there are also some indications that technological and other changes also may be rendering those in the latter occupational groups increasingly vulnerable; a front-page headline in a recent *New York Times* proclaimed, "Skilled Workers Watch Their Jobs Migrate Overseas. A Blow to Middle Class: College Educated Foreigners Are Doing High Technology Tasks for Far Less Pay." (August 28, 1995, A:1, C-6). Should such trends persist for any significant period, we might well expect that the coalitions supporting and opposing trade liberalization will also change.

In short, although there has been a good deal of stability in the background correlates of foreign policy beliefs during the period since the end of the Vietnam War, including the growth and persistence of partisan and ideological cleavages that have survived the dramatic international changes since the late 1980s, those patterns could change in response to future developments, some of which can only dimly be perceived today.

Finally, it may be worth speculating about the linkages between leaders and the general public, with special emphasis on the impact of partisanship and ideology on foreign policy beliefs. This discussion assumes that the relationship between decision makers, opinion leaders, and the general public is better characterized as complex and interactive rather than simple and unidirectional, as depicted by either a "bottom-up" or a "top-down" model. The latter model has dominated analyses of public opinion and the media at least since Walter Lippmann's early writings, cited in chapter 1, challenged the ability and willingness of ordinary citizens to meet the requirements of classical democratic theory. The central premises of the "top-down" model are that the general public takes its cues from elites, and the media take theirs from the government. A number of recent studies have raised some serious questions about the adequacy of this model. For example, based on his analysis of the Persian Gulf War, Zaller (1994, 271–72) concluded that "many exaggerated reports of its demise to the contrary, the democratic interplay between leaders and followers was alive and well in the Gulf Crisis." Similarly, a careful analysis of leaders, the media, and public opinion on the 1989 Tiananmen Square massacre and the coup attempt against Mikhail Gorbachev two years later also revealed that the public is capable of taking autonomous positions on foreign policy issues that do not merely reflect the views of leaders or the media (Isaacs 1994).

For purposes of illustrating at least one way of linking leaders and the general public, the hypothesis to be explored here is this:

> Significant divisions on major issues of national security are usually rooted in ideological differences arising from competing views about the proper U.S. role in the world, the major source of threats to national security, and the most effective means and strategies for coping with them; the divisions are only secondarily partisan in origin, depending, first, on whether leaders believe that framing the issues in partisan terms will enable them to achieve their goals and, second, on public opinion, actual and anticipated, on these issues.

Leaders may have better informed and more sophisticated worldviews, but they cannot neglect those of the general public. Zaller's

(1994, 251) concept of "anticipated future opinions"—leaders take policy positions based on their anticipation of future public opinions—serves as a useful way to link leaders and the general public. (See also Stimson, MacKuen, and Erikson 1994, 1995). Three examples, sketched in broad strokes rather than fine-grained detail, will illustrate but not adequately test this hypothesis.

During the decade leading up to Pearl Harbor, there were sharp differences about whether and how the United States should deal with the growing military power and increasingly transparent ambitions of expansionist dictatorships in Europe and the Far East. To oversimplify, some (including President Roosevelt) feared that aggressive German and Japanese ambitions represented long-term threats to the country's security and the survival of democracy; it was thus vital for the United States to support those resisting these dictatorships. Critics of this position countered that an active internationalist foreign policy is incompatible with democracy at home. War itself, not the European or Asian balance of power, most directly threatened America's interests and democratic institutions; thus, every effort should be made to avoid once again being drawn into distant conflicts that pose no clear and present danger to the preservation of the Republic or its key institutions. (For an excellent and more detailed analysis of public opinion during this period, see Hinckley 1992.)

But these competing worldviews were very imperfectly correlated with party identification, either among leaders or the general public. For example, at the time of his 1937 speech advocating an international "quarantine" of the expansionist powers, President Roosevelt's Democratic Party held overwhelming majorities of 75 to 17 (with 4 "others") in the Senate and 333 to 89 (with 13 "others") in the House. Three years later, when Roosevelt consummated the "destroyer deal" that transferred fifty aged warships to Great Britain by doing an end run around Congress, the Democrats still outnumbered Republicans by three to one in the Senate and by ninety-three seats in the House. Despite these handsome majorities, because foreign policy beliefs in Congress cut across rather than along party lines, Roosevelt repeatedly found himself stymied by various forms of "neutrality legislation" in his efforts to assist the beleaguered allies, even after the collapse of France in the face of the German blitzkrieg in May 1940. Among his efforts to build an effective foreign policy coalition across party lines was the replacement in 1940 of his isolationist Secretaries of War and the Navy with two distinguished Republicans, Henry Stimson and Frank Knox.

The absence of strictly partisan divisions on foreign policy issues was also reflected in the character of several major foreign policy interest groups—the isolationist America First and its internationalist counterparts, the Non-Partisan Committee for Peace through Revision of the Neutrality Laws and the Committee to Defend America by Aiding the Allies. The latter organizations were led by a newspaper editor with impeccable Republican credentials. Although Roosevelt was never reticent about attacking the GOP when it served his political purposes, it would have been self-defeating to frame the key foreign policy issues in partisan terms. Finally, Roosevelt's manifest skill in using the new medium of radio notwithstanding, his efforts to mold public opinion on foreign policy were calculatedly cautious. He interpreted reactions to his "quarantine" speech as unfavorable on balance and, anticipating that the public would be even more critical of concrete steps to help Britain and France, he emphasized repeatedly that he had no intention of permitting the United States to be drawn into war. Thus, despite Roosevelt's personal popularity and public relations skills, his efforts to influence the public on international affairs had a relatively modest impact. As I noted in chapter 1, almost to the eve of Pearl Harbor strong majorities among the general public favored a wide array of legislative and constitutional efforts to prevent the country from again being pulled into any war for purposes other than defense of the home territory.

The early Cold War period also revealed ideological differences that were less than perfectly correlated with party. Divisions within the GOP pitted such staunch critics of a broadly internationalist foreign policy as Senator Robert Taft and former President Herbert Hoover against the Vandenburg-Dewey-Eisenhower-Dulles faction within the party. Democrats were similarly divided between those supporting Harry Truman, J. William Fulbright, Dean Acheson, and other internationalists and such critics of the U.S. foreign defense policies as Henry Wallace, who bolted the Democrats in 1948 to run for president on the Progressive Party ticket.

The important point, however, is that the internationalists were generally dominant within the leadership of both parties; for example, between 1948 and 1960, presidential candidates of both major parties shared a broad internationalist ideology on foreign affairs. Although there were often sharp partisan differences on which party was best suited to implement that worldview, the principle of active American engagement in world affairs was rarely the basis of partisan debates. That fact no doubt contributed to the absence of striking partisan differences among the general public, at least on many of the important foreign policy issues of the period (see table 5.1). Moreover, most of the major foreign policy interest groups, including the Foreign Policy Association, the United Nations Association, and the Council on Foreign Relations, were largely bipartisan in membership and generally offered support for the internationalist foreign policies of the Truman and Eisenhower administrations. There were, of course, also some critics of internationalism, including the Congress of Industrial Organizations (CIO) prior to its merger with the American Federation of Labor (AFL) in 1955, but some of the more vocal ones—for example the John Birch Society or supporters of Senator Joseph McCarthy—were not primarily partisan in character. Their shotgun charges of treason were aimed at targets in both political parties, and they appealed mostly to those who were prepared to believe in a global communist conspiracy that counted Dwight Eisenhower and George Marshall among its cat's-paws.

The late Cold War period, encompassing the two decades prior to demolition of the Berlin Wall, featured sharp divisions within the major political parties. The presidential nomination of George McGovern by Democrats in 1972 represented a repudiation by many Democrats of the Truman-Kennedy-Johnson internationalist policies that, McGovern argued, had ineluctably led to the disaster in Vietnam; it was, therefore, time to "Come Home, America." For them, the most important "lesson of Vietnam" was that the United States should avoid military engagement in the Third World. Even a stalwart architect and supporter of post–World War II foreign policies, Democratic Senator J. William Fulbright, called for rejection of an internationalism that, in his view, had failed to distinguish adequately between vital and peripheral interests.

The Vietnam War and the Nixon-Kissinger policies of trying to contain the USSR by offering carrots (arms control agreements, crisis control measures, expanded trade and credits) as well as sticks (containment and deterrence) also divided Republicans. The Goldwater-Reagan wing of the party narrowly failed to capture the GOP presidential nomination in 1976, but it succeeded in doing so four years later. Charging that the détente and arms control policies of his predecessors in the White House, including Republicans Nixon and Gerald Ford, had severely crippled the United States—if not endangered its very survival—Reaganites were no less reluctant than the McGovernites to challenge some foundations of post–World War II foreign and defense policies, albeit from a distinctly different perspective. For them, the lessons of Vietnam included the imperatives of a major military buildup, removal of undue restrictions on the uses of military force, and the desirability of challenging the USSR on the peripheries of its empire (the "Reagan Doctrine").

Thus, whereas, the core leadership of the Democratic and Republican parties during the two decades prior to Vietnam shared some basic axioms about the appropriate U.S. role in world affairs, critics of those premises came to dominate the two major parties in the post-Vietnam years. As a consequence, the partisan cleavages came to be more closely aligned with ideological ones. The Democratic Party tended to be the most congenial home for *accommodationists*, whereas *hard-liners* were usually found in the Republican Party. Some prominent hard-line Democrats, including Paul Nitze, Eugene Rostow, and Jeane Kirkpatrick, accepted high positions in the Reagan administration. The convergence of ideological and partisan cleavages was also reflected in some of the major foreign policy interest groups of the period, including the hawkish Committee on the Present Danger, more than three dozen of whose members served in key foreign and defense policy positions in the Reagan administration, and more dovish groups such as the Arms Control Association.

In line, then, with the hypothesis on the ideological origins of foreign policy differences presented previously, partisan cleavages should have widened under these circumstances because, as each of the two major parties was becoming more ideologically homogeneous, differences between them were becoming more pronounced. As indicated in tables 5.4 and 5.6, that has been true of opinion leaders. Other evidence also reveals that this has also been true among the general public; for example, the data in table 5.2 reveal sharp partisan cleavages on many foreign policy issues. Finally, this hypothesis appears to offer at least a tentative and partial explanation for the tendency of ideology to dominate party identification among both the opinion leaders (see table 5.7) and the general public (Wittkopf 1990, 1995).

In summary, these brief and sketchy interpretations suggest that major international developments, especially those that revolve around questions of war and peace, often give rise to divergent policy prescriptions rooted in different worldviews. Whether they also divide the country along partisan lines depends on complex interactions between leaders and the public. Despite the dominance of FDR's own party, for example, ideological divisions among leaders and the lack of public support for even modest forms of engagement in emerging conflicts in Europe and Asia required Roosevelt to work toward a bipartisan leadership coalition and to avoid framing foreign policy issues in partisan terms. During the Truman and Eisenhower years, the dominance of an internationalist ideology within both political parties, as well as a public that was prepared to accept major international undertakings, muted sharp partisan clashes on the fundamental nature of American foreign and defense policies. In contrast, controversies over the Vietnam War gave rise to two internally consistent but mutually exclusive interpretations for why the United States became involved in that conflict, why it lost, and what "lessons" should be learned from it. According to one view, an undiscriminating internationalism drew the United States into an unwinnable conflict that never engaged important national interest. According to the other, the United States appropriately viewed the defense of South Vietnam as a vital interest, its war effort fulfilled a solemn treaty obligation, and it could have been victorious but for the media, protests at home, and unwise restrictions on military force imposed by political leaders. These Vietnam postmortems, which also yielded divergent lessons about the future conduct American foreign and defense policies, tended to fall largely along partisan lines (Holsti and Rosenau 1984). Although that conflict ended more than two decades ago, the continued convergence of partisan and ideological cleavages appears to be one of its more enduring residues.

It bears repeating, in conclusion, that this discussion has only illustrated one of the ways that analyses of public opinion can attempt to link leaders and the general public. Moreover, even if the foregoing hypothesis seems plausible, the sketchy and anecdotal evidence is not an adequate substitute for the kind of systematic testing that has not been possible here.

CHAPTER 6

Public Opinion and Foreign Policy: Where Do We Go from Here?

A few days before President Clinton ordered American troops to invade Haiti in September 1994, Jeff MacNelly of the *Chicago Tribune* published an editorial cartoon depicting a loaded military landing craft approaching the coast of Haiti. Among those on board was President Clinton, who was depicted as saying, "Shouldn't the pollsters go in first?" To be sure, in the case of Haiti President Clinton did take action in the face of substantial evidence of public and congressional opposition to any military intervention there. But the cartoon reflects the widely held belief that the Clinton administration's frequent threats of strong action, followed by retreats, over Somalia, Bosnia, Haiti, and Most Favored Nation trade status for China were significantly influenced by public opinion, and especially, in the first three cases, by widespread disquiet about deployment of American troops abroad. Indeed, at about the same time another cartoonist, Gary Trudeau, began depicting President Clinton as a disembodied "waffle" in his *Doonesbury* comic strip.

Whether or not these cartoons accurately or fairly depicted the Clinton administration's approach to international issues, there is a good deal of evidence that, for better or worse, public opinion had a substantial impact on the foreign policies of Clinton's predecessors. Some of this evidence was reviewed in chapter 3. This chapter will focus on two related points. First, I will develop the thesis that, whatever may have been true in earlier periods, during the post–Cold War era public opinion is likely to become a more rather than less potent force in shaping American foreign policy. If the reverse were true, then there would be scant reason for students of international relations and foreign policy to direct additional attention to public opinion. On the other hand, if the hypothesis about an increasing role for public opinion is valid, it leads to the second point to be considered in this chapter: what might be done in order to better understand the relationship between public opinion and foreign policy? The second part of the chapter will consider several approaches that might contribute to that goal, including case studies to assess causal relationships, cross-national comparative analyses, and standardized questions.

Public Opinion in the Post–Cold War Era

The realist thesis, some features of which were described in chapter 1, is that public opinion can contribute very little to the effective conduct of foreign affairs. In some versions of the realist position, public opinion is depicted as an ill-informed, volatile, and mood-driven force that, if heeded, would often deflect statesmen from the steady pursuit of the long-range interests and goals that constitute the essence of the country's national interests. In other contexts, the realist position views public opinion as pushing the government into ill-considered undertakings that have little, if any, relationship to those national interests. Other critiques agree that the public is poorly informed about international affairs, but they also focus on the alleged rigidity rather than the volatility of public opinion. The public is described as so firmly set in its ways of thinking that serious attention to public preferences would make it impossible for policymakers to act with sufficient flexibility and dexterity to cope effectively with international opportunities and challenges. In his classic *Study of War* (1942), published when the Axis powers had reached the outer limits of their conquests in Europe and Asia, Quincy Wright wrote that democracies were hampered in their attempts to cope with the imperatives of an anarchical international environment.

> Executive freedom of action has been hampered by an active and independent public opinion, by indirect checks on the control of appropriations, by certain direct checks, such as legislative participation in treaty-making and general responsibility of the executive to parliament and the electorate. These limitations have seriously affected the capacity of the more democratic nations to conduct foreign policy efficiently when that policy must be conducted in a balance of power system. (Wright 1965, 265)

More specifically, the essence of the case against public opinion is that effective diplomacy requires three important features, none of which is enhanced by a more active public participation: *secrecy, speed,* and *flexibility.* All of these requirements are deemed by critics, not all of whom are realists, to be essential to bargaining and negotiating effectively with other countries, meeting challenges and taking advantage of opportunities as they arise, maneuvering adroitly in a rapidly changing global system and, most importantly, avoiding war. Senator J. William Fulbright expressed some of these reservations. "Statesmen and scholars have long since discovered that the kind of thinking which makes for the successful conduct of foreign-policy is all too often diametrically opposed to prevailing public attitudes." He went on to assert that the public prefers "a hero to a horsetrader and, knowing this, the diplomat is under the strongest pressure to strike postures rather than bargains" (Battle 1995, private communication).

The case for the importance of these features in the conduct of foreign affairs is most plausible in times of war, crisis, and confrontation. Without in any way suggesting that traditional security concerns have vanished with the end of the Cold War and the disintegration of the Soviet Union, it seems increasingly likely that the top echelons of the U.S. foreign policy agenda during the post–Cold War era will encompass some issues on which it is difficult to make a compelling case for excluding the public and its representatives from involvement in the policy process. This agenda will probably include but not be limited to a number of issues on which the public is likely to have strong views and on which the thesis that "the president knows best" may appear less compelling than, for example, during World War II or the Cold War (Yankelovich 1978; Clough 1994).

Trade. As I noted in chapter 4, the general public has diverged sharply from the views of elites on questions of trade liberalization versus protectionism, as well as on such specific trade agreements as the NAFTA and GATT/World Trade Organization pact. Moreover, because such a varied array of opponents of trade liberalization, from Ross Perot, Patrick Buchanan, and Ralph Nader to Senators Ernest Hollings and Jesse Helms, have consistently argued that there is a direct negative relationship between trade liberalization and the number of good jobs in the United States, the issue is likely to continue to engage the interest of the public, especially when major trade agreements or other trade-related issues are being negotiated or are before Congress for ratification. Patrick Buchanan's vehement attacks on free trade and his promise to cancel the NAFTA agreement if elected president appear to have contributed to his successes in the early 1996 Republican presidential primary elections. At the minimum, his strong showing ensured that trade would remain a contentious issue throughout the entire election—and probably well beyond it.

Refugees and immigration. Few international issues in recent years have aroused as many public passions as those of immigration and refugees, especially in states and regions that have been the more popular destinations of those entering the United States—the Southeast for those arriving from Haiti and Cuba, and the Southwest for those arriving from Mexico and from Central America.[1] Several states have sued the federal government to recover the alleged costs of providing services to illegal immigrants, and immigration was probably the most potent issue in the 1994 California gubernatorial election. The overwhelming support for California Proposition 187, which would deny educational, medical, and social services to all persons who have entered the United States illegally, even if declared unconstitutional, is not likely to be the last such effort to deal with the issue. The response to Proposition 187 encouraged California Governor Pete Wilson to make immigration control the centerpiece of his 1996 presidential campaign; Patrick Buchanan proposed even more restrictive measures—including erection of a high wall on the Mexican border—to stem the flow of immigrants into the United States. Although Wilson's presidential bid was aborted soon after its inception, the issue will almost surely survive well beyond the 1996 election, if only because President Clinton's 1996 State of the Union message included a call for immigration reform.

Environmental issues. Environment-related issues, especially those that may involve further regulation of major industries or trigger NIMBY (not in my back yard) responses, are likely to remain controversial. Environmental and trade issues also have been linked, especially by opponents of the NAFTA in 1993 and the GATT/World Trade Organization agreement a year later. Many environmental groups and activists charged that these agreements would prevent the United States from enforcing environmental standards that are more stringent than those of its trade partners.

Ethnic, racial, religious, and nationalist conflicts and civil wars. It is also clear, however, that post–Cold War foreign policy leaders will not have the luxury of focusing all of their energies on international economic, social, and environmental issues, if only because of the persistence of ethnic, racial, religious, nationalist, and tribal civil wars in many regions. The disintegration of the Soviet Union and its withdrawal from its Eastern European empire have also opened up opportunities for sometimes ancient rivalries and hatreds to resurface as civil wars. At least some of these intrastate conflicts are also likely to stimulate political activity by ethnic and other interest groups in the United States, thereby magnifying the impact of at least parts of the public. Efforts of the American-Israeli Political Action Committee (AIPAC) on behalf of Israel, of Greek-Americans following the Turkish invasion of Cyprus, of TransAfrica in connection with conflicts within South Africa and Haiti, and of Irish-Americans with respect to Northern Ireland illustrate forms of political activity that are likely to become more rather than less frequent. According to such realists as George Kennan (1993), internal conflicts abroad are often precisely the types of issues on which the public, aroused by television images of unspeakable suffering at the hands of local tyrants or competing warlords, may push the United States and international organizations into well-intentioned but hopeless and probably dangerous undertakings—for example, "nation-building" in Somalia or "restoring democracy" in Haiti.

If we are indeed entering a period of fewer crises and confrontations among the major powers with greater attention paid to post–Cold War issues such as those just listed—and ample survey data demonstrates that much of the American public believed this was true even before the end of the Cold War (Americans Talk Security 1987–90)—it is also likely to be an era in which public opinion plays a more autonomous role. Even those who do not fully subscribe to the thesis that the public is merely the hapless object of elite manipulations would acknowledge that crises and confrontation abroad provide a setting in which opportunities and temptations for elite manipulation of the public are far greater than on nonsecurity issues. The latter are typically resolved over a longer time period, thus providing greater opportunities for the public, interest groups, the media, Congress, and other domestic actors to play a significant role. But nonsecurity issues also tend to be more resistant to claims that the needs for secrecy, flexibility, and speed of action, as well as the president's constitutional role as commander-in-chief of the armed forces, make it both necessary and legitimate for the executive to have a relatively free hand. In short, we may be moving into a period in which the relationship between public opinion and foreign policy takes on added rather than diminished significance.

Public Opinion in the Foreign Policy Process

The argument that public opinion is likely to play a more potent role in the future than in the past, however plausible, is a hypothesis to be tested rather than a firmly established fact. This raises some questions about research strategies for accomplishing this. Important elements of the strategy will include continuing performance of the tasks that have dominated public opinion research during the past half century, including gathering and summarizing data about public attitudes, correlating them with important international events and foreign policy decisions, depicting major trends, describing the concepts around which attitudes are structured, identifying the demographic correlates of attitudes, and the like. No doubt there is room for important substantive and technical developments that will enable us to have more confidence in the validity and reliability of the resulting data; for example, devising survey methods to provide a better sense of what the public is thinking (Yankelovich 1991; Yankelovich and Destler 1994; Kay 1992a, 1992b; Fishkin 1991, 1992, 1994), dealing with the problem of nonresponses to surveys (Brehm 1993), improving the quality of longitudinal analyses (Taylor 1980; Stimson 1991), combining survey research with experimental designs (Sniderman 1993), and bringing new theoretical perspectives and concepts to the study of public opinion (Gaubatz 1995).

However, as I noted in chapter 3, by far the least well developed of the areas of public opinion research has been the opinion-policy link. This is also arguably the most important aspect of the topic. We have some impressive correlational studies revealing that when public policies change, the shifts are in fact predominantly in the direction favored by the public, but these do not exhaust the relevant questions. These include, but are not limited to, the following:

> Did policymakers rule out certain courses of action because of a belief that lack of public support would reduce or eliminate the prospects of success?
> Did policymakers decide upon certain foreign policy undertakings, even when the chances of success were deemed very slight, because of a belief that the public demanded some form of action?
> How, if at all, did expectations of future public reactions affect the appraisal of policy options by decision makers?
> How, if at all, did calculations about the electoral consequences of certain decisions restrain or motivate policymakers?
> What indicators, if any, of public sentiments did leaders rely upon?
> Were the timing of foreign policy decisions and the choice of means to carry out an undertaking influenced by beliefs about what the public would or would not accept, would or would not demand?

Answers to these and related questions require more substantial evidence of a causal nature. Case studies employing archival research, interviews with policymakers, or both, are virtually indispensable for assessing the impact of public opinion. But as noted earlier, those employing interviews and archives must also be sensitive to possible validity problems. Moreover, the brief review of some case studies in chapter 3 revealed quite mixed results; in some instances, the evidence indicated that public opinion had a negligible impact, whereas in others its effects were highly significant. These varied findings, while scarcely surprising, suggest the need for research strategies and designs that can capture adequately the variations that may be found across cases and that can also help to explain the sources of those differences. The case studies will also need to be designed in ways that will enhance cross-case comparisons by employing, for example, the method of "structured, focused comparison" (George 1979).

Case studies designed to assess the impact of public opinion on foreign policy are likely to be enhanced by sensitivity to certain distinctions in research designs; these include not only the *type of issue,* as noted earlier, but also the *stage of the policy process,* the *decision context* and policymakers' *beliefs about and sensitivity to public opinion.* Although all administrations since World War II have had access to immense amounts of survey data about public attitudes, it should not be assumed that this information is taken uniformly into account in policy deliberations. Just as policymakers may vary substantially in their sensitivity to public opinion, they also may have quite different conceptions of the most relevant and useful indicators of public attitudes. Moreover, decision makers at varying levels of the government hierarchy may be sensitive to public opinion to different degrees. Political appointees are more likely than civil servants to pay attention to it, and elected officials are likely to be even more sensitive to public sentiments.

Stage in the policy process. Thomas Graham (1989, 1994) analyzed the impact of public opinion on four arms control issues spanning seven American administrations from Presidents Truman through Carter. The four cases—international control of atomic energy, the Limited Test Ban Treaty, the SALT I/ABM treaties, and SALT II— varied in outcomes, ranging from unsuccessful negotiations with the USSR to negotiated treaties that received approval by the Senate and were successfully implemented. Graham distinguished between four stages in the policy process: getting the issue on the agenda, negotiating the issue, ratification, and implementation. Although the evidence revealed that public opinion had an important impact in all of the cases, it also varied according to the stage in the policy process.

Public opinion had a direct impact on getting the issues on the agenda and on ratification of agreements, but only an indirect effect on negotiations and implementation.

Graham's study focused on strategic nuclear arms control, but an intensive analysis by Douglas Foyle (1996) of four cases spanning a broader range of foreign and defense policy episodes during the Eisenhower administration provided further support for the proposition that a distinction between stages in the policy process is important for understanding the ways in which public opinion may affect the policy process. In the four Eisenhower cases, public opinion had limited impact on problem representation, but it became a focus of policymakers' concern during consideration of policy options.

Decision context. The cases in the Foyle study just cited included four decision contexts: *crisis* (the 1954 Formosa Straits confrontation with China), *reflexive* (the 1954 Dien Bien Phu case), *innovative* (the 1957–58 response to the successful Soviet launching of the Sputnik space satellite), and *deliberative* (the 1954 "New Look" defense policy).[2] The impact of public opinion varied across the four cases. In the Formosa Straits crisis, for instance, decision makers focused their attention on fears about how the public eventually would react to developments in the episode rather than upon specific indicators of current public views. During the deliberative cases, in contrast, Eisenhower administration officials anticipated the need to confront the issue and, having a long time to cope with it, were more comfortable with making efforts to generate public support for their preferred policy options.

Beliefs about public opinion. Even a cursory reading of memoirs, biographies, and accounts of many important decisions reveals that top-ranking American leaders have shown wide variations in their assessments of, sensitivity to, and strategies for dealing with public opinion. Moreover, although elected officials never can be utterly indifferent to public opinion, they may have quite different assessments of what constitute the most valid and politically significant indicators of those attitudes.

The latter point has become more relevant during recent years because the number of potential sources of information about the public has increased sharply. The menu of choices available in earlier eras may have included little more than legislative sentiments, newspapers, conversations with influential citizens, mail, and some limited contacts with the general public. Policymakers have often regarded newspapers as the best indicator of public opinion. A former newspaper editor, Warren G. Harding relied heavily on the press as a gauge of public sentiments, as did his key advisers. Secretary of State Charles Evans Hughes asserted that "The sentiment of our people is expressed by our press, which gives the point of view of our composite population, the fidelity of the general picture making up for inaccuracies in the detail of the drawing." The Harding administration established a Subcommittee on Public Opinion during the Washington Conference of 1921–22; it used newspaper editorials and letters from the public as sources of information (Williams 1996). Some policymakers may still regard newspapers as important indicators of public sentiments, but the range of potential sources of public opinion data has expanded dramatically during the past half century. The most important innovation during that period clearly has been the advent of systematic polling, but the electronic age also has opened up new possibilities that have yet to be fully developed.

These innovations have, of course, also opened up vast new opportunities for official efforts to influence the public. Theodore Roosevelt's description of the White House as a "bully pulpit" (which could apply equally well to 10 Downing Street and many other official executive residences), does not fully capture the range of tools available to top leaders today. Roosevelt's distant cousin Franklin revealed an uncanny ability to deal with the public, but the means at his disposal were quite limited compared to those available to one of his successors. Ronald Reagan asserted that the most important lesson he learned as governor of California was the value of "making an end run around the legislature by going directly to the people" (Reagan 1990, 234). According to two observers, the "Reagan entourage possessed an unprecedented sophistication in the technology of discerning what the public wanted and then giving it to them." Assisted by pollster Richard Wirthlin, the Reagan presidency revealed that "influencing public opinion by broadly based appeals and image building has become not only a way of campaigning but a way of governing" (Weiler and Pearce 1992, 39, 94). This assessment was validated by two White House "insiders," who wrote that "opinion polls are at the core of presidential decision making" (Beal and Hinckley 1984, 74).

Even the nature of polling has undergone significant changes since the pioneering surveys conducted by George Gallup, Archibald Crossley, and Elmo Roper. These developments include a vast increase in the number of polls and countries where they can be conducted, the ability to get almost instantaneous public reactions to developing situations and, perhaps most important, the widespread publicity accorded poll results. As noted earlier, major newspapers and television networks are today among the major producers of information about public opinion (see Mann and Orren 1992, especially the essay by Ladd and Benson [1992]). Consequently, their news reports not only describe major events, but they also can insert data on public opinion directly into even the most rapidly breaking crises. Moreover, the extensive use of polls to assess presidential performance and popularity—as against surveys that focus on specific issues—may add to the influence of public opinion. Even presidents who may be reluctant to place much weight on how the public feels about foreign policy issues are not likely to be indifferent to surveys that assess their own performance. Yet it would be a mistake to assume that technical improvements in polling have uniformly increased the impact of survey data on policymakers. An anecdotal examination of some evidence about the uses of information about public opinion by a few American presidents suggests the need for skepticism on that score.

Most accounts of the Franklin Roosevelt administration depict the president as intensely interested in public opinion. He relied on multiple sources of information, including analyses of mail to the White House (Sussman 1963), press opinion, and conversations with visitors. Roosevelt's long tenure coincided with the advent of scientific polling, however, and he was the first president to make extensive use of the resulting information. Indeed, few of his successors appear to have matched FDR's intense interest in public opinion surveys. This interest was especially manifest in the areas of foreign and defense policy, including such issues as aid to Britain during the period between the outbreak of World War II and the attack on Pearl Harbor that brought the United States into the conflict. He took a special interest in charts that plotted trends in public opinion.

FDR was not merely a consumer of data produced by Gallup and other surveys, however. In order to meet his desire for frequent information about public attitudes, he commissioned Hadley Cantril to conduct nationwide surveys. With all expenses covered by financial support from Gerald Lambert, a drug company heir, Cantril established a secret organization, Research Council, Inc., to conduct surveys for the president. Both admirers and critics agree that FDR's actions were strongly influenced by public opinion. A passionate critic, Congresswoman Claire Booth, contemptuously compared FDR to Churchill, asserting that whereas the latter's symbol was two upheld fingers in the form of a *V*, Roosevelt's was a wet finger held to the wind. But even a sympathetic biographer concluded that "Roosevelt would lead—but not by more than a step. He seemed beguiled by public opinion, by its strange combination of fickleness and rigidity, ignorance and comprehension, by rapidly shifting optimism and pessimism" (Burns 1970, 66).

Roosevelt's successor, Harry S. Truman, provides an interesting contrast to FDR. Both presidents were confronted with a predominantly Republican press that was less than supportive, especially on domestic issues, and thus they shared a somewhat skeptical view about newspapers as indicators of public attitudes. Truman also paid close attention to mail and telegrams after his speeches, but in contrast to FDR, his enthusiasm for polls was very limited. In one of his more colorful observations, he asserted:

> Some people think that public relations should be based on polls. That is nonsense. I wonder how far Moses would have gone if he had taken a poll in Egypt? What would Jesus Christ have preached if he had taken a poll in the land of Israel? Where would the reformation have gone if Martin Luther had taken a poll? It isn't polls or public opinion of the moment that counts. It is right and wrong, and leadership—men with fortitude, honesty and a belief in the right that makes epochs in the history of the world (Hechler 1982, 219–20).

In an assessment of ten presidents between Roosevelt and George Bush, Roosevelt received an "extensive" rating on two criteria: levels of presidential understanding of public opinion and successful presidential use of public opinion (Graham 1994, 198). In contrast, Graham gave Truman a "poor" score on both counts. These ratings seem valid, but they may also underscore the limits of focusing on a single dimension of leadership. His modest public relations abilities notwithstanding, Truman's administration achieved what has sometimes been called the "revolution in American foreign policy," including such innovative undertakings as membership in the United Nations, the Marshall Plan, and NATO. Perhaps a president more cowed by the fear that the public would not tolerate broad international commitments—as predicted in pollster Hadley Cantril's 1945 report to President Roosevelt—or by the congressional elections of 1946 that gave the Republicans control of both the House and Senate, might not have attempted such undertakings.

Although the differences between Roosevelt and Truman were a reflection of different leadership styles, their attitudes toward public opinion polls perhaps also were reinforced by their different experi-

ences with election surveys. George Gallup had established his reputation as a pollster by forecasting that Roosevelt would win his 1936
reelection bid with a landslide victory over Republican nominee Alf
Landon. Gallup's prediction was especially noteworthy because it
flew in the face of a contrary forecast, by the established and re-
spected *Literary Digest* poll, that Landon would be swept into the
presidency by a large margin. In contrast to Roosevelt's experience in
1936, Truman had seen Gallup and the other polls confidently confirm
the widespread expectation that Thomas Dewey would ride a Republican tidal wave into the White House in the 1948 presidential election.
Although Gallup's forecast missed the size of the Democratic vote by
a greater margin in 1936 (6.8 percent) than in 1948 (5.4 percent), is it
any wonder that Truman never came to share his predecessor's fas-
cination with public opinion surveys?

Even within a single administration there may be quite different
views about representations of public opinion. President Eisenhower
relied on multiple indicators, including informal dinner meetings with
leaders from government, business, publishing, the professions, agri-
culture, the arts, labor, and education "as a means of gaining information and intelligent opinion" (Eisenhower 1965, 265). He also relied
on polls conducted by the U.S. Information Agency. In contrast, his
Secretary of State, John Foster Dulles, felt that although "We can't get
too far ahead of public opinion and we must do everything we can to
bring it along with us," polls were of limited value. The State Department under Dulles discontinued the use of survey questions on foreign
affairs; evidence about public opinion was derived from articles and
editorials in one hundred daily newspapers, columnists, radio and
television commentators, letters to the editor, materials from nongovernmental organizations, and speeches in Congress (Berding
1965, 140).[3]

Leaders also may have quite varied reasons for being interested
in evidence about public opinion. In some cases it may be used as a
lever for dealing with governments abroad. Midway through the crisis
precipitated by Egyptian nationalization of the Suez Canal in 1956,
President Eisenhower attempted to head off the use of force by the
British. In a letter to Anthony Eden, he wrote:

> I regard it as indispensable that if we are to proceed to the
> solution of this [Suez] problem, public opinion in our several
> countries must be overwhelmingly in its support. I must tell you
> frankly that American public opinion flatly rejects the thought of
> using force. . . . I must say frankly that there is as yet no public

opinion in this country which is prepared to support such a move, and the most significant public opinion that there is seems to think that the United Nations was formed to prevent this very thing (Eisenhower 1965, 667–70).

Similarly, Paul Warnke reported that he used survey data as a bargaining instrument in arms control negotiations with his counterparts from the Soviet Union.

> He [Soviet Deputy Foreign Minister Semenov] would always take the position that we were asking too much in the way of verification, and I would continually point out that as indicated by the polls and not necessarily reflecting my own feeling, there still was a wide distrust within the American public; therefore, verification and their acceptance of our verification position was a *sine qua non* to getting a SALT Treaty approved. (Quoted in Cantril 1980, 133).

In other cases, public opinion may tip the balance in favor of one policy option or rule out another that seems destined to arouse strong public disapproval. Despite John Kennedy's doubts about the realism of U.S. policy toward China, according to Dean Rusk, "Fearing the issue might divide Congress and the American people, he decided that potential benefits of a more realistic China policy didn't warrant risking a severe political confrontation" (Rusk 1990, 283). The anticipation of public responses also appears to have played a role in President Bush's decision to use military force to drive Iraq out of Kuwait because he feared that the public would be unwilling to accept the deployment of American forces in Saudi Arabia for a sufficient time to ensure the success of economic sanctions.

In still other cases, policymakers may undertake visible efforts to seek guidance from the public on decisions that, in fact, were already made for reasons that had little if anything to do with public preferences. According to one of his biographers, a "favorite technique" of Richard Nixon's was "pretending to canvass public opinion on a decision on which he had already made up his mind" (Ambrose 1989, 258). A variant of that technique is to use public opinion data for guidance on the best ways to depict the rationale for decisions that have been arrived at for reasons that do not necessarily reflect public sentiments. The surveys conducted during the period immediately following Iraq's invasion of Kuwait helped the administration to identify the public's strongest concern about Iraq—its nuclear weapons program—but it appears to have had limited impact on the decision to launch a war against the Baghdad regime when it failed to comply with an ultimatum to withdraw its forces from Kuwait.

This brief survey is by no means a comprehensive analysis of the role that public opinion may play in the foreign policy process. It may, however, illustrate the important general point that the public opinion-policy relationship is usually complex, variable, and interactive rather than simple, constant, and unidirectional. Research designs that fail to take into account the possible impact of issue, decision context, stage of the policy process, and policymakers' beliefs about public opinion are thus likely to overlook important aspects of the relationship.

Cross-National Research

Because of the focus of this book, the theories and findings discussed here are almost wholly confined to the United States. But many of the questions addressed here are obviously of much broader concern. Debates between supporters and critics of the Tocqueville thesis that democracies are at an inherent disadvantage in the conduct of foreign policy often revolve around competing conceptions of the contribution of public opinion to the quality of foreign policy; these debates clearly have implications for countries other than the United States, especially in an era of expanding democracy.

Another issue also points to the need for public opinion research in which evidence about the United States is placed in a broader comparative context. The role of public opinion in foreign policy is often a central aspect of the contemporary debates about the "democratic peace"—the finding that democracies rarely if ever go to war against each other (Doyle 1986). It is at least a plausible working hypothesis that the nature of public opinion, the channels through which it enters the policy process, and its impact may vary across countries and political systems. A good many other issues that have been discussed in the preceding chapters, including questions about how foreign policy attitudes are structured, would benefit from comparative research designed to identify common elements and differences.

Examples of innovative comparative research on public opinion include studies by Abravanel and Hughes (1973); Munton (1989, 1991, 1992); Eichenberg (1989); Mandel (1991); Jacobs (1992); Hurwitz, Peffley, and Seligson (1993); Rattinger (1993); Brandes (1994); Asmus (1995); and Risse-Kappen (1991). The latter found that although public opinion was important in each of four countries—France, Japan, West Germany, and the United States—its impact was significantly affected by domestic institutions and coalition-building processes among elites. Distinctions of this kind clearly take us a substantial distance toward a fuller and finer-grained understanding of opinion-policy linkages. Dramatic political changes, notably in Eastern Europe and the former Soviet Union, open up possibilities for a range of comparative analyses that would have been quite unthinkable as recently as a decade ago (Miller, Reisinger, and Hesli 1993; Gibson 1994; Miller, Hesli, and Reisinger 1995). Studies by Zimmerman and his colleagues in Russia, in some cases posing questions identical to those used in American studies, exemplify some of the interesting possibilities (Zimmerman and Stam n.d.).

Jacobs and Shapiro (1994) have provided a useful framework for comparative research, both across countries and across issues or administrations within a single country, based on the divergent ways in which opinion and leadership responsiveness can be combined. *Responsive leadership* is characterized by strong impact of opinions on leaders and of leaders on opinion. *Bureaucratic rule* takes place when opinion provides low direction and there is a low leadership response. When leaders defer to strong, sustained public preferences, the result is *democratic responsiveness*. The fourth combination, when leaders pursue their own convictions and the role of the public is restricted, is described as *charismatic direction*.

Standard Questions

There is ample evidence that the wording of questions and even the context in which they are posed can significantly affect responses; for example, the nature of the immediately preceding questions in a survey may "prime" respondents to perceive a certain issue in a specific way.[4] An example of the importance of wording emerges from two questions that were frequently asked during the crisis arising from Iraq's invasion of Kuwait. One question, "All in all, is the current situation in the Mideast worth going to war over, or not?" yielded an almost even division between positive and negative answers in each of nine Gallup surveys during the five months preceding the start of Operation Desert Storm. Another survey organization posed a slightly different question: "Do you agree or disagree that the United States should take all action necessary, including the use of military force, to make sure that Iraq withdraws its forces from Kuwait?" Responses to the latter question in sixteen ABC-*Washington Post* surveys resulted in majorities ranging between two to one and more than three to one in favor of the use of force (Mueller 1994, 208, 217).

Moreover, the suspicion that pollsters can craft questions so as to elicit whatever results their clients prefer is not wholly without merit (Moore 1992). Indeed, rare is the voter who has not at some time received a "questionnaire" asking such challenging questions as these: "Do you believe that the administration should squander your hard-earned tax dollars for wasteful programs that have never worked?" or "Do you believe that the government should restrict the right of law-abiding citizens to protect themselves so that only the criminals will be able to get guns?"—along with a request for a contribution to pay for "tabulating the results." More seriously, one might question the disinterestedness of Louis Harris, a prominent pollster who has been closely associated with Democratic candidates and who is reported to have boasted, "I elected one President, one prime minister, about 28 governors and maybe close to 60 U.S. Senators" (Moore 1992, 78). These are, of course, extreme examples, but they underscore the point that surveys may be used to generate data in support of virtually any predetermined position. The issue of bias in constructing survey instruments may not be limited to commercial firms. The questions raised by Philip Tetlock (1994a) in a broader context—"political psychology or politicized psychology?"—are not irrelevant to survey research (see also the further discussion by Sniderman 1994, Sears 1994, Kroeger and Sapiro 1994, and Tetlock 1994b). Aside from the issue of bias, a skeptical position on survey data validity has been summarized by John Mueller's observation that "the poll interview is a rather primitive stimulus-response social situation in which poorly-thought out responses are casually fitted to questions that are overly ingenuous" (Mueller 1973, 265; see also Mueller 1994, 1–11; Zaller 1992, 76–96).

Even if this warning may be somewhat overstated with respect to the best surveys, it appropriately reminds us to be cautious about drawing conclusions from any single datum on public opinion. It is permissible to be more venturesome in making inferences about trends on specific issues, but doing so assumes that the questions from which the trends are adduced have remained constant, providing control over at least one potential threat to valid results. Gallup and other major polling organizations have asked certain standard political questions at quite regular intervals; for example, queries asking respondents to assess presidential performance. However, as noted in chapter 3, even slight variations in the wording of this question brought forth consistently different results in Gallup and Harris surveys about President Reagan's performance in dealing with the Soviet Union.

Questions focusing on foreign or defense policy issues have not been posed with comparable regularity. During and immediately after World War II, the public was regularly asked about the desirability of an active U.S. role in the world, but interest in that issue appears to have waned by the mid-1950s, perhaps because by then the United States seemed to be firmly committed to a broadly internationalist foreign policy; it was asked only once during the 1960s (see fig. 3.1). The question was revived in the wake of the war in Vietnam, when U.S. global activism once again became controversial; since 1973, it has been posed quite regularly except for a four-year gap between 1978 and 1982.

Many other important foreign and defense policy issues that might well have been the subject of surveys at regular intervals were in fact ignored for long periods. For example, the Gallup poll asked the public to assess the appropriate level of defense spending in 1950 and 1953. During the next sixteen years, the question was asked only once—in 1960, when presidential candidate John F. Kennedy criticized the Eisenhower administration for allegedly having neglected defense needs and for being dangerously complacent about the development of a "missile gap" that supposedly favored the Soviet Union. Since 1969 the question has been asked quite regularly, with a frequency largely determined by the extent to which the defense budget has been controversial. For example, Gallup asked questions about the Pentagon budget five times in 1982–83, when public support for the massive Reagan administration defense buildup was waning. In still other cases, promising time series data have been rendered suspect by wording changes. In 1956, the Gallup survey made a "minor" alteration to its standard item asking about support for U.S. foreign aid programs by adding the phrase "to prevent their [the recipients of aid] from going communistic" at the end of the question, giving it a quite different tenor than it had previously.

Among the many useful features of the six quadrennial CCFR studies (Rielly 1975–95) has been a carryover of certain questions from survey to survey. The cluster of items asking respondents to rate the importance of a series of possible U.S. foreign policy goals has been especially useful for analysts with an interest in tracing trends in public opinion (table 3.2). Responses to these questions have played a central role in several secondary analyses of the CCFR data (for example, Wittkopf 1990).

With a few exceptions, however, the independent surveys that

have been undertaken in recent years appear to have taken little note
of questions in other studies that might provide the basis for comparative analyses. In one sense this is understandable; the rationale for an
independent survey is to undertake probes that have been overlooked
by others. But it is also regrettable that there appears to have been
rather limited communication at the planning stage between those
who are designing surveys. The development of even a handful of
standard foreign and defense policy questions that would be included
in all such surveys is highly desirable.

Richard Sobel (1995a) has made a useful contribution toward this
end with a proposed list of thirty standard questions for polling on
foreign policy crises. The questions are clustered into nine groups that
deal with respondents' opinions on the importance of the issue, attention to the issue, U.S. interests at stake, presidential approval on
dealing with it, responsibility for coping with the crisis, policy options, likely outcomes, the impact of costs and casualties, and retrospective appraisals. The focus on crises makes these questions more
appropriate for commercial or news organizations that are capable of
conducting surveys with little advance notice. Surveys that are undertaken at regular and more distant intervals—for example, the American National Election Study or the CCFR studies—are less suited to
dealing with crises. It would be useful for them to use a somewhat
different set of standard questions. They might, for example, focus on:

Foreign policy goals (the CCFR cluster of goal items, cited several times above, is a good starting point).
U.S. interests in various areas and countries.
Threats to vital interests and security (the questions should include a broader list than military threats by including trade,
immigration, the environment, drug trafficking, etc.).
Assessment of institutions such as the United Nations.
Proper allocation of resources for recurring lines in the budget,
including the Defense Department, foreign aid, international
peacekeeping, and the like.
Questions that pose trade-offs (for example, reducing the budget
deficit versus the defense budget and allocations for other programs).

Widespread use of such questions, using standard wording, would go
a long way toward improving a less than outstanding record of cu-
mulative findings.

In summary, although recent decades have witnessed a remarkable and productive renaissance of interest in public opinion, a number of steps could further enhance our understanding of the topic, especially on the most important and least well-developed areas of systematic knowledge. As noted several times, many of these questions center on the *impact* of public opinion on foreign policy.

Public Opinion and Foreign Policy after the Cold War

Not only has most of the evidence cited here come from the United States, but the bulk of it also emerged from a period dominated first by World War II and soon thereafter by the Cold War. One can make a plausible case that this period is sufficiently atypical to raise questions about at least some generalizations relating to public opinion. Ronald Hinckley has argued persuasively that some discussions about the post-Vietnam breakdown of a foreign policy consensus are misdirected if they assume that broad disagreement about international affairs is an abnormal state of affairs in American politics. As he put it, "what has appeared since Vietnam is not dissensus but the reemergence of the basic and fundamentally different attitudinal beliefs that Americans have held and debated for some time" (Hinckley 1992, 10; see also Schneider 1992).

More generally, we need to address questions about whether and how the end of the Cold War may have affected or even rendered obsolete much of what we have learned about public opinion and foreign policy. At the most obvious level, there has been a sea change in public attitudes toward virtually all of the issues and some of the key actors that dominated the Cold War era. Indeed, one could make a plausible case that in many respects changing public attitudes *preceded* rather than followed those at the pinnacles of government on such issues as the appropriate level of defense spending, the primary threats to American national security, assessments of Mikhail Gorbachev's goals, and the motivations underlying Soviet foreign policy (Americans Talk Security 1987–90; Holsti 1991). Well before the demolition of the Berlin Wall or the disintegration of the Soviet Union, the public ranked the danger to American national security from the USSR in seventh place, tied with the greenhouse effect (Americans Talk Security 1988, No. 9: 51–54).

The end of the Cold War also raises some questions about the structuring of the foreign policy attitudes. Substantial evidence indicates that assessments of the Soviet Union have played a key role in foreign policy belief structures; for example, they are a central element in the hierarchical model developed by Hurwitz and Peffley

(1990), as well as in Wittkopf's (1986, 1990) militant internationalism dimension. Some interesting questions arise from the collapse of
the Soviet Union and the dramatic change in relations between Washington and Moscow. Will these events result for many in a loss of
structure and a consequent disorientation about foreign affairs? Are
the structures of foreign policy beliefs likely to differ among the many
democracies that joined forces to contain the USSR? Will there be a
search for a replacement of the Soviets by another adversary such as
Japan? Are there segments of the public or leadership groups who, if
deprived of one enemy, will seek to find another? Alternatively, are
the key concepts that structured beliefs about foreign affairs during the
Cold War era sufficiently generic and robust that they will survive the
dramatic international changes of the past decade? Will they be adequate for an expanded agenda of post–Cold War issues?

   There is some evidence that such dimensions as militant internationalism, cooperative internationalism, and unilateralism-multilateralism may continue to structure foreign policy attitudes, but the
changes we have witnessed since the late 1980s are of such unprecedented magnitude that this must be treated as a hypothesis that requires systematic testing. In short, we may be entering into a period in
which the relationship between public opinion and foreign policy
takes on added significance, but we should also be wary of assumptions that the theories, evidence, and linkages that emerged from
research during the World War II and Cold War eras are sufficiently
robust to be transported intact into a period of strikingly different
circumstances. It will not be possible for some years to undertake
archival research on the impact of public opinion during the post–
Cold War era, but judicious use of open sources, memoirs, and interviews should make it possible at least to explore the hypothesis that
public sentiments are playing a greater role than they did during the
half century between Pearl Harbor and the disintegration of the Soviet
Union.

Some Concluding Thoughts

Chapters 1 and 2 summarized very briefly the competing positions in
the venerable and persisting differences between realists and liberals
on the proper role of public opinion in international affairs. It was
noted that critical events, including two world wars and the long,
controversial conflict in Vietnam, have often played an important role
in igniting debates and framing the terms of the discourse between
these schools of thought. The end of the Cold War has been no less

significant in stimulating interest in and arousing controversies about the topic. The debate about the "democratic peace" is but one such example. These are not merely continuations of prior disputes in the memoirs of retired Cold War policymakers—for example, between George Shultz (1993) and Caspar Weinberger (1990)—or esoteric debates carried on between the covers of obscure academic journals. The democratic peace issue has found its way into the press (*Economist* 1995) as well as into official foreign policy blueprints (White House 1994). Such post–Cold War events as conflicts in Bosnia, Somalia, and Haiti have also brought forth a flurry of op-ed articles and rejoinders in mass circulation newspapers, lamenting or defending the impact of the public in shaping foreign policies (for example, Kennan 1993; Koppel 1994; Wines 1994; and the rejoinders to them in the "letters to the editor" columns).

This conclusion is not intended to bring definitive evidence to bear on these issues, nor would it be possible to do so within the confines of a few pages, but perhaps a few general observations are appropriate. First, debates about the proper role of public opinion on foreign policy ought not be framed in terms that posit, on the one hand, a bottom-up, direct democracy model in which public officials are merely the agents for carrying out whatever public preferences emerge from the latest Gallup poll, versus, on the other hand, a vision of skilled and knowledgeable elites, shielded from the television-aroused passions of an ill-informed public, carefully deliberating the great international issues of the day. Unfortunately, even such thoughtful observers of international affairs as George Kennan (1993) sometimes slip into this style of discourse. Framing the alternatives in such a dichotomous fashion trivializes an important issue in democratic theory, precluding the considered discussion that it deserves.

Second, a cursory—and admittedly selective—sample of foreign and defense policy episodes to be discussed below suggests that perhaps the realist thesis against public participation in international affairs is somewhat less persuasive than some of its staunchest advocates would have us believe—or at least it is not so compelling that the case should be considered closed. A list of the more successful American international undertakings since World War II might, arguably, include the Marshall Plan (1947), NATO (1949), and the Limited Test Ban Treaty (1963). In each instance the administration made a forceful case for the policies in question, but without gross distortions or suppression of vital information, tactics that are unfortunately not unknown in such cases. Before approving these undertakings, Congress engaged in extensive debates about each of them and, ultimately, substantial majorities of the public were persuaded that the policies were in the national interest. Whether public opinion played a significant role in these undertakings is certainly open to debate, but the outcomes hardly square with Walter Lippmann's charges (1955, 20), leveled soon after the Marshall Plan and NATO debates and a few years before the test ban treaty, that the proper balance between the executive and the legislature in Washington had been destroyed, and that the public "has shown itself to be a dangerous master of decision when the issues are life and death."

Conversely, a list of the foreign policy disasters of the Cold War period would almost surely include the Vietnam War and the Iran-contra episode. In the former case, evidence that the Johnson and Nixon administrations were less than forthright with the public—or even with the Congress—is not hard to find. Nor did prescient warnings about public opinion have an impact. Clark Clifford (1991, 412) recounts one such episode:

> During the summer of 1965, as the Johnson Administration was moving toward fateful decisions regarding Vietnam, George Ball warned: "We can't win," he said, his deep voice dominating the Cabinet Room. "The war will be long and protracted, with heavy casualties. The most we can hope for is a messy conclusion. We must measure the longterm price against the short-term loss that will result from withdrawal." Producing a chart that correlated public opinion with American casualties in Korea, Ball predicted that the American public would not support a long and nonconclusive war.

Ball's warnings were dismissed, perhaps because they were viewed as the predictable gloomy diagnoses of the "house devil's advocate."

The central figures in the Iran-contra affair, notably Lieutenant Colonel Oliver North, repeatedly engaged in secret and patently illegal maneuverings. Not only did they fail to achieve any of their stated goals with respect to establishing links with "moderates" in Iran or in freeing the American hostages who were believed to be held by groups under control of the Teheran government, but when the facts of the arms deliveries to Iran undertaking became known, they resulted in a powerful public backlash against the Reagan administration, reflected most dramatically in a record decline in the president's performance ratings. Even a heavy-handed public relations campaign by the president to gain support for assistance to the contras in Nicaragua— at one point the rebel group was described as "the moral equivalent of the [U.S.] Founding Fathers"—failed to arouse substantial public enthusiasm. Would a more realistic appreciation of the public's disapproval of shipping arms to Iran or negotiating with terrorists have averted a policy disaster? It is, of course, impossible to answer this question definitively, or, more broadly, to establish beyond reasonable doubt a causal link between inattention to or contempt for public opinion and policy decisions and outcomes.

Such a highly selective group of cases, focusing on a small sample of successes and failures, does not constitute an adequate discussion of the public's role in foreign policy. Nor does it address at least one other aspect of the relationship between public opinion and foreign policy that merits some discussion. Almost all public officials succumb at one time or another to a temptation to engage in "oversell" with a view to gaining public support, be it for an election or a specific policy objective. Leaders who ascribe the most importance to public opinion and are most sensitive to public preferences may also be the most likely to engage in oversell. The temptation may appear all the more attractive if the costs of hyperbolic or misleading rhetoric are not adequately appreciated at the time or, even if they are, if it is believed that they will not have to be paid until much later. Examples from several episodes involving relations with the Soviet Union can be used to illustrate a problem that is not confined to the three administrations in question.

Throughout much of World War II, Franklin Roosevelt was often less than frank with the American public in describing the nature of the Soviet regime or in acknowledging divergent American and Soviet interests on such issues as the future of Poland. For example, after the Nazi invasion of its erstwhile Soviet ally in 1941 but before the Japanese attack on Pearl Harbor had brought the United States into World War II, Roosevelt depicted the Stalin regime's policy toward religion in glowing but quite inaccurate terms in order to defuse arguments used by opponents of American aid to Moscow. For example, at a press conference on September 30, 1941, the president asserted that the constitution of the USSR guaranteed freedom of conscience: "Freedom equally to use propaganda against religion, which is essentially what is the rule in this country, only we don't put it quite the same way" (Dallek 1979, 297; see also Beschel 1991). Roosevelt's optimistic public expressions with respect to the Soviet Union no doubt contributed to maintenance of the Allied coalition against Hitler—perhaps they were even necessary to prevent it from fracturing before the defeat of the Third Reich—but they also may have poorly prepared the public to face realistically the policy differences between Washington and Moscow that would almost inevitably emerge when the guns of World War II had stopped firing.

Two years after the defeat of Germany, the Truman administration faced an urgent request to provide assistance to beleaguered Greek and Turkish governments in the wake of a British decision to reduce its traditional commitments in that area. When Senator Arthur Vandenberg told Truman that it would be necessary to "scare the hell" out of Congress in order to assure appropriation of the funds for Greece and Turkey, the president did so in his "Truman Doctrine" address to that body on March 12, 1947. The $400 million aid package was quickly approved by Congress, and Gallup polls revealed that a majority of both Republicans and Democrats supported the program. Nevertheless, the open-ended commitments implied by Truman's rhetoric may have served longer-term national interests less well.

The final example of oversell also involves American relations with the USSR. As part of a broad effort to restructure American foreign policy, the Nixon administration pursued a policy of détente with the Soviet Union by which carrots would supplement sticks as strategies aimed at stabilizing relations between the superpowers and creating incentives for the Soviet Union to contain itself. President Nixon and national security adviser Henry Kissinger succumbed to the temptation to oversell détente during the 1972 presidential campaign with such declarations as "the Cold War is over." While this may have proved an effective short-run strategy for Nixon's successful reelection campaign, it also set the stage for a public backlash against détente when subsequent events, including the Yom Kippur War in 1973, revealed that Washington and Moscow held quite different conceptions of the meaning of détente, especially in connection with rivalries in the Third World. According to the author of the most comprehensive study of American-Soviet relations during the period in question:

> One reason for the disintegration of consensus in favor of détente in the United States was the failure of leadership to explain its limitations as well as its promisees to the public. . . .When the expectations of the public, aroused by the hyperbole about the benefits of peace and détente, were not met, disillusion set in—and so did the natural temptation to blame the other side (Garthoff 1985, 1088; see also Homet 1990).

A few anecdotes do not constitute definitive analyses, nor do they give rise to timeless prescriptions about such complex and enduring issues as the proper role of public opinion in the formulation and implementation of American foreign policy. Nevertheless, if we are indeed entering into a period in which the public will be increasingly vocal in expressing its policy preferences, especially on a growing agenda of issues that fall at the intersection of domestic and foreign affairs, perhaps it is worth contemplating whether there is less to be gained by tactics for bypassing, manipulating, or misleading the public to ease the short-term tasks of policymakers than by frank efforts to engage the public in constructive debates about the proper American role in the world, definitions of the national interest, and the appropriate strategies (if not necessarily the tactics) for pursuing them. Is such a suggestion evidence of terminal woolly-headed idealism or of a realistic appraisal of the necessary conditions for the effective pursuit of long-range interests? Opponents and skeptics will no doubt play their strongest card against such proposals by pointing to the indisputable fact that the American public is poorly informed on even some of the most basic facts about the world and international affairs. In fairness, however, it should be pointed out that some of these critics also take a very broad view of what information it is permissible to withhold from the public because of national security concerns.

Can efforts to provide the public with better international education improve what Yankelovich (1991) calls "public judgment?" If international education consists primarily of providing more factual information of the kind that might improve students' performances on a television game show, then one might well share Kay's (1992b, 14) pessimistic conclusion that "efforts to remedy this situation by educational programs of any kind clearly seem headed for failure." It is not clear that knowing the name of the prime minister of Israel, all the members of NATO, or the nations that have held democratic elections in Africa during the 1990s will add substantially to the public's ability to render more informed judgments on major international issues.

Yet one cannot help but be sobered by the most consistent finding to emerge from the vast literature on public opinion—Americans are poorly informed about most aspects of international affairs. Despite the proliferation of new technologies and information sources available to most Americans—or maybe because of them—publics in other democracies are significantly better informed (Dimock and Popkin 1995). As shown in many studies cited earlier, publics are capable of making coherent judgments ("low information rationality") and, in the aggregate, public opinion is marked by a good deal of stability. But when many Americans are unable to identify a single nation bordering on the Pacific Ocean, there would not appear to be much warrant for complacency about the state of American education. A detailed discussion of international education is clearly beyond the scope of this book, but perhaps it is appropriate to suggest that a single educational reform—the restoration of geography to standard curricula—might well be an important step toward coping with one of the most significant gaps in knowledge.

But even if we acknowledge that the public is not well informed, is it fruitless to engage the public with a view to a better understanding of at least some aspects of foreign policy? Foreign aid may provide a case in point. Two facts—foreign aid accounts for less than 1 percent of the federal budget (it is not the largest item in the budget, as believed by 27 percent of those taking part in a recent poll) and most of the foreign assistance funds are spent in the United States—may be relevant (Greenhouse 1994). But these facts alone may not be sufficient for engaging the public on the issue or for raising the discussion above the "foreign aid is money down the rathole" thesis propounded by Senate Foreign Relations Committee Chairman Jesse Helms. When respondents are provided with additional information about actual foreign aid outlays, their attitudes toward assistance programs become substantially more favorable (Kull 1995a). Moreover, when discussions of foreign aid are linked to other vital concerns of the American public—for example, immigration, jobs supported by foreign purchases in the United States, stability in the Middle East, and the dismantling of nuclear weapons in parts of the former Soviet Union—the discourse may take a different tone. No doubt there would still be intense skepticism about some forms of foreign assistance, especially to regimes that exhibit a callous disregard for the most basic human rights, but such distinctions do not seem beyond the capabilities of the public.

Perhaps it is appropriate to give the final word on this point, not to ivory tower idealists but to a hardheaded conservative whose career was spent in the rough-and-tumble arenas of a Wall Street law firm, the War Department, the State Department, and the U.S. Senate.

That way to prevent a people from having an erroneous opinion is to furnish the whole people, as a part of their ordinary education, with correct information about their relations to other peoples, about the limitations upon their own rights, about their duties to respect the rights of others, about what has happened and is happening in international affairs, and about the effects upon national life of the things that are done or refused as between nations; so that the people themselves will have the means to test misinformation and appeals to prejudice and passion based upon error. (Root 1922, 5)

Notes

Chapter 1

1. CBS conducts surveys with the *New York Times,* ABC with the *Washington Post,* and NBC with the *Wall Street Journal.*

2. Bevin, speech to the House of Commons, November 1945. The liberal position on questions of international relations is effectively summarized and analyzed in Doyle 1986.

3. Locke argued that issues of security and foreign affairs properly are a function of the executive. Foreign policy requires a consistency that derives only from the vision of one person rather than from the diverse interests of the public. Locke 1988, 365–66.

4. These efforts stimulated the creation of a new field of inquiry—propaganda analysis—which engaged the interest of such leading social scientists as Harold Lasswell and Alexander L. George.

5. Woodrow Wilson, quoted in Carr 1941, 44. Carr cites volume 1, page 259, of the R. S. Baker edition of Wilson's papers as the source. However, I was unable to find it in that source.

6. The role of liberals, Protestants, Irish-Americans, and public culture in the League of Nations debate has been examined in Helbich (1967–68), Lancaster (1967–68), Maxwell (1967–68), and Levering (1991).

7. Root 1922, 5. Root was not unmindful of the realist thesis that the passions and prejudices of the mass public can complicate international negotiations and contribute to conflict. For example, he wrote in 1907 (nine years after the Spanish-American War), that "it sometimes happens that governments are driven into war against their will by the pressure of strong popular feeling . . . because a large part of the people in both countries maintain an uncompromising and belligerent attitude, insisting upon the supreme and utmost views of their own right in a way which, if it were to control national actions, would render peaceable settlement impossible" (Root 1907, 1). See also Root (1917).

8. An indication of Lippmann's continuing influence is the fact that *Public Opinion* was republished in a paperback edition in 1965 and by the 1990s was in its fifteenth printing. Evidence of his influence as a columnist emerged during the tensest days of the Cuban missile crisis. His *Washington Post* column on October 25, 1962, the fourth day of the public phase of the crisis, proposed a trade of U.S. missiles in Turkey for the Soviet missiles in Cuba. Although many in President Kennedy's ExComm opposed the swap, that proposal became a crucial part of the deliberations in the final stages of the crisis.

9. Although it is widely recognized that an unrepresentative sample led the

Literary Digest astray in 1936, scholars and pollsters still debate the specific details of the debacle. See, for example, Squire 1988.

10. For an excellent history and analysis of survey research in the United States, see Jean Converse 1987.

11. Even before U.S. entry into World War II, a majority of the public supported the Soviet Union rather than Germany. In 1938, the margin was 83 to 17 percent, and after the Nazi attack on its erstwhile ally the margin was 72 to 4 percent. In July 1941, Gallup asked whether respondents favored a peace in which Germany would keep "only territory won from Russia" and give up its other conquests; only 34 percent accepted that proposition.

12. All of the survey results reported below are drawn from Gallup 1972, vol. 1.

Chapter 2

1. This report is undated, but internal evidence indicates that the survey was conducted in September 1947.

2. Almond's use of the term *mood* differs from that of Frank Klingberg. Almond refers to short-term shifts of attention and preferences, whereas Klingberg has used the term to explain American foreign policy in terms of generation-long societal swings between introversion and extroversion. For the latter usage of the term, see Klingberg (1952, 1979, 1983) and Holmes (1985).

3. By 1960, Almond himself was backing away from his most pessimistic diagnoses. See his new introduction to a reprinting of *The American People and Foreign Policy.*

4. Some of the more notable examples include Jones (1955) on the Truman Doctrine and Marshall Plan, Wohlstetter (1962) on Pearl Harbor, George (1955) and Paige (1968) on the decision to resist aggression in Korea, Neustadt (1970) on the Suez crisis and cancellation of the Skybolt missile program, Allison (1971) on the Cuban missile crisis, and George and Smoke (1974) on challenges to U.S. deterrence policy.

5. The exceptions include Cohen 1957; Bauer, Pool, and Dexter 1963; and Cottam 1977.

Chapter 3

1. Studies of the general public include: Rielly 1975; Hurwitz and Peffley 1987, 1990; Americans Talk Security 1987–91; and Americans Talk Issues 1991–95. Six Chicago Council on Foreign Relations (CCFR) surveys have been conducted in 1974, 1978, 1982, 1986, 1990, and 1994, and each of them has been summarized in a monograph edited by Rielly. A series of surveys on post–Cold War foreign policy issues has been summarized in Kull 1995a, 1995b and Kull and Ramsay 1993, 1994a, 1994b, and 1994c.

Studies of opinion leaders include Barton 1974–75; Russett and Hanson 1975; Chittick and Billingsley 1989; Chittick, Billingsley, and Travis 1990; Koopman, Snyder, and Jervis 1989, 1990; Holsti and Rosenau 1984; and Times Mirror Center for the People and the Press 1993. In addition, each of the CCFR surveys cited in the preceding paragraph included a small elite sample.

2. Valuable book-length, post-Vietnam works that explore the nature, sources, trends, and other important aspects of public opinion include Levering 1978, Foster 1983, Deibel 1987, Wittkopf 1990, Mayer 1992, Page and Shapiro 1992, Price 1992, Zaller 1992, and Murray 1996.

3. For additional evidence from this research program, see Page and Shapiro 1983, 1984, 1992; Page, Shapiro, and Dempsey 1987; and Shapiro and Page 1988, 1994. A somewhat different assessment of stability and change in American public opinion appears in Mayer 1992.

4. For additional evidence about the "rational public," the stability of policy preferences, and issue voting, see Bennett 1972; Free and Watts 1980; Graham 1988, 1989, 1994; Krosnick 1988a, 1988b, 1990, 1991; Russett 1990; Popkin 1991; Peffley and Hurwitz 1992; and Marcus and Hanson 1993.

5. For a somewhat similar effort to categorize the American public in the post–Cold War era, see Kohut and Toth (1994). Using questions on the approval or disapproval of using force abroad for oil security and humanitarian assistance, they classified respondents as *interventionists* (approve the use of force for both purposes), *noninterventionists* (disapprove force for both), *oneworlders* (approve for humanitarian, disapprove for oil), and *U.S.-centrics* (approve for oil, disapprove for humanitarian).

6. Good starting points are Bauer, Pool, and Dexter 1963; Rosenau 1963, 1974; Hughes 1978; and Zaller 1992.

7. Not surprisingly, many of the existing studies have been conducted by historians. In addition to those cited in the following pages, see May 1959, 1964; Benson 1967–68; Small 1970; Levering 1978, 1989; and Williams 1996.

8. Note that the public differences between Defense Secretary Weinberger and Secretary of State Shultz, described in the opening pages of chapter 1, were also evident in private policy discussions.

9. Public opinion analysts have long focused on American attitudes toward the Soviet Union. See, for example, Walsh (1944), Levering (1976), Smith (1983), and Richman (1991).

10. A study by Russian, Chinese, and American scholars, based on recently opened archives in Moscow, confirms the hypothesis that Stalin knew of and in 1950 approved Kim Il Sung's plan to invade South Korea, although he had earlier refused to give Kim the go-ahead for an invasion (Goncharov, Lewis, and Xue Litai 1993).

11. The thesis that Ronald Reagan won the 1980 election despite rather than because of his foreign policy positions is developed in Schneider 1983.

12. Table 3.2 includes only those goals that appeared in the 1990 or 1994 CCRF survey. A number of others were included in the earlier studies, and some of them received more "very important" ratings than did "containing communism" or "matching Soviet military power."

Chapter 4

1. For example, Sussman 1976; Barton 1974–75, 1980; Russett and Hanson 1975; Kinnard 1975; Chittick, Billingsley, and Travis 1990; Koopman, Snyder, and Jervis 1989, 1990; Times Mirror Center for the People and the Press 1993.

2. The occupations listed in table 4.1 are those specifically targeted by the sampling design. This list does not include other occupations or groups that may also be represented in the samples. For example, in the course of sampling among

various occupational groups, the Times-Mirror sample included substantial numbers of women, as well as some military officers. Thus, it should not be assumed that the Times-Mirror data preclude analyses directed at possible gender-based differences. Similarly, the FPLP survey includes lawyers who may have been included as part of a random sample of leaders drawn from general directories (*Who's Who in America*) or because they qualified for inclusion by other criteria, such as foreign policy experts who have published in major foreign affairs journals.

3. For a scathing critique of what the 1994 CCFR survey reveals about the American public, see Schlesinger (1995, 7), who writes: "The latest public opinion survey by the Chicago Council on Foreign Relations and the Gallup Organization shows that, while Americans are still ready to endorse euphonious generalities in support of internationalism, there is a marked drop-off when it comes to committing not just words but money and lives." Schlesinger is among several articulate liberals who criticized expansive definitions of American national interests two decades ago but are now strong proponents of a more active U.S. leadership role in such areas as Bosnia. *New York Times* columnist Anthony Lewis shares these views.

4. I am indebted to Ronald Hinckley for the 1812 example.

5. The question about using U.S. troops was also included in the 1974 CCFR survey, but its wording seems sufficiently different to raise questions about comparability with the four subsequent surveys. Hence, table 4.3 begins with data from the 1978 CCFR survey.

6. Unfortunately, the "cooperation" question was dropped from the CCFR surveys of the public after 1974. In that survey, the gap in "very important" ratings between leaders and the public was 19 percent (86 and 67 percent, respectively).

A comparison of responses to the CCFR and FPLP surveys reveals that consistently higher proportions of leaders in the former studies accorded arms control a "very important" rating. That gap may largely be the result of one significant difference in the CCFR and FPLP samples. The latter included military officers, an occupational group that has generally expressed somewhat less enthusiasm for arms control than most others, whereas descriptions of the six CCFR samples indicate that they did not include military officers

7. The centrality of attitudes toward the Soviet Union in structuring foreign policy beliefs emerges from many studies, including those cited in chapter 3.

8. In order to take the intensity of attitudes into account, each response was transformed into a scale of 1.00 to -1.00 in this manner: "agree strongly" (1.00) to "disagree strongly" (-1.00), or "very important" (1.00) to "not at all important" (-1.00). Scores were then summed in order to place each leader on the two scales.

9. A more extensive analysis that assesses the relationship of the MI/CI scheme to a broader set of issues appears in Holsti and Rosenau 1993.

10. For a critique of international relations theorists and their failure to predict the end of the Cold War, see Gaddis 1992–93. However, Gaddis could perhaps equally well have aimed his critique at students of comparative politics. For an especially clear example of misprediction by a comparative politics scholar, see Hough 1990.

11. As with the militant and cooperative internationalism scales (see note 8 for this chapter), each response was given a score between 1.00 and -1.00, depend-

ing on the intensity of the attitude: "agree strongly" (1.00) to "disagree strongly" (−1.00). Responses to the twelve items were then summed to place each leader on the social and economic issues scales.

12. Ronald Hinckley has taken this classification scheme and expanded it into a two-by-two-by-two scheme by categorizing respondents according to their answers to three questions—whether or not the government should be more or less involved in economic, social, and value engineering. The resulting eight groups range from *libertarians* (who believe that the government is doing too many things in all three areas) to *statists* (who believe that the government should do more in all of them). The other six groups are: *conservatives, egalitarians, materialists, populists, moralists,* and *liberals.*

As this book was going to press, I became aware of a very similar classification scheme using two dimensions to describe *liberals, conservatives, populists,* and *libertarians* (Janda, Berry, and Goldman 1994, 26). In the next edition of their book, these authors plan to replace the term *populist* with *communitarian.*

Still another effort to classify respondents on domestic politics is described in *U.S. News and World Report* (1995). The seven groups are described as *populist traditionalists, stewards, liberal activists, dowagers, conservative activists, ethnic conservatives,* and *agnostics.*

For one of the earliest efforts of this kind, see Lowell (1923, 271–89) on "classification of dispositions."

13. A detailed examination of how the four domestic policy groups assessed a broad range of foreign policy issues sustains the overall conclusion from table 4.10: domestic and foreign policy attitudes are systematically and very closely linked. See Holsti 1994.

Chapter 5

1. See chapter 3, including figures 3.2 and 3.3 for evidence of changing public attitudes toward the Soviet Union.

2. Responses to almost three hundred questions on the Persian Gulf War, many of which were asked several times, are reported and analyzed in Mueller 1994. Almost half of the book consists of tables reporting aggregate responses to these questions. However, neither the tables nor the text examine the demographic correlates of opinions on the war. Other studies that deal with public opinion during the Persian Gulf War include Idelson 1991, Kagay 1992, Renshon 1993, Bennett and Paletz 1994, and Nacos 1994.

3. For effective summaries of the circumstances when the "rally round the flag" phenomenon is likely to occur, see Brody and Shapiro 1989; and Lian and Oneal, 1993.

4. These measures received strong support in Congress. In each case, votes in support exceeded 70 percent and, in the cases of the Marshall Plan and NATO, the favorable votes ranged from 80 to 86 percent.

5. Foster 1983, 112. For evidence of partisan differences on foreign policy during the period immediately following Truman's dismissal of MacArthur, see Belknap and Campbell 1951–52.

6. For the most detailed assessment of public support for the wars in Korea and Vietnam, see Mueller 1973. Verba et al. 1967 report that even after the

Vietnam War became controversial, party identification was not an important determinant of attitudes on the war.

7. Gaubatz (1995) also found important intransitivities in public preferences on the various U.S. policy options for responding to the Iraqi invasion of Kuwait: withdrawal, multilateral economic sanctions, unilateral military intervention, and multilateral military intervention.

8. Gallup special survey of leaders listed in *Who's Who in America*, May 22, 1955.

9. The following paragraphs discuss only some highlights of similarities and differences between Democrats and Republicans who participated in the 1992 leadership survey. For tables that provide more detailed data, see Holsti and Rosenau 1994.

10. Drew 1978, 116–17. Many others regarded the views of the "Vietnam generation" as the best hope for this nation's future. "What the country may have learned is that it should listen to its young. They never saw the cables. They read the handwriting on the wall. The Vietnam generation was 'the best and the brightest,' the term David Halberstam applies to the glittering Kennedyites who got us into the war in the first place" (McGrory 1975).

11. An article on the African policy staff of the State Department described its leading members in this way; "The four are in the same age group—39–46—and they share a common experience of disillusionment with and then opposition to the Vietnam War. All remain highly skeptical about United States military involvement, direct and indirect, in areas where they feel the national interest is not obviously at stake" (Hovey 1978; see also, Roberts 1982).

12. See, for example, comments by Samuel P. Huntington in Hoffmann 1981, 3–27; and Representative Thomas Downey's assertion that "The children of Vietnam are the adults of El Salvador" (Roberts 1983).

13. The percentages in the text are recalculated from the date in table 1 of Mandelbaum and Schneider 1979.

14. The data in this paragraph are drawn from Gallup surveys, January 24–26, February 12–14, and February 26–28, 1993 (Gallup 1993, 41, 43).

15. Neumann has defined a political generation as all those who underwent essentially similar historical experiences during the crucial formative years between seventeen and twenty-five (Neumann 1942, 235–36). The importance of this period in the life cycle is emphasized by many others; for example, Barber 1972.

16. In the five FPLP surveys, the correlations (*phi*) between generation and foreign policy orientation were consistently weak: .19, .09, .12, .08, and .10.

17. In two-way analyses of variance, occupational differences were significant at the .001 level for all four of these questions. None of the differences across generations reached that level, although those for the United Nations question approached it.

18. For further evidence on this point, see Holsti and Rosenau 1984, 153–63.

19. Other relevant studies on gender include Smith 1984; Zur and Morrison 1989; Rapaport, Stone, and Abramowitz 1990; Cook and Wilcox 1991; Bardes 1992; and Gallagher 1992.

20. The data in this paragraph are drawn from Americans Talk Security surveys numbers 2, 3, and 6 (1988), and Gallup polls in February, May, June, and July 1992.

21. The correlations between gender and foreign policy orientations (*phi*) for the five surveys are .11, .06, .03, .08, and .06.

22. For an extensive presentation and analysis of the impact of gender in the 1976–88 FPLP data, see Holsti 1990. A greatly abbreviated version appears in Holsti and Rosenau 1995.

23. Data on racial differences with respect to these issues were drawn from the following sources: South Africa, Gallup 1991, 133–34; Haiti, Gallup 1992, 32–33; Somalia, Gallup 1993, 175; and Bosnia, Gallup 1993, 41–42.

Chapter 6

1. For a study that links attitudes toward immigration to broader aspects of U.S. identity and nationalism, see Citrin, Haas, Muste, and Reingold (1994).

2. This distinction between decision contexts is drawn from Hermann 1969.

3. If congressional moods are viewed by the executive as expressions of public opinion, then it opens up another very large body of evidence on intervening variables between public opinion and foreign policy. For recent studies that explore these linkages on the Strategic Defense Initiative, weapons procurement, and sanctions on South Africa, see Lindsay 1990, 1991; and Hill 1993. Other issues are considered in Ripley and Lindsay 1993.

4. The literature on these questions is enormous. See, for example, Bishop, Tuchfarber, and Oldendick 1978; Bishop, Oldendick, and Tuchfarber 1984; and Kagay and Elder 1992. A somewhat different view on the importance of identically worded questions is presented in Graham 1989.

Bibliography

Abramson, Paul, John H. Aldrich, and John Rohde. *Change and Continuity in the 1988 Election.* Washington, DC: Congressional Quarterly Press, 1990.

Abravanel, Martin, and Barry Hughes. "The Relationship Between Public Opinion and Governmental Foreign Policy: A Cross-National Study." In *Sage International Yearbook of Foreign Policy Studies,* vol. 4, 107–33. Edited by Charles W. Kegley, Jr. and Patrick J. McGowan. Beverly Hills, CA: Sage Publications, 1973.

Achen, Christopher H. "Mass Political Attitudes and the Survey Response." *American Political Science Review* 69 (1975): 1218–31.

Aldrich, John H., John L. Sullivan, and Eugene Borgida. "Foreign Affairs and Issue Voting: Do Presidential Candidates 'Waltz before a Blind Audience?'" *American Political Science Review* 83 (1989): 123–41.

Allison, Graham T. *The Essence of Decision: Explaining the Cuban Missile Crisis.* Boston: Little, Brown, 1971.

Allison, Graham T. "Cool It: The Foreign Policy of Young America." *Foreign Policy,* no. 1 (winter 1970–71): 144–60.

Almond, Gabriel. "Public Opinion and National Security." *Public Opinion Quarterly* 20 (1956): 371–78.

Almond, Gabriel. *The American People and Foreign Policy.* New York: Harcourt, Brace, 1950. Reprinted with a new introduction, New York: Praeger, 1960.

Altschuler, Bruce E. "Lyndon Johnson and the Public Polls." *Public Opinion Quarterly* 50 (1986): 285–99.

Ambrose, Stephen. *Nixon: The Triumph of a Politician.* New York: Simon and Schuster, 1989.

Americans Talk Issues: Serial National Surveys of Americans on Public Policy Issues. Washington, DC: Americans Talk Issues Foundation, 1991–95.

Americans Talk Security: Fourteen National Surveys on National Security Issues. Winchester, MA: Americans Talk Security, October 1987 to September 1990.

Angle, Paul M., ed. *The Complete Lincoln-Douglas Debates of 1858.* Chicago: University of Chicago Press, 1991.

Asmus, Ronald D. *Germany's Geopolitical Maturation: Public Opinion and Security Policy in 1994.* Santa Monica, CA: RAND Corporation, 1995.

Bailey, Thomas A. *A Diplomatic History of the American People.* 4th ed. New York: Appleton-Century-Crofts, 1950.

Bailey, Thomas A. *The Man in the Street: The Impact of American Public Opinion on Foreign Policy.* New York: Macmillan, 1948.

Barber, James David. *The Presidential Character.* Englewood Cliffs, NJ: Prentice-Hall, 1972.

Bardes, Barbara A. "Women and the Persian Gulf War: Patriotism and Emotion."
    Paper presented to the Brookings Institution Conference on Public Opinion
    and the Persian Gulf Crisis, Washington, DC, February 28, 1992.
Bardes, Barbara A., and Robert W. Oldendick. "Public Opinion and Foreign
    Policy: A Field in Search of a Theory." *Research in Micropolitics* 3 (1990):
    227–47.
Bardes, Barbara A., and Robert W. Oldendick. "Beyond Internationalism: A
    Case for Multiple Dimensions in the Structure of Foreign Policy Attitudes."
    Social Science Quarterly 59 (1978): 496–508.
Bartels, Larry M. "Constituency Opinion and Congressional Policy Making: The
    Reagan Defense Buildup." *American Political Science Review* 85 (1991):
    457–74.
Barton, Allen H. "Fault Lines in American Elite Consensus." *Daedalus* 109
    (1980): 1–24.
Barton, Allen H. "Conflict and Consensus among American Leaders." *Public
    Opinion Quarterly* 38 (1974–75): 507–30.
Battle, Joseph. Private communication with author, July 7, 1995.
Bauer, Raymond A., Ithiel deSola Pool, and Lewis A. Dexter. *American Busi-
    ness and Public Policy: The Politics of Foreign Trade*. New York: Atherton
    Press, 1963.
Baxter, Sandra, and Marjorie Lansing. *Women and Politics: The Invisible Major-
    ity*. Ann Arbor: University of Michigan Press, 1980.
Beal, Richard S., and Ronald H. Hinckley. "Presidential Decision Making and
    Opinion Polls." *Annals* 472 (1984): 1272–84.
Beckman Peter R., and Francine D'Amico, eds. *Women, Gender, and World
    Politics: Perspectives, Policies, and Prospects*. Westport, CT: Bergin and
    Garvey, 1994.
Belknap, George, and Angus Campbell. "Political Party Identification and Atti-
    tudes toward Foreign Policy." *Public Opinion Quarterly* 15 (1951–52):
    601–23.
Bennett, Stephen Earl. "The Persian Gulf War's Impact on Americans' Political
    Information." Paper presented to the National Election Studies Conference
    on the Political Consequences of the War, Washington, DC, February
    28, 1992.
Bennett, Stephen Earl. "Attitude Structure and Foreign Policy Opinions." *Social
    Science Quarterly* 55 (1972): 732–42.
Bennett, W. Lance, and David L. Paletz, eds. *Taken by Storm: The Media, Public
    Opinion, and U.S. Foreign Policy in the Gulf War*. Chicago: University of
    Chicago Press, 1994.
Benson, Lee. "An Approach to the Scientific Study of Past Public Opinion."
    Public Opinion Quarterly 31 (1967–68): 522–67.
Bentham, Jeremy. *Works of Jeremy Bentham*. 11 vols. New York: Russell and
    Russell, 1962.
Berding, Andrew H. *Dulles on Diplomacy*. Princeton, NJ: Van Nostrand, 1965.
Berelson, Bernard R., Paul F. Lazarsfeld, and William N. McPhee. *Voting: A
    Study of Opinion Formulation in a Presidential Campaign*. Chicago: Univer-
    sity of Chicago Press, 1954.
Beschel, Robert P., Jr. "Morality, Ideology, Legitimacy, and American Soviet
    Policy." Ph.D. diss., Government Dept., Harvard University, 1991.
Bevin, Ernest. Speech to the House of Commons, United Kingdom, November

1945. Quoted in John Bartlett, *Familiar Quotations*. 13th edition. Boston: Little, Brown and Co., 1955, 926.

Billington, James H. "Realism and Vision in American Foreign Policy." *Foreign Affairs* 65 (1987): 630–52.

Bishop, George F., Robert W. Oldendick, and Alfred J. Tuchfarber. "Interest in Political Campaigns: The Influence of Question Order and Electoral Context." *Political Behavior* 6 (1984): 159–69.

Bishop, George F., Alfred J. Tuchfarber, and Robert W. Oldendick. "Change in the Structure of American Political Attitudes: The Nagging Question of Question Wording." *American Journal of Political Science* 22 (1978): 250–69.

Bobrow, Davis, and Neal E. Cutler. "Time-Oriented Explanations of National Security Beliefs: Cohort, Life-Stage and Situation." *Peace Research Society (International) Papers* 8 (1967): 31–57.

Boyce, Louis. "The Role of Gender in Recent Presidential Elections: Reagan and the Reverse Gender Gap." *Presidential Studies Quarterly* 15 (1985): 372–85.

Brace, Paul, and Barbara Hinckley. *Follow the Leader: Opinion Polls and Modern Presidents*. New York: Basic Books, 1992.

Brandes, Lisa Catherine Olga. "Public Opinion, International Security Policy, and Gender." Ph.D. diss., Political Science Dept., Yale University, 1994.

Brehm, John. *The Phantom Respondents: Opinion Surveys and Political Representation*. Ann Arbor: University of Michigan Press, 1993.

Brody, Richard A., and Catherine R. Shapiro. "A Reconsideration of the Rally Phenomenon in Public Opinion." In *Political Behavior Annual*, vol. 2, 77–102. Edited by Samuel Long. Boulder, CO: Westview, 1989.

Bruner, Jerome S. *Mandate from the People*. New York: Duell, Sloan and Pearce, 1944.

Buchanan, Patrick. "America First—and Second, and Third." *National Interest* 19 (spring 1990): 77–92.

Bundy, McGeorge, transcriber, and James G. Blight, ed. "October 27, 1962: Transcript of the Meetings of the ExComm." *International Security* 12 (winter 1987–88): 30–92.

Burns, James M. *Roosevelt: the Soldier of Freedom*. New York: Harcourt, Brace, Jovanovich, 1970.

Campbell, Angus, Philip E. Converse, Warren E. Miller, and Donald E. Stokes. *The American Voter*. New York: John Wiley, 1964.

Cantril, Albert H. *Polling on the Issues: Twenty-One Perspectives on the Role of Opinion Polls in the Making of Public Policy*. Cabin John, MD: Seven Locks Press, 1980.

Cantril, Hadley. *The Human Dimension: Experiences in Policy Research*. New Brunswick, NJ: Rutgers University Press, 1967.

Carr, Edward Hallett. *The Twenty Years' Crisis, 1919–1939: An Introduction to the Study of International Relations*. London: Macmillan, 1941.

Caspary, William R. "The 'Mood Theory': A Study of Public Opinion and Foreign Policy." *American Political Science Review* 64 (1970): 536–47.

Chittick, William O. *State Department, Press, and Pressure Groups: A Role Analysis*. New York: John Wiley, 1970.

Chittick, William O., and Keith R. Billingsley. "The Structure of Elite Foreign Policy Beliefs." *Western Political Quarterly* 42 (1989): 201–24.

Chittick, William O., Keith R. Billingsley, and Rick Travis. "A Three-Dimensional Model of American Foreign Policy Beliefs." *International Studies Quarterly* 39 (1995): 313–31.

Chittick, William O., Keith R. Billingsley, and Rick Travis. "Persistence and Change in Elite and Mass Attitudes toward U.S. Foreign Policy." *Political Psychology* 11 (1990): 385–402.

Citrin, Jack, Ernst B. Haas, Christopher Muste, and Beth Reingold. "Is American Nationalism Changing? Implications for Foreign Policy." *International Studies Quarterly* 38 (1994): 1–32.

Clifford, Clark, with Richard Holbrooke. *Counsel to the President: A Memoir.* New York: Random House, 1991.

Clough, Michael. "Grass-Roots Policymaking." *Foreign Affairs* 73 (January-February 1994): 191–96.

Cohen, Bernard C. *The Public's Impact on Foreign Policy.* Boston: Little, Brown, 1973.

Cohen, Bernard C. *The Political Process and Foreign Policy: The Making of the Japanese Peace Settlement.* Princeton, NJ: Princeton University Press, 1957.

Conover, Pamela Johnston. "Feminists and the Gender Gap." *Journal of Politics* 50 (1988): 985–1010.

Conover, Pamela Johnston, and Stanley Feldman. "How People Organize the Political World: A Schematic Model." *American Journal of Political Science* 28 (1984): 95–126.

Converse, Jean. *Survey Research in the United States: Roots and Emergence 1890–1960.* Berkeley and Los Angeles: University of California Press, 1987.

Converse, Philip E. "The Enduring Impact of the Vietnam War on American Public Opinion." In *After the Storm: American Society a Decade after the Vietnam War,* 53–75. Taipei, R.O.C.: Academic Sinica, 1987a.

Converse, Philip E. "Changing Conceptions of Public Opinion in the Policy Process." *Public Opinion Quarterly* 51 (1987b): S12–S24.

Converse, Philip E. "Public Opinion and Voting Behavior." In *Handbook of Political Science,* vol. 4, 75–169. Edited by Fred Greenstein and Nelson Polsby. Reading, MA: AddisonWesley, 1975.

Converse, Philip E. "Attitudes and Non-Attitudes: Continuation of a Dialogue." In *The Quantitative Analysis of Social Problems,* 168–89. Edited by Edward R. Tufte. Reading, MA: Addison-Wesley, 1970.

Converse, Philip E. "The Nature of Belief Systems in Mass Publics." In *Ideology and Discontent,* 206–61. Edited by David E. Apter. New York: Free Press, 1964.

Converse, Philip E., and Howard Schuman. "Silent Majorities and the Vietnam War." *Scientific American* 222 (1970): 17–25.

Cook, Elizabeth Adell, and Clyde Wilcox. "Feminism and the Gender Gap—A Second Look." *Journal of Politics* 53 (1991): 1111–22.

Cornwell, Elmer E. "Wilson, Creel, and the Presidency." *Public Opinion Quarterly* 23 (1959): 189–202.

Cottam, Richard. *Foreign Policy Motivation.* Pittsburgh: University of Pittsburgh Press, 1977.

Cottrell, Leonard S., Jr. and Sylvia Eberhart. *American Opinion on World Affairs in the Atomic Age.* Princeton, NJ: Princeton University Press, 1948.

Crabb, Cecil. *Policy-Makers and Critics: Conflicting Theories of American Foreign Policy.* New York: Praeger, 1976.

Cutler, Neal E. "Generational Succession as a Source of Foreign Policy Attitudes: A Cohort Analysis of American Opinion, 1946–1966." *Journal of Peace Research* 7 (1970): 33–47.

Dallek, Robert. *The American Style of Foreign Policy: Cultural Politics and Foreign Affairs.* New York: Alfred A. Knopf, 1983.

Dallek, Robert. *Franklin D. Roosevelt and American Foreign Policy, 1932–1945.* New York: Oxford University Press, 1979.

D'Amico, Francine, and Peter R. Beckman, eds. *Women in World Politics.* Westport, CT: Bergin and Garvey, 1995.

Davies, Joseph E. *Mission to Moscow.* New York: Simon and Schuster, 1941.

Davis, James A. "The Future Study of Public Opinion: A Symposium." *Public Opinion Quarterly* 51 (1987): S178–S179.

DeConde, Alexander. *Ethnicity, Race, and American Foreign Policy: A History.* Boston: Northeastern University Press, 1992.

Deese, David. *The New Politics of American Foreign Policy.* New York: St. Martin's Press, 1994.

Deibel, Terry L. *Presidents, Public Opinion, and Power: The Nixon, Carter, and the Reagan Years.* New York: Foreign Policy Association, 1987.

De Stefano, Linda "Looking Ahead to the Year 2000." Princeton, NJ. Gallup Organization, 1990.

Destler, I. M., Leslie H. Gelb, and Anthony Lake. *Our Own Worst Enemy.* New York: Simon and Schuster, 1984.

Devine, Donald J. *The Attentive Public: Polyarchical Democracy.* Chicago: Rand McNally, 1970.

Dimock, Michael A., and Samuel L. Popkin. "Who Knows?: Political Knowledge in a Comparative Perspective." Paper presented to the annual meeting of the Midwest Political Science Association, Chicago, April 3, 1993.

Doyle, Michael W. "Liberalism and World Politics." *American Political Science Review* 80 (1986): 1151–70.

Drew, Elizabeth. "A Reporter at Large (Zbigniew Brzezinski)." *New Yorker,* May 1, 1978, 90–130.

"Democracies and War: The Politics of Peace." *Economist,* vol. 335, April 1, 1995, 17–18.

Ehrenreich, Barbara. "The Real and Ever-Widening Gender Gap." *Esquire,* vol. 101, no. 6, June 1984, 213–17.

Eichenberg, Richard. *Public Opinion and National Security in Western Europe.* Ithaca, NY: Cornell University Press, 1989.

Eisenhower, Dwight D. *Waging Peace, 1956–1961.* Garden City, NY: Doubleday, 1965.

Elder, Robert E. "The Public Studies Division of the Department of State: Public Opinion Analysts in the Formulation and Conduct of American Foreign Policy." *Western Political Quarterly* 10 (1957): 783–92.

Erikson, Robert S. "Constituency Opinion and Congressional Behavior: A Reexamination of the Miller-Stokes Data." *American Journal of Political Science* 22 (1978): 511–35.

Erskine, Hazel. "The Polls: Pacifism and the Generation Gap." *Public Opinion Quarterly* 36 (1972): 617–27.

Erskine, Hazel. "The Polls: Is War a Mistake?" *Public Opinion Quarterly* 34 (1970): 134–50.

Fagen, Richard R. "Some Assessments and Uses of Public Opinion in Diplomacy." *Public Opinion Quarterly* 24 (1960): 448–57.

Ferguson, Thomas. "The Right Consensus." *International Studies Quarterly* 30 (1986): 411–23.

Fiorina, Morris P. *Retrospective Voting in American National Elections.* New Haven, CT: Yale University Press, 1981.

Fishkin, James S. "Britain Experiments with the Deliberative Poll." *Public Perspective* 5 (July-August 1994): 27–29.

Fishkin, James S. "The Idea of a Deliberative Opinion Poll." *Public Perspective* 3 (January-February 1992): 26–34.

Fishkin, James S. *Democracy and Deliberation: New Directions for Democratic Reform.* New Haven, CT: Yale University Press, 1991.

Fite, David, Marc Genest, and Clyde Wilcox. "Gender Differences in Foreign Policy Attitudes: A Longitudinal Analysis." *American Politics Quarterly* 18 (1990): 492–513.

Foster, H. Schuyler. *Activism Replaces Isolationism: U.S. Public Attitudes, 1940–1975.* Washington, DC: Foxhall Press, 1983.

Foyle, Douglas. "The Influence of Public Opinion on American Foreign Policy Decision Making: Context, Beliefs, and Process." Ph.D. diss., Political Science Dept., Duke University, 1996.

Free, Lloyd, and William Watts. "Internationalism Comes of Age . . . Again." *Public Opinion* 3 (April-May 1980): 46–50.

Friedman, Thomas L. "The No-Dead War." *New York Times,* August 23, 1995. A-21:1.

Gaddis, John L. "International Relations Theory and the End of the Cold War. *International Security* 17 (1992–93): 5–58.

Gallagher, Nancy W. "The Gender Gap in Popular Attitudes toward the Use of Force." In *Women and the Use of Military Force,* 23–37. Edited by Ruth Howes and Michael Stevenson. Boulder, CO: Lynn Reiner, 1993.

Gallup, George, H. *The Gallup Poll* (annual, 1978–1983). Wilmington, DE: Scholarly Resources, 1979–84.

Gallup, George H. *The Gallup Poll: Public Opinion 1972–1977.* 2 vols. Wilmington, DE: Scholarly Resources, 1978.

Gallup, George H. *The Gallup Poll: Public Opinion 1935–1971.* 3 vols. New York: Random House, 1972.

Gallup, George H., and Saul Rae. *The Pulse of Democracy.* New York: Simon and Schuster, 1940.

Gallup, George, Jr. *The Gallup Poll* (annual, 1984–1993). Wilmington, DE: Scholarly Resources, 1985–94.

Gamson, William A., and Andre Modigliani. "Knowledge and Foreign Policy Opinions: Some Models for Consideration." *Public Opinion Quarterly* 30 (1966): 187–99.

Garthoff, Raymond L. *Détente and Confrontation: American-Soviet Relations from Nixon to Reagan.* Washington, DC: Brookings Institution, 1985.

Gaubatz, Kurt Taylor. "Intervention and Intransitivity: Public Opinion, Social Choice, and the Use of Military Force Abroad." *World Politics* 47 (1995): 534–54.

Genco, Stephen J. "The Attentive Public and American Foreign Policy." Ph.D. diss., Political Science Dept., Stanford University, 1984.

George, Alexander L. "Case Studies and Theory Development: The Method of Structured, Focused Comparison." In *Diplomacy: New Approaches in History, Theory, and Policy,* 43–68. Edited by Paul Gordon Lauren. New York: Free Press, 1979.

George, Alexander L., and Richard Smoke. *Deterrence in American Foreign Policy: Theory and Practice.* New York: Columbia University Press, 1974.

George, Alexander L. "American Policy-Making and the North Korean Aggression." *World Politics* 2 (1955): 209–32.

Gergen, Kenneth J., and Kurt W. Back. "Aging, Time Perspective and Preferred Solutions to International Conflicts." *Journal of Conflict Resolution* 9 (1965): 177–86.

Gibson, James L. "Survey Research in the Past and Future USSR: Reflections on the Methodology of Mass Opinion Surveys." *Research in Micropolitics* 4 (1994): 87–114.

Ginsberg, Benjamin. *The Captive Public: How Mass Opinion Promotes State Power.* New York: Basic Books, 1986.

Goncharov, Sergei, John W. Lewis, and Xue Litai. *Uncertain Partners: Stalin, Mao, and the Korean War.* Stanford, CA: Stanford University Press, 1993.

Graber, Doris A. *Public Opinion, the President, and Foreign Policy: Four Case Studies from the Formative Years.* New York: Holt, Rinehart and Winston, 1968.

Graebner, Norman A. "Public Opinion and Foreign Policy: A Pragmatic View." In *Interaction: Foreign Policy and Public Policy,* 11–34. Edited by E. D. Piper and R. J. Tercheck. Washington, DC: American Enterprise Institute, 1983.

Graham, Thomas W. "Public Opinion and U.S. Foreign Policy Decision Making." In *The New Politics of American Foreign Policy,* 190–215. Edited by David A. Deese. New York: St. Martin's Press, 1994.

Graham, Thomas W. " The Politics of Failure: Strategic Nuclear Arms Control, Public Opinion, and Domestic Politics in the United States—1945–1980." Ph.D. diss., Political Science Dept., MIT, 1989.

Graham, Thomas W. "The Pattern and Importance of Public Knowledge in the Nuclear Age." *Journal of Conflict Resolution* 32 (1988): 319–34.

Greenhouse, Steven. "Foreign Aid and G.O.P.: Deep Cuts." *New York Times,* December 21, 1994, A3.

Hamill, Ruth, Milton Lodge, and Frederick Blake. "The Breadth, Depth, and Utility of Class, Partisan, and Ideological Schemata." *American Journal of Political Science* 29 (1985): 850–70.

Hamilton, Alexander, John Jay, and James Madison. *The Federalist.* 1787–88. New York: Modern Library, 1937.

Handberg, Roger B., Jr. "The 'Vietnam Analogy': Student Attitudes on War." *Public Opinion Quarterly* 36 (1972–73): 612–15.

Hartley, Thomas, and Bruce Russett. "Public Opinion and the Common Defense: Who Governs Military Spending in the United States?" *American Political Science Review* 86 (1992): 905–15.

Hechler, Ken. *Working with Truman: A Personal Memoir of the White House Years.* New York: Putnam, 1982.

Helbich, Wolfgang J. "American Liberals in the League of Nations Controversy." *Public Opinion Quarterly* 31 (1967–68): 568–96.

Herman, Edward S., and Noam Chomsky. *Manufacturing Consent: The Political Economy of the Mass Media*. New York: Pantheon, 1988.

Hermann, Charles F. "International Crisis as a Situational Variable." In *International Politics and Foreign Policy,* 409–21. Edited by James N. Rosenau. New York: Free Press, 1969.

Herrmann, Richard. "The Power of Perceptions in Foreign Policy Decision Making." *American Journal of Political Science* 30 (1986): 841–75.

Hero, Alfred O., Jr. "Liberalism-Conservatism Revisited: Foreign vs. Domestic Federal Policies, 1937–1967." *Public Opinion Quarterly* 33 (1969): 399–408.

Hero, Alfred O., Jr. *Americans in World Affairs*. Boston: World Peace Foundation, 1959.

Higgs, Robert, and Anthony Kilduff. "Public Opinion: A Powerful Predictor of U.S. Defense Spending." *Defense Economics* 4 (1992): 227–38.

Hildebrand, Robert C. *Power and the People: Executive Management of Public Opinion in Foreign Affairs, 1897–1921*. Chapel Hill: University of North Carolina Press, 1981.

Hill, Kevin A. "The Domestic Sources of Foreign Policymaking: Congressional Voting and American Mass Attitudes toward South Africa." *International Studies Quarterly* 37 (1993): 195–214.

Hinckley, Ronald H. Private communication with author, July 26, 1995.

Hinckley, Ronald H. "Public Opinion and Foreign Policy in Comparative Perspective." Paper presented to the annual meeting of the International Studies Association, Acapulco, Mexico, March 24–28, 1993.

Hinckley, Ronald H. *People, Polls, and Policy-Makers: American Public Opinion and National Security*. New York: Lexington Books, 1992.

Hinckley, Ronald H. "Public Attitudes toward Key Foreign Policy Events." *Journal of Conflict Resolution* 32 (1988): 295–318.

Hoffmann, Stanley, et al. "Vietnam Reappraised." *International Security* 6 (summer 1981): 3–27.

Holmes, Jack E. *The Mood/Interest Theory of American Foreign Policy*. Lexington: University Press of Kentucky, 1985.

Holsti, Ole R. "The Domestic and Foreign Policy Beliefs of American Leaders, during and after the Cold War." Paper presented to the annual conference of the International Studies Association, Washington, DC, March 29–April 1, 1994.

Holsti, Ole R. "American Reactions to the USSR: Public Opinion." In *Soviet-American Relations after the Cold War,* 23–47. Edited by Robert Jervis and Seweryn Bialer. Durham, NC: Duke University Press, 1991.

Holsti, Ole R. "Gender and the Political Beliefs of American Leaders, 1976–1988." Paper presented to the annual meeting of the International Studies Association, Washington, DC, April 10–14, 1990. A greatly abbreviated version appears in Ole R. Holsti and James N. Rosenau, "Gender and the Political Beliefs of American Opinion Leaders," in *Women and World Politics*, edited by Francine D'Amico and Peter Beckman (Amherst, MA: Bergin and Garvey, 1995).

Holsti, Ole R. "What Are the Russians Up to Now: The Beliefs of American Leaders about the Soviet Union and Soviet-American Relations, 1974–

1984." In *East-West Conflict: Elite Perceptions and Political Options*, 45–105. Edited by Michael D. Intriligator and Hans-Adolf Jacobsen. Boulder, CO: Westview, 1988.

Holsti, Ole R. "The Three-Headed Eagle: The United States and System Change." *International Studies Quarterly* 23 (1979): 339–59.

Holsti, Ole R., and James N. Rosenau. "Gender and the Political Beliefs of American Opinion Leaders." In *Women and World Politics*, 113–42. Edited by Francine D'Amico and Peter Beckman. Amherst, MA: Bergin and Garvey, 1995.

Holsti, Ole R., and James N. Rosenau. "The Post–Cold War Foreign Policy Beliefs of American Leaders: Persistence or Abatement of Partisan Cleavages?" In *The Future of American Foreign Policy*, 127–47. Edited by Eugene R. Wittkopf. New York: St. Martin's Press, 1994.

Holsti, Ole R., and James N. Rosenau. "The Structure of Foreign Policy Beliefs among American Opinion Leaders—After the Cold War." *Millennium* 22 (1993): 235–78.

Holsti, Ole R., and James N. Rosenau. "The Structure of Foreign Policy Attitudes among American Leaders." *Journal of Politics* 52 (1990): 94–125.

Holsti, Ole R., and James N. Rosenau. "The Domestic and Foreign Policy Beliefs of American Leaders." *Journal of Conflict Resolution* 32 (1988): 248–94.

Holsti, Ole R., and James N. Rosenau. "The Foreign Policy Beliefs of American Leaders: Some Further Thoughts on Theory and Method." *International Studies Quarterly* 30 (1986): 473–84.

Holsti, Ole R., and James N. Rosenau. *American Leadership in World Affairs: Vietnam and the Breakdown of Consensus*. London: Allen and Unwin, 1984.

Holsti, Ole R., and James N. Rosenau. "The Foreign Policy Beliefs of Women in Leadership Positions." *Journal of Politics* 43 (1981): 326–47.

Holsti, Ole R., and James N. Rosenau. "Vietnam, Consensus, and the Belief Systems of American Leaders." *World Politics* 32 (1979): 1–56.

Homet, Roland S., Jr. *The New Realism*. New York: HarperCollins, 1990.

Hough, Jerry F. "Gorbachev's Endgame." *World Policy Journal* 7 (1990): 639–72.

House, Karen Elliott. "Reagan's World: Republican's Policies Stress Arms Buildup, A Firm Line to Soviet." *Wall Street Journal*, June 3, 1980, 1.

Hovey, Graham. "Architects of U.S. African Policy Privately Worried by Carter's Attacks on Moscow." *New York Times*, June 4, 1978, A3.

Howe, Neil, and William Strauss. "The New Generation Gap." *Atlantic*, vol. 270, December 1992, 67–89.

Hughes, Barry B. *The Domestic Context of American Foreign Policy*. San Francisco: Freeman, 1978.

Hughes, Thomas L. "The Crack-Up: The Price of Collective Irresponsibility." *Foreign Policy*, no. 40 (1980): 33–60.

Hugick, Larry, and Alec H. Gallup. "Rally Events and Presidential Approval." *Gallup Poll Monthly* (June 1991): 15–31.

Hull, Cordell. Speech at the Pan American Conference, Buenos Aires, December 5, 1936. Reprinted in the *New York Times*, December 6, 1936, 47: 1.

Huntington, Samuel P. "Paradigms of American Politics: Beyond the One, the Two, and the Many." *Political Science Quarterly* 89 (1974): 1–26.

Hurwitz, Jon, and Mark Peffley. "Public Images of the Soviet Union and Its

Leaders: The Impact on Foreign Policy Attitudes." *Journal of Politics* 52 (1990): 3–28.

Hurwitz, Jon, and Mark Peffley. "How Are Foreign Policy Attitudes Structured? A Hierarchical Model." *American Political Science Review* 81 (1987): 1099–120.

Hurwitz, Jon, Mark Peffley, and Mitchell A. Seligson. "Foreign Policy Belief Systems in Comparative Perspective: The United States and Costa Rica." *International Studies Quarterly* 37 (1993): 245–70.

Idelson, Holly. "National Opinion Ambivalent as Winds of War Stir Gulf." *Congressional Quarterly Weekly*, January 5, 1991, 14–17.

Isaacs, Maxine. "The Independent American Public: The Relationship between Elite and Mass Opinions on American Foreign Policy in the Mass Communication Age." Ph.D. diss., School of Public Affairs, University of Maryland, 1994.

Jacobs, Lawrence R. "The Recoil Effect: Public Opinion and Policy Making in the U.S. and Britain." *Comparative Politics* 24 (January 1992): 199–217.

Jacobs, Lawrence R., and Robert Y. Shapiro. "The Rise of Presidential Polling: The Nixon White House in Historical Perspective." *Public Opinion Quarterly* 59 (1995): 163–95.

Jacobs, Lawrence R., and Robert Y. Shapiro. "Issues, Candidate Image, and Priming: The Use of Private Polls in Kennedy's 1960 Presidential Campaign." *American Political Science Review* 88 (1994): 527–40.

Jacobs, Lawrence R., and Robert Y. Shapiro. "Studying Substantive Democracy." *PS: Political Science and Politics* 27 (March 1994): 9–17.

Janda, Kenneth, Jeffrey M. Berry, and Jerry Goldman. *The Challenge of Democracy: Government in America*. 4th ed. Boston: Houghton Mifflin Co., 1994.

Jennings, M. Kent. "Ideological Thinking among Mass Publics and Political Elites." *Public Opinion Quarterly* 56 (1992): 419–41.

Jennings, M. Kent. "Residues of a Movement: The Aging of the American Protest Generation." *American Political Science Review* 81 (1987): 367–82.

Jentleson, Bruce W. "Who, Why, What, and How: Debates over Post-Cold War Military Intervention." In *Eagle Adrift: American: American Foreign Policy at the End of the Century*. Edited by Robert J. Lieber. New York: HarperCollins, 1996.

Jentleson, Bruce W. "The Pretty Prudent Public: Post-Vietnam American Opinion on the Use of Military Force." *International Studies Quarterly* 36 (1992): 49–73.

Jones, Joseph M. *Fifteen Weeks*. New York: Viking, 1955.

Kagay, Michael R. "Variability without Fault: Why Even Well-Designed Polls Can Disagree." In *Media Polls in American Politics*. Edited by Thomas E. Mann and Gary R. Orren. Washington, DC: Brookings Institution, 1992.

Kagay, Michael R., and Janet Elder. "Numbers Are No Problem for Pollsters. Words Are." *New York Times*, August 9, 1992, K-5.

Kant, Immanuel. *Perpetual Peace and Other Essays on Politics, History, and Morals*. Translated with an introduction by Ted Humphrey. 1796. Reprint, Indianapolis: Hackett Publishing, 1983.

Katz, Elihu. "The Two-Step Flow of Communication: An Up-To-Date Report on an Hypothesis." *Public Opinion Quarterly* 21 (1957): 61–78.

Katz, Elihu, and Paul F. Lazarsfeld. *Personal Influence*. Glencoe, IL: The Free Press, 1955.

Kay, Alan F. "Discovering the Wisdom of the People." *World Business Academy Perspectives* 6 (1992a): 19–28.

Kay, Alan F. *Uncovering the Public View on Policy Issues: Evidence that Survey Research Can Address Intractable Problems in Governance.* Washington, DC: Americans Talk Issues Foundation, 1992b.

Kegley, Charles W., Jr. "The Neoidealist Moment in International Studies? Realist Myths and the New International Realities." *International Studies Quarterly* 37 (1993): 131–46.

Kegley, Charles W., Jr. "Assumptions and Dilemmas in the Study of Americans' Foreign Policy Beliefs: A Caveat." *International Studies Quarterly* 30 (1986): 447–71.

Kelman, Herbert C. "Social-Psychological Approaches to the Study of International Relations: The Question of Relevance." In *International Behavior: A Social-Psychological Analysis,* 565–607. Edited by Herbert C. Kelman. New York: Holt, Rinehart and Winston, 1965.

Kelman, Steven J. "Youth and Foreign Policy." *Foreign Affairs* 48 (1970): 414–26.

Kennan, George F. "Somalia, Through a Glass Darkly." *New York Times,* September 30, 1993, A25.

Kennan, George F. *American Diplomacy, 1900–1950.* New York: Mentor Books, 1951.

Kennan, George F ["X"]. "Sources of Soviet Conduct." *Foreign Affairs* 25 (1947): 566–82.

Key, V. O., Jr. *Public Opinion and American Democracy.* New York: Alfred A. Knopf, 1961.

Kinder, Donald R. "Diversity and Complexity in American Public Opinion." In *Political Science: The State of the Discipline,* 389–425. Edited by Ada W. Finifter. Washington, DC: American Political Science Association, 1983.

Kinder, Donald R., and David O. Sears. "Public Opinion and Political Action." In *Handbook of Social Psychology,* 3d ed., 659–741. Edited by Elliott Aronson and Gardner Lindzey. New York: Random House, 1985.

Kinnard, Douglas. "Vietnam Reconsidered: An Attitudinal Survey of U.S. Army General Officers." *Public Opinion Quarterly* 39 (1975): 445–56.

Kissinger, Henry. *Diplomacy.* New York: Simon and Schuster, 1994.

Klein, Ethel. *Gender Politics: From Consciousness to Mass Politics.* Cambridge, MA: Harvard University Press, 1984.

Klingberg, Frank L. *Cyclical Trends in American Foreign Policy Moods: The Unfolding of America's World Role.* Lanham, MD: University Press of America, 1983.

Klingberg, Frank L. "Cyclical Trends in American Foreign Policy Moods and Their Policy Implications." In *Challenges to America: United States Foreign Policy in the 1980s,* 37–56. Edited by Charles W. Kegley Jr. and Patrick J. McGowan. Beverly Hills, CA: Sage Publications, 1979.

Klingberg, Frank L. "The Historical Alternation of Moods in American Foreign Policy." *World Politics* 4 (1952): 239–73.

Knight, Thomas J. "The Passing of the Cold War Generation." *Intellect* 105 (February 1977): 236–41.

Kohut, Andrew, and Robert C. Toth. "Arms and the People." *Foreign Affairs* 73 (1994): 47–61.

Kolko, Gabriel, and Joyce Kolko. *The Limits of Power: The World and United States Foreign Policy, 1945–1954*. New York: Harper and Row, 1972.

Koopman, Cheryl, Jack Snyder, and Robert Jervis. "Theory-Driven versus Data-Driven Assessment in a Crisis." *Journal of Conflict Resolution* 34 (1990): 694–722.

Koopman, Cheryl, Jack Snyder, and Robert Jervis. "American Elite Views of Relations with the Soviet Union." *Journal of Social Issues* 45 (1989): 119–38.

Koppel, Ted. "The Perils of Info-Democracy." *New York Times*, July 1, 1994, A5.

Krauthammer, Charles. "The Unipolar Moment." *Foreign Affairs* 70 (1990–91): 23–33.

Kriesberg, Martin. "Dark Areas of Ignorance." In *Public Opinion and Foreign Policy*. Edited by Lester Markel. New York: Harper, 1949.

Kroeger, Brian, and Virginia Sapiro. "Oh, Ye of Little Faith: Philip Tetlock's Road to Hell." *Political Psychology* 15 (1994): 557–66.

Krosnick, Jon A. "The Stability of Political Preferences: Comparisons of Symbolic and Nonsymbolic Attitudes." *American Journal of Political Science* 35 (1991): 547–76.

Krosnick, Jon A. "American's Perceptions of Presidential Candidates: A Test of the Projection Hypothesis." *Journal of Social Issues* 46 (1990): 159–82.

Krosnick, Jon A. "Attitude Importance and Attitude Change." *Journal of Experimental Social Psychology* 24 (1988a): 240–55.

Krosnick, Jon A. "The Role of Attitude Importance in Social Evaluation: A Study of Policy Preferences, Presidential Candidate Evaluations, and Voting Behavior." *Journal of Personality and Social Psychology* 55 (1988b): 196–210.

Krosnick, Jon, and Catherine Carnot. *Identifying the Foreign Affairs Attentive Public in the U.S.: A Comparison of Competing Theories*. Columbus: Ohio State University, 1988. Mimeograph.

Kull, Steven. "What the Public Knows that Washington Doesn't." *Foreign Policy*, no. 101 (1995–96): 102–15.

Kull, Steven. *American and Foreign Aid: A Study of American Public Attitudes*. College Park, MD: Center for International and Security Studies, 1995a.

Kull, Steven. *Americans on Bosnia: A Study of U.S. Public Attitudes*. College Park, MD: Center for International and Security Studies, 1995b.

Kull, Steven. "American Public Attitudes on Sending U.S. Troops to Bosnia." College Park, MD: Center for International and Security Studies, 1995c.

Kull, Steven, and Clark Ramsay. *U.S. Public Attitudes on Involvement in Bosnia*. College Park, MD: Center for International Security Studies, 1994a.

Kull, Steven, and Clark Ramsay. *U.S. Public Attitudes on Involvement in Haiti*. College Park, MD: Center for International and Security Studies, 1994b.

Kull, Steven, and Clark Ramsay. *U.S. Public Attitudes on UN Peacekeeping: Part I, Funding*. College Park, MD: Center for International and Security Studies, 1994c.

Kull, Steven, and Clark Ramsay. *U.S. Public Attitudes on Involvement in Somalia*. College Park, MD: Center for International and Security Studies, 1993.

Kusnitz, Leonard A. *Public Opinion and Foreign Policy: America's China Policy 1949–1979*. Westport, CT: Greenwood Press, 1984.

Ladd, Everett Carll, and John Benson. "The Growth of News Polls in American Politics." In *Media Polls in American Politics*, 19–31. Edited by Thomas E. Mann and Gary R. Orren. Washington, DC: Brookings Institution, 1992.

LaFeber, Walter. "American Policy-Makers, Public Opinion, and the Outbreak of the Cold War, 1945–1950." In *The Origins of the Cold War in Asia*, 43–65. Edited by Yonosuke Nagai and Akira Iriye. New York: Columbia University Press, 1977.

Lancaster, James L. "The Protestant Churches and the Fight for Ratification of the Versailles Treaty." *Public Opinion Quarterly* 31 (1967–68): 597–619.

Larson, Eric V. "Ends and Means in the Democratic Conversation: Understanding the Role of Casualties in Support of U.S. Military Operations." Ph.D. diss, RAND Graduate School of Public Policy Analysis, 1995.

Lazarsfeld, Paul F., Bernard R. Berelson, and Hazel Gaudet. *The People's Choice*. New York: Duell, Sloan and Pearce, 1944.

Leigh, Michael. *Mobilizing Consent: Public Opinion and American Foreign Policy*. Westport, CT: Greenwood Press, 1976.

Levering, Ralph B. "Public Culture and Public Opinion: The League of Nations Controversy in New Jersey and North Carolina." In *The Wilson Era: Essays in Honor of Arthur S. Link*, 159–97. Edited by John Milton Cooper and Charles E. Neu. Arlington Heights, IL: Harlan Davidson, 1991.

Levering, Ralph. "Public Opinion, Foreign Policy, and American Politics since the 1960s." *Diplomatic History* 13 (1989): 383–93.

Levering, Ralph B. *The Public and American Foreign Policy, 1918–1978*. New York: Morrow, 1978.

Levering, Ralph B. *American Opinion and the Russian Alliance, 1939–1945*. Chapel Hill: University of North Carolina Press, 1976.

Lian, Bradley, and John R. Oneal. "Presidents, the Use of Military Force and Public Opinion." *Journal of Conflict Resolution* 37 (1993): 277–300.

Lindsay, James. "Testing the Parochial Hypothesis: Congress and the Strategic Defense Initiative." *Journal of Politics* 53 (1991): 860–76.

Lindsay, James. "Parochialism, Policy, and Constituency Constraints: Congressional Voting on Strategic Weapons Systems." *American Journal of Political Science* 34 (1990): 936–60.

Lippmann, Walter. *Essays in the Public Philosophy*. Boston: Little, Brown, 1955.

Lippmann, Walter. *The Phantom Public*. New York: Harcourt Brace, 1925.

Lippmann, Walter. *Public Opinion*. New York: Macmillan, 1922.

Lippmann, Walter. *Liberty and the News*. New York: Harcourt, Brace and Howe, 1920.

Lippmann, Walter, and Charles Merz. "A Test of the News." *New Republic*, special supplement, 23 (1920): 1–42.

Lipset, Seymour Martin, and Everett Carll Ladd, Jr. "College Generations from the 1930s to the 1960s." *Public Interest* 25 (1971): 99–113.

Lipset, Seymour Martin. "The President, the Polls and Vietnam." *Trans-action* (September-October 1966): 19–24.

Literary Digest 122 (October 31, 1936): 5–6.

Locke, John. *Two Treatises of Government*. Edited by Peter Laslett. 1690. Reprint, New York: Cambridge University Press, 1988.

Lowell, A. Lawrence. *Public Opinion in War and Peace*. Cambridge, MA: Harvard University Press, 1923.

Lowi, Theodore J. "Making Democracy Safe for the World: National Politics and Foreign Policy." In *Domestic Sources of Foreign Policy,* 295–331. Edited by James N. Rosenau. New York: Free Press, 1967.

Lunch, William, and Peter W. Sperlich. "American Public Opinion and the War in Vietnam." *Western Political Quarterly* 32 (1979): 21–44.

Luttbeg, Norman R. "The Structure of Beliefs among Leaders and the Public." *Public Opinion Quarterly* 32 (1968): 398–409.

Luttbeg, Norman R., and Michael M. Gant. "The Failure of Liberal/Conservative Ideology as a Cognitive Structure." *Public Opinion Quarterly* 49 (1985): 80–93.

Luttwak, Edward N. "Where Are the Great Powers?" *Foreign Affairs* 73 (July-August 1994): 23–29.

Mandel, Robert. "Public Opinion and Superpower Strategic Arms." *Armed Forces and Society* 17 (1991): 409–27.

Mandelbaum, Michael. "Foreign Policy as Social Work." *Foreign Affairs* 75 (January-February 1996): 16–32.

Mandelbaum, Michael, and William Schneider. "The New Internationalism." In *Eagle Entangled: U.S. Foreign Policy in a Complex World,* 40–63. Edited by Kenneth A. Oye, Robert J. Lieber, and Donald Rothchild. New York: Longman, 1979.

Mann, Thomas E., and Gary R. Orren, eds. *Media Polls in American Politics.* Washington, DC: Brookings Institution, 1992.

Mannheim, Karl. *Essays in the Sociology of Knowledge.* Edited by Paul Kecskemeti. London: Routledge and Kegan Paul, 1952.

Marcus, George E., and Russell L. Hanson, eds. *Reconsidering the Democratic Public.* University Park: Pennsylvania University Press, 1993.

Margolis, Michael, and Gary A. Mauser, eds. *Manipulating Public Opinion.* Pacific Grove, CA: Brooks/Cole, 1989.

Markel, Lester. "Opinion—A Neglected Instrument." In *Public Opinion and Foreign Policy,* 3–46. Edited by Lester Markel et al. New York: Harper and Brothers, 1949.

Marra, R. F., C. W. Ostrom, and D. M. Simon. "Foreign Policy and Presidential Popularity." *Journal of Conflict Resolution* 34 (1990): 588–623.

Maxwell, Kenneth R. "Irish-Americans and the Fight for Treaty Ratification." *Public Opinion Quarterly* 31 (1967–68): 620–41.

May, Ernest R. "An American Tradition in Foreign Policy: The Role of Public Opinion." In *Theory and Practice in American Politics,* 101–22. Edited by William H. Nelson. Chicago: University of Chicago Press, 1964.

May, Ernest R. *The World War and American Isolation, 1914–1917.* Cambridge, MA: Harvard University Press, 1959.

Mayer, William G. *The Changing American Mind: How and Why American Public Opinion Changed between 1960 and 1988.* Ann Arbor: University of Michigan Press, 1992.

McCloskey, Herbert, Paul J. Hoffmann, and Rosemary O'Hara. "Issue Conflict and Consensus among Party Leaders and Followers." *American Political Science Review* 54 (1960): 406–27.

McGrory, Mary. "The Young People Had It Right." *Boston Globe,* May 1, 1975, 31.

Mill, James. "On Liberty of the Press for Advocating Resistance to Government:

Being Part of an Essay Written for the Encyclopedia Britannica." 6th ed. 1821. Reprint, New York: Free Speech League, 1913.

Miller, Arthur H., Vicki L. Hesli, and William M. Reisinger. "Mass and Elite Belief Systems in Russia/Ukraine." *Public Opinion Quarterly* 59 (1995): 1–40.

Miller, Arthur H., William M. Reisinger, and Vicki L. Hesli, eds. *Public Opinion and Regime Change: The New Politics of Post-Soviet Societies*. Boulder, CO: Westview, 1993.

Miller, Warren E. "Voting and Foreign Policy." In *Domestic Sources of Foreign Policy*, 213–30. Edited by James N. Rosenau. New York: Free Press, 1967.

Miller, Warren E., and Donald E. Stokes. "Constituency Influence in Congress." *American Political Science Review* 57 (1963): 45–56.

Molyneux, Guy. "NAFTA Revisited: Unified 'Public Opinion' Best a Reluctant Public." *Public Perspective* 5 (January-February 1994): 28–30.

Monroe, Alan D. "Consistency between Public Preferences and National Policy Decisions." *American Politics Quarterly* 7 (1979): 3–19.

Moore, David W. *The Superpollsters: How They Measure and Manipulate Public Opinion in America*. New York: Four Walls and Eight Windows Press, 1992.

Morgenthau, Hans J. *Politics among Nations*. 5th ed. New York: Alfred A. Knopf, 1978.

Mueller, John E. *Policy and Opinion in the Gulf War*. Chicago: University of Chicago Press, 1994.

Mueller, John E. *War, Presidents, and Public Opinion*. New York: John Wiley, 1973.

Munton, Don. "Up (or Down) on Arms: American and Canadian Public Attitudes in the Mid-1980s." In *East-West Arms Control: Challenges for the Western Alliance*, 212–44. Edited by David Dewitt and Hans Rattinger. London and New York: Routledge, 1992.

Munton, Don. "NATO Up against the Wall: Changing Security Attitudes in Germany, Britain, and Canada, 1960s to the 1980s." In *Debating National Security: The Public Dimension*, 343–77. Edited by Hans Rattinger and Don Munton. Frankfurt am Main: Peter Lang, 1991.

Munton, Don. "Threat Perceptions and Shifts of Public Attitudes, 1960s–1980s." In *Western Perceptions of Soviet Goals: Is Trust Possible?* 97–134. Edited by Klaus Gottstein. Frankfurt am Main and Boulder, CO: Campus Verlag and Westview, 1989.

Murray, Shoon. *Anchors Against Change: American Opinion Leaders' Beliefs After the Cold War*. Ann Arbor: University of Michigan Press, 1996.

Nacos, Brigitte Lebens. "Presidential Leadership during the Persian Gulf War." *Presidential Studies Quarterly* 24 (summer 1994): 543–61.

National Opinion Research Center. " Cincinnati Looks at the United Nations." Report No. 37. Chicago National Opinion Research Center, 1947.

Neuman, W. Russell. *The Paradox of Mass Politics: Knowledge and Opinion in the American Electorate*. Cambridge, MA: Harvard University Press, 1986.

Neumann, Sigmund. *Permanent Revolution: The Total State in a World at War*. New York: Harper and Brothers, 1942.

Neustadt, Richard. *Alliance Politics*. New York: Columbia University Press, 1970.

Nevitte, Neil, and Roger Gibbins. "The Ideology of Gender." Paper presented to the tenth annual meeting of the International Society of Political Psychology, San Francisco, July 4–7, 1987.

Newport, Frank. "Presidential Address on Bosnia Changed Few Minds." Princeton, NJ: Gallup Organization, November 30, 1995.

New York Times, November 29, 1984, A5:1.

Newsweek, November 20, 1989, 90.

Nie, Norman H., and Kristi Anderson. "Mass Belief Systems Revisited: Political Change and Attitude Structure." *Journal of Politics* 36 (1974): 540–91.

Nie, Norman H., Sidney Verba, and John R. Petrocik. *The Changing American Voter.* Cambridge, MA: Harvard University Press, 1976.

Niemi, Richard G. "The Dynamics of Public Opinion." In *Political Science: The Science of Politics,* 225–40. Edited by Herbert Weisberg. New York: Agathon Press, 1986.

Nincic, Miroslav. *Democracy and Foreign Policy: The Fallacy of Political Realism.* New York: Columbia University Press, 1992.

Nincic, Miroslav. "The United States, the Soviet Union, and the Politics of Opposites." *World Politics* 40 (1988): 452–75.

Oldendick, Robert W., and Barbara Ann Bardes. "Mass and Elite Foreign Policy Opinions." *Public Opinion Quarterly* 46 (1982): 368–82.

Page, Benjamin I. "Democratic Responsiveness? Untangling the Links Between Public Opinion and Policy." *PS: Political Science and Politics* 27 (March 1994): 17–21.

Page, Benjamin I., and Robert Y. Shapiro. *The Rational Public: Fifty Years of Trends in Americans' Policy Preferences.* Chicago: University of Chicago Press, 1992.

Page, Benjamin I., and Robert Y. Shapiro. "Presidents as Opinion Leaders: Some New Evidence." *Policy Studies Journal* 12 (1984): 649–61.

Page, Benjamin I., and Robert Y. Shapiro. "Effects of Public Opinion on Policy." *American Political Science Review* 77 (1983): 175–90.

Page, Benjamin I., and Robert Y. Shapiro. "Changes in Americans' Policy Preferences, 1935–1979." *Public Opinion Quarterly* 46 (1982): 24–42.

Page, Benjamin I., Robert Y. Shapiro, and G. R. Dempsey. "What Moves Public Opinion." *American Political Science Review* 81 (1987): 23–43.

Paige, Glenn D. *The Korean Decision: June 24–30, 1950.* New York: Free Press, 1968.

Parry, R., and P. Kornbluh. "Iran-Contra's Untold Story." *Foreign Policy,* no. 72 (1988): 3–30.

Paterson, Thomas G. "Presidential Foreign Policy, Public Opinion, and Congress: The Truman Years." *Diplomatic History* 3 (1979): 1–18.

Peffley, Mark A., and Jon Hurwitz. "International Events and Foreign Policy Beliefs: Public Responses to Changing Soviet-U.S. Relations." *American Journal of Political Science* 36 (1992): 431–61.

Percy, Charles. "The Partisan Gap." *Foreign Policy,* no. 45 (1981–82): 3–15.

Popkin, Samuel L. *The Reasoning Voter.* Chicago: University of Chicago Press, 1991.

Powlick, Philip J. "Public Opinion and the Lebanon Intervention." In *Mass Communication, Democratization, and the Political Process.* Westport, CT: Greenwood Press, forthcoming.

Powlick, Philip J. "The Sources of Public Opinion for American Foreign Policy Officials. *International Studies Quarterly.* 39 (1995): 427–52.

Powlick, Philip J. "The Attitudinal Bases for Responsiveness to Public Opinion among American Foreign Policy Officials." *Journal of Conflict Resolution* 35 (1991): 611–41.

Price, Vincent. *Public Opinion*. Newbury Park, CA: Sage Publications, 1992.

Prothro, James, and Charles Grigg. "Fundamental Principles of Democracy: Bases of Agreement and Disagreement." *Journal of Politics* 22 (1960): 276–94.

Randall, Vicky. *Women and Politics: An International Perspective*. New York: St. Martin's Press, 1982.

Rapaport, Ronald B., Walter J. Stone, and Alan I. Abramowitz. "Sex and the Caucus Participant: The Gender Gap and Presidential Nominations." *American Journal of Political Science* 34 (1990): 725–40.

Rattinger, Hans. "Causal Models of German Public Attitudes on Foreign Policy and Security after Reunification." Paper presented to the annual meeting of the International Studies Association, Acapulco, Mexico, March 24–28, 1993.

Reagan, Ronald W. *An American Life*. New York: Simon and Schuster, 1990.

Renshon, Stanley A., ed. *The Political Psychology of the Gulf War: Leaders, Publics, and the Process of Conflict*. Pittsburgh: University of Pittsburgh Press, 1993.

Richman, Alvin. "When Should We Be Prepared to Fight?" *Public Perspective* 6 (April-May 1995): 44–47.

Richman, Alvin. "The Polls: Poll Trends: Changing American Attitudes toward the Soviet Union." *Public Opinion Quarterly* 55 (1991): 135–48.

Rielly, John E., ed. *American Public Opinion and U.S. Foreign Policy, 1995*. Chicago: Chicago Council on Foreign Relations, 1995.

Rielly, John E., ed. *American Public Opinion and U.S. Foreign Policy, 1991*. Chicago: Chicago Council on Foreign Relations, 1991.

Rielly, John E., ed. *American Public Opinion and U.S. Foreign Policy, 1987*. Chicago: Chicago Council on Foreign Relations, 1987.

Rielly, John E., ed. *American Public Opinion and U.S. Foreign Policy, 1983*. Chicago: Chicago Council on Foreign Relations, 1983.

Rielly, John E., ed. *American Public Opinion and U.S. Foreign Policy, 1979*. Chicago: Chicago Council on Foreign Relations, 1979.

Rielly, John E., ed. *American Public Opinion and U.S. Foreign Policy, 1975*. Chicago: Chicago Council on Foreign Relations, 1975.

Rintala, Marvin. *Three Generations: The Extreme Right in Finnish Politics*. Bloomington: Indiana University Publications: Russian and East European Series, Vol. 22, 1962.

Ripley, Randall B., and James M. Lindsay, eds. *Congress Resurgent: Foreign and Defense Policy on Capitol Hill*. Ann Arbor: University of Michigan Press, 1993.

Risse-Kappen, Thomas. "Public Opinion, Domestic Structure, and Foreign Policy in Liberal Democracies." *World Politics* 43 (1991): 479–512.

Roberts, Steven V. "The Focus Turns to Foreign Policy." *New York Times*, May 3, 1983, D26.

Roberts, Steven V. "A Critical Coterie on Foreign Policy." *New York Times*, April 5, 1982, A20.

Rogers, William C., Barbara Stuhler, and Donald Koenig. "A Comparison of Informed and General Public Opinion on U.S. Foreign Policy." *Public Opinion Quarterly* 31 (1967): 242–52.

Root, Elihu. "A Requisite for the Success of Popular Diplomacy." *Foreign Affairs* 1 (1922): 1–10.

Root, Elihu. "The Effects of Democracy on International Law." *Proceedings of the American Society of International Law* (1917): 2–11.

Root, Elihu. "The Need of Popular Understanding of International Law." *American Journal of International Law* 1 (1907): 1–3.

Rosenau, James N. *Turbulence in World Politics: A Theory of Change and Continuity.* Princeton, NJ: Princeton University Press, 1990.

Rosenau, James N. *Citizenship between Elections: An Inquiry into the Mobilizable American.* New York: Free Press, 1974.

Rosenau, James N., ed. *Domestic Sources of Foreign Policy.* Free Press: New York, 1967.

Rosenau, James N. *National Leadership and Foreign Policy: A Case Study in the Mobilization of Public Support.* Princeton, NJ: Princeton University Press, 1963.

Rosenau, James N. *Public Opinion and Foreign Policy: An Operational Formulation.* New York: Random House, 1961.

Rosenberg, Milton J. "Attitude Change and Foreign Policy in the Cold War Era." In *Domestic Sources of Foreign Policy,* 111–60. Edited by James N. Rosenau. New York: Free Press, 1967.

Roskin, Michael. "From Pearl Harbor to Vietnam: Shifting Generational Paradigms and Foreign Policy." *Political Science Quarterly* 89 (1974): 563–88.

Rosner, Jeremy D. "The Know-Nothings Know Something." *Foreign Policy,* no. 101 (1995–96): 116–29.

Rusk, Dean. *As I Saw It.* As told to Richard Rusk, edited by Daniel S. Papp. New York: W. W. Norton, 1990.

Russett, Bruce M. *Controlling the Sword: The Democratic Governance of National Security.* Cambridge, MA: Harvard University Press, 1990.

Russett, Bruce M. "The Americans' Retreat from World Power." *Political Science Quarterly* 90 (1975): 1–21.

Russett, Bruce M., and Elizabeth C. Hanson. *Interest and Ideology: The Foreign Policy Beliefs of American Businessmen.* San Francisco: Freeman, 1975.

Russett, Bruce, Thomas Hartley, and Shoon Murray. "The End of the Cold War, Attitude Change, and the Politics of Defense Spending." *PS: Political Science and Politics* 27 (March 1994): 17–21.

Russett, Bruce, and Samuel Shye. "Aggressiveness, Involvement, and Commitment in Foreign Policy Attitudes." In *Diplomacy, Force, and Leadership: Essays in Honor of Alexander L. George.* Edited by Dan Caldwell and Timothy J. McKeown. Boulder, CO: Westview, 1993.

Saad, Lydia. "Americans Back Clinton's Plan to Keep the Peace in Bosnia." Princeton, NJ: Gallup Organization, October 27, 1995.

Saad, Lydia, and Frank Newport. "Americans Want To Keep At Arms Length From Bosnian Conflict." *The Gallup Monthly,* no. 358 (July 1995): 16–18.

Schlesinger, Arthur, Jr. "Back to the Womb?" *Foreign Affairs* 74 (July-August 1995): 2–8.

Schlesinger, James R. "Now—a Tougher U.S." *U.S. News and World Report,* May 26, 1975, 25.

Schneider, William. "The Old Politics and the New World Order." In *Eagle in a New World.* Edited by Kenneth A. Oye, Robert J. Lieber, and Donald Rothchild. New York: HarperCollins, 1992.

Schneider, William. "Conservatism, not Interventionism: Trends in Foreign Policy Opinion, 1974–1982." In *Eagle Defiant: United States Foreign Policy in the 1980s.* Edited by Kenneth Oye, Robert J. Lieber, and Donald Rothchild. Boston: Little, Brown, 1983.

Schuman, Howard, and Cheryl Rieger. "Historical Analogies, Generational Effects, and Attitudes toward War." *American Sociological Review* 57 (1992): 315–26.

Schwarzkopf, H. Norman, with Peter Petre. *It Doesn't Take a Hero.* New York: Bantam Books, 1992.

Sears, David. "Ideological Bias in Political Psychology: The View from Scientific Hell." *Political Psychology* 15 (1994): 547–56.

Shapiro, Robert Y., and Lawrence R. Jacobs. "The Relationship between Public Opinion and Public Policy: A Review." In *Political Behavior Annual,* vol. 2, 149–79. Edited by Samuel Long. Boulder, CO: Westview, 1989.

Shapiro, Robert Y., and Harpreet Mahajan. "Gender Differences in Policy Preferences: A Summary of Trends from the 1960s to the 1980s." *Public Opinion Quarterly* 50 (1986): 42–61.

Shapiro, Robert Y., and Benjamin I. Page. "Foreign Policy and Public Opinion." In *The New Politics of American Foreign Policy,* 216–35. Edited by David A. Deese. New York: St. Martin's Press, 1994.

Shapiro, Robert Y., and Benjamin I. Page. "Foreign Policy and the Rational Public." *Journal of Conflict Resolution* 32 (1988): 211–47.

Shogan, Robert. *Hard Bargain.* New York: Scribner, 1995.

Shultz, George P. *Turmoil and Triumph: My Years as Secretary of State.* New York: Charles Scribner's, 1993.

Sigelman, Lee, and Pamela Johnston Conover. "Knowledge and Opinions about the Iran Crisis: A Reconsideration of Three Models." *Public Opinion Quarterly* 45 (1981): 477–91.

Small, Melvin, ed. *Public Opinion and Historians: Interdisciplinary Perspectives.* Detroit: Wayne State University Press, 1970.

Smith, Tom W. "The Polls: America's Most Important Problems: National and International." *Public Opinion Quarterly* 49 (1985): 264–74.

Smith, Tom W. "The Polls: Gender and Attitudes toward Violence." *Public Opinion Quarterly* 48 (1984): 384–96.

Smith, Tom W. "The Polls: American Attitudes toward the Soviet Union and Communism." *Public Opinion Quarterly* 47 (1983): 277–92.

Sniderman, Paul M. "Burden of Proof." *Political Psychology* 15 (1994): 541–46.

Sniderman, Paul M. "The New Look in Public Opinion Research." In *Political Science: The State of the Discipline II,* 219–45. Edited by Ada W. Finifter. Washington, DC: American Political Science Association, 1993.

Sniderman, Paul M., and Philip E. Tetlock. "Interrelationship of Political Ideology and Public Opinion." In *Political Psychology,* 62–96. Edited by Margaret G. Hermann. San Francisco: Jossey-Bass, 1986.

Sobel, Richard. "Polling on Foreign Policy Crises: Ascertaining the Questions to Ask." Princeton University, 1995a. Typescript.

Sobel, Richard. "What People Really Say About Bosnia." *New York Times,* November 22, 1995b, A23:2.

Sobel, Richard. "Public Opinion about United States Intervention in El Salvador and Nicaragua." *Public Opinion Quarterly* 53 (1989): 114–28.

Sobel, Richard, ed. *Public Opinion and Foreign Policy: The Controversy over Contra Aid*. Lanham, MD: Rowman and Littlefield, 1993.

Spitzer, Alan B. "The Historical Problem of Generations." *American Historical Review* 78 (1973): 1353–85.

Spivak, Jonathan. "Generation Gap: Polish Crisis Is a Clash of Old and Entrenched with Impatient Youth." *Wall Street Journal*, February 11, 1981a, 1, 20.

Spivak, Jonathan. "Changes in Poland's Communist Party Shows Switch to a Younger Generation." *Wall Street Journal* , September 3, 1981b, 26.

Squire, Peverill. "Why the 1936 *Literary Digest* Poll Failed." *Public Opinion Quarterly* 52 (1988): 125–33.

Steel, Ronald. *Walter Lippmann and the American Century*. Boston: Little Brown, 1980.

Steele, Richard W. "The Pulse of the People: Franklin D. Roosevelt and the Gauging of American Public Opinion." *Journal of Contemporary History* 9 (1974): 195–216.

Steele, Richard W. *Propaganda in an Open Society: The Roosevelt Administration and the Media, 1933–1941*. Westport, CT: Greenwood, 1985.

Stimson, James A. *Public Opinion in America: Moods, Cycles and Swings*. Boulder, CO: Westview, 1991.

Stimson, James A., Michael B. MacKuen, and Robert S. Erikson. "Dynamic Representation." *American Political Science Review* 89 (1995): 543–65.

Stimson, James A., Michael B. MacKuen, and Robert S. Erikson. "Opinion and Policy: A Global View." *PS: Political Science and Politics* 27 (March 1994): 29–35.

Stouffer, Samuel A. et al. *The American Soldier,* vol. 1. New York: John Wiley, 1949; vol. 2, Princeton, NJ: Princeton University Press, 1949.

Strauss, William, and Neil Howe. *Generations: The History of America's Future, 1584 to 2069*. New York: Morrow, 1991.

Sullivan, John L., J. E. Pierson, and George E. Marcus. "Ideological Constraint in the Mass Public: A Methodological Critique and Some New Findings." *American Journal of Political Science Review* 22 (1978): 234–49.

Sussman, Barry. *Elites in America*. Washington, DC: Washington Post, September 26–30, 1976.

Sussman, Leila A. *Dear FDR: A Study of Political Letter Writing*. Totowa, NJ: Bedminster Press, 1963.

Sussman, Leila. "FDR and the White House Mail." *Public Opinion Quarterly* 20 (1956): 5–15.

Taylor, D. Garth. "Procedure for Evaluating Trends in Public Opinion." *Public Opinion Quarterly* 44 (1980): 86–100.

Taylor, Stan A., and Robert S. Wood. "Image and Generation: A Social-Psychological Analysis of the Sino-Soviet Dispute." *Brigham Young University Studies* 7 (1966): 143–57.

Tetlock, Philip. "Political Psychology or Politicized Psychology: Is the Road to Scientific Hell Paved with Good Moral Intentions?" *Political Psychology* 15 (1994a): 509–30.

Tetlock, Philip. "How Politicized Is Political Psychology and Is There Anything We Should Do about It?" *Political Psychology* 15 (1994b): 567–77.

"The New Americans: A New *U.S. News* Poll Shatters Old Assumptions about American Politics." *U.S. News and World Report*, July 10, 1995, 18–23.

Times Mirror Center for the People and the Press. *America's Place in the World: An Investigation of the Attitudes of American Opinion Leaders and the American Public about International Affairs.* Washington, DC: Times Mirror Center for the People and the Press, 1993.

Tocqueville, Alexis de. *Democracy in America.* Vol. 1. New York: Vintage, 1958.

Trubowitz, Peter. "Sectionalism and American Foreign Policy: The Political Geography of Consensus and Conflict." *International Studies Quarterly* 36 (1992): 173–90.

Turner, Henry A. "Woodrow Wilson and Public Opinion." *Public Opinion Quarterly* 21 (1957): 505–20.

U.S. Department of Commerce. *Statistical Abstract of the United States.* Washington, DC: U.S. Government Printing Office, 1994.

U.S. Strategic Bombing Survey. *The Effects of Strategic Bombing on German Morale.* Vol. 1. Washington, DC: U.S. Strategic Bombing Survey, 1947.

Vandenberg, Arthur H., Jr., ed. *The Private Papers of Senator Vandenberg.* Boston: Houghton Mifflin, 1952.

Verba, Sidney, and Richard A. Brody. "Participation, Policy Preferences, and the War in Vietnam." *Public Opinion Quarterly* 34 (1970): 325–32.

Verba, Sidney, et al. "Public Opinion and the War in Vietnam." *American Political Science Review* 61 (1967): 317–33.

Walsh, Warren B. "What the American People Think of Russia." *Public Opinion Quarterly* 8 (1944): 513–22.

Waltz, Kenneth N. "Electoral Punishment and Foreign Policy Crises." In *Domestic Sources of Foreign Policy,* 263–94. Edited by James N. Rosenau. New York: Free Press, 1967.

Watts, William, and Lloyd A. Free. *State of the Nation.* New York: Universe Books, 1973.

Weiler, Michael, and W. Barnett Pearce, eds. *Reagan and Public Discourse in America.* Tuscaloosa: University of Alabama Press, 1992.

Weinberger, Caspar. *Fighting for Peace: Seven Critical Years in the Pentagon.* New York: Warner Books, 1990.

White House. *A National Security Strategy of Engagement and Enlargement.* Washington, DC: U.S. Government Printing Office, 1994.

White, Lincoln. "The News Division of the Department of State." *Department of State Bulletin,* 40 (June 22, 1959): 921–25.

Wildavsky, Aaron. "The Two Presidencies." *Trans-Action* 4 (December 1966): 7–14.

Williams, Erin M. "Sources of New Era Foreign Policy: Public Opinion, Congress, and the Harding Administration, 1921–1923." Ph.D. diss., History Dept., Emory University, 1996.

Williams, Frederick W. "Regional Attitudes on International Cooperation." *Public Opinion Quarterly* 9 (1945): 38–50.

Willkie, Wendell L. *One World.* New York: Simon and Schuster, 1943.

Wilson, Woodrow. "Text of the President's Address." *New York Times,* April 3, 1917, 1:1.

Wines, Michael. "Washington Is Really in Touch: We're the Problem." *New York Times,* October 16, 1994, sec. 4, 1, 6.

Wirls, Daniel. "Reinterpreting the Gender Gap." *Public Opinion Quarterly* 50 (1986): 316–30.

Wittkopf, Eugene R. "The Faces of Internationalism Revisited." Paper presented to the annual meeting of the American Political Science Association, Chicago, August 31–September 3, 1995.

Wittkopf, Eugene R. *Faces of Internationalism: Public Opinion and American Foreign Policy.* Durham, NC: Duke University Press, 1990.

Wittkopf, Eugene R. "On the Foreign Policy Beliefs of the American People: A Critique and Some Evidence." *International Studies Quarterly* 30 (1986): 425–45.

Wohlstetter, Roberta. *Pearl Harbor: Warning and Decision.* Stanford, CA: Stanford University Press, 1962.

Wood, Floris E., ed. *An American Profile: Opinions and Behavior, 1972–1989.* Detroit: Gale Research, 1990.

Woodward, Julian L. "Public Opinion Polls as an Aid to Democracy." *Political Science Quarterly* 61 (1945): 238–46.

Wright, Quincy. *A Study of War.* 2d ed. 1942. Reprint, Chicago: University of Chicago Press, 1965.

Yankelovich, Daniel. *Coming to Public Judgment: Making Democracy Work in a Complex World.* Syracuse, NY: Syracuse University Press, 1991.

Yankelovich, Daniel. "Farewell to 'the President Knows Best,'" *Foreign Affairs* 57 (1978): 670–93.

Yankelovich, Daniel, and I. M. Destler, eds. *Beyond the Beltway: Engaging the Public in U.S. Foreign Policy.* New York: W. W. Norton, 1994.

Zaller, John R. "Strategic Politicians, Public Opinion, and the Gulf Crisis." In *Taken by Storm: The Media, Public Opinion, and U.S. Foreign Policy in the Gulf War,* 250–76. Edited by W. Lance Bennett and David L. Paletz. Chicago: University of Chicago Press, 1994.

Zaller, John R. *The Nature and Origins of Mass Opinion.* New York: Cambridge University Press, 1992.

Zimmerman, William, and Allan Stam. "Constrained Belief Systems, Rational Publics, and Russian Foreign Policy in the 1990s." University of Michigan, n.d. Typescript.

Zur, Ofer, and Andrea Morrison. "Gender and War: Reexamining Attitudes." *American Journal of Orthopsychiatry* 59 (1989): 528–33.

Index